101
No-Huddle Spread Offense Plays

Brent Eckley

ISBN: 978-1-60679-047-2
Library of Congress Control Number: 2009929113
Cover design: Studio J Art & Design
Book layout: Studio J Art & Design
Front cover photo: Otto Greule Jr/Getty Images

Coaches Choice
P.O. Box 1828
Monterey, CA 93942
www.coacheschoice.com

Dedication

This book is dedicated to my wife, Sherene, and children, Hannah, Emily, Madison, and Hillary, and Marquis. My family has always been supportive and involved in my endeavors as a coach.

This book is also dedicated to my father Dallas, who passed away in 2008. He did not understand football to any great depth but grasped the concept of hard work and making the people around him feel good, which I admire and miss the most.

Acknowledgments

The information in this book is a reflection of all the coaches that have been gracious enough to share with me their best schemes or techniques. As many of us know, football coaches are the best "borrowers" around, and I am no different.

I'd like to thank the following, in no particular order, for sharing with me: Hal Mumme, Mike Emendorfer, Eric Thomas, Ben Blank, Jeff Wallace, Dan Robinson, Andrew Coverdale, Cliff Ice, Phil Lite, Gus Malzahn, Ken Leonard, David Yost, Shawn Jackson, Paul Day, Steve Rampy, Rick Jones, Greg Nesbitt, and Gene Gladstone among many others.

Also, I'd like to thank the Union High School football staff, both past and present: Brad Julius, Keith Janssen, Gary Vogel, Chris Kelley, Erick Webster, Pat Luck, Nick Kelley, Isaac Arand, George Hinkle, and Paul Brake.

Finally, and most importantly, I'd like to acknowledge my high school football coach, Tom Stone, who has won well over 300 games in over 35 years of service as a head coach. Coach Stone was a true father figure to me from the time I was an elementary school student until well after I finished college. Coach Stone is the reason I coach, which is one of the best gifts I've ever received.

Contents

Section 1
The Quick Passing Game

1

Hitch Routes

Introduction

The quarterback will pick a side of the formation to which he will throw the ball. His decision is based on finding the shortest throw that is the most open. He makes this decision pre-snap.

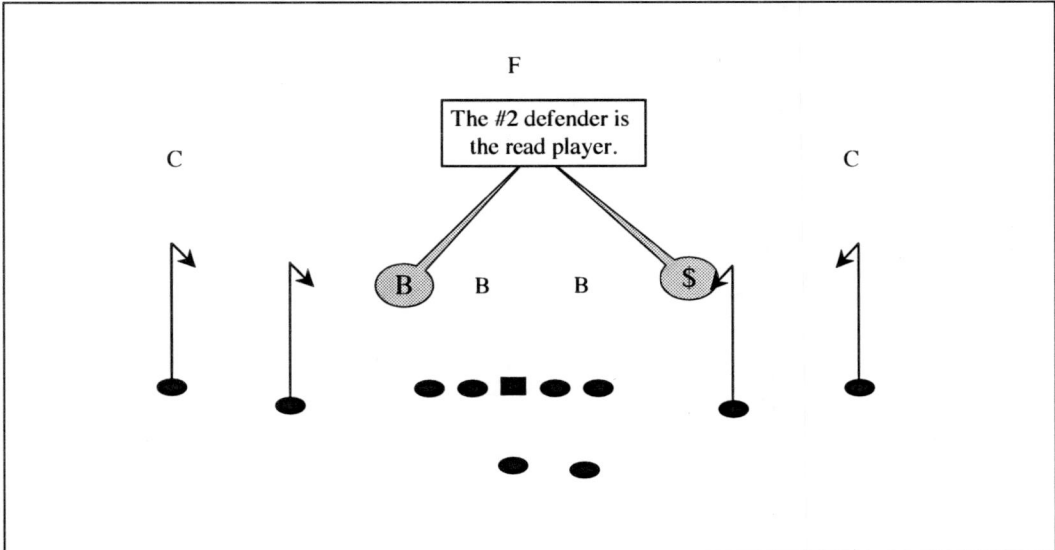

Figure 1-1. Finding the #2 defender

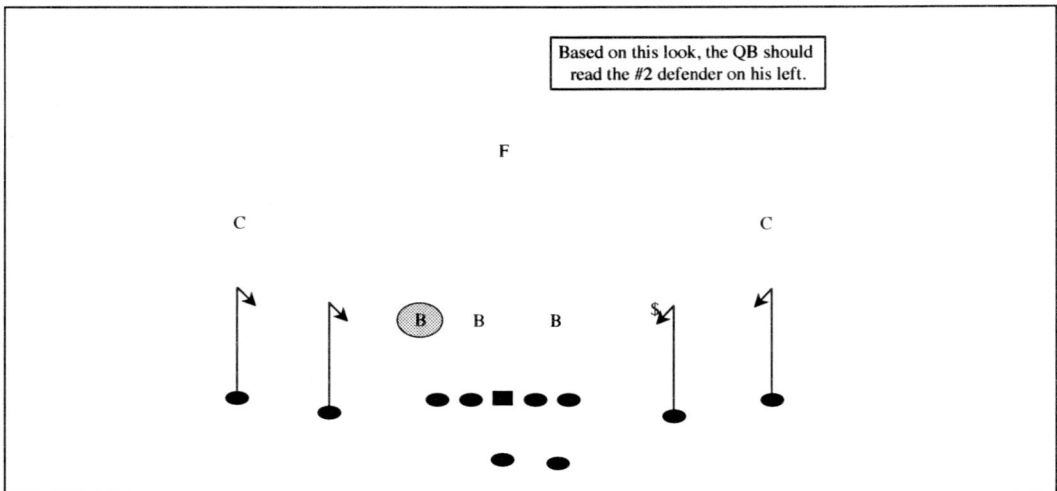

Figure 1-2. The quarterback must determine which #2 defender has the least advantageous leverage.

It is beneficial to have a consistent defender-counting system. The counting system that is used in this book is an outside-in system, as shown in Figure 1-3.

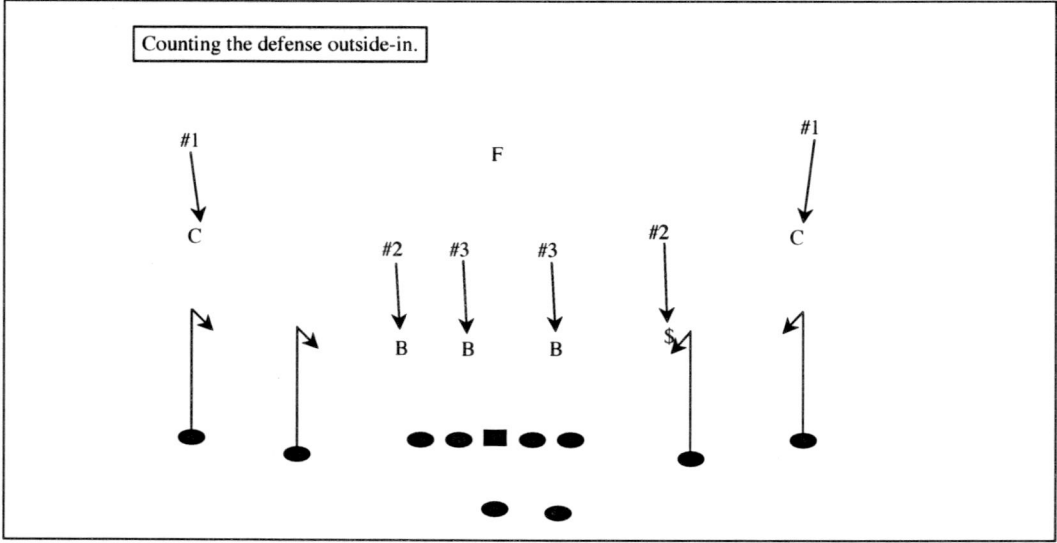

Figure 1-3. Count system

Play #1: The Hitch Route

The hitch route has become a staple of the spread offense over the years. It has been very easy to teach and learn. The hitch route has many different applications.

After the ball is snapped, the quarterback will read the #2 defender to the side of the formation he picked before the snap. He wants to make the defender wrong. If the defender backpedals or gets width immediately, the quarterback will throw the ball to the inside receiver. If the defender stays in place or holds on the stem of the #2 receiver, the quarterback will throw to the outside receiver.

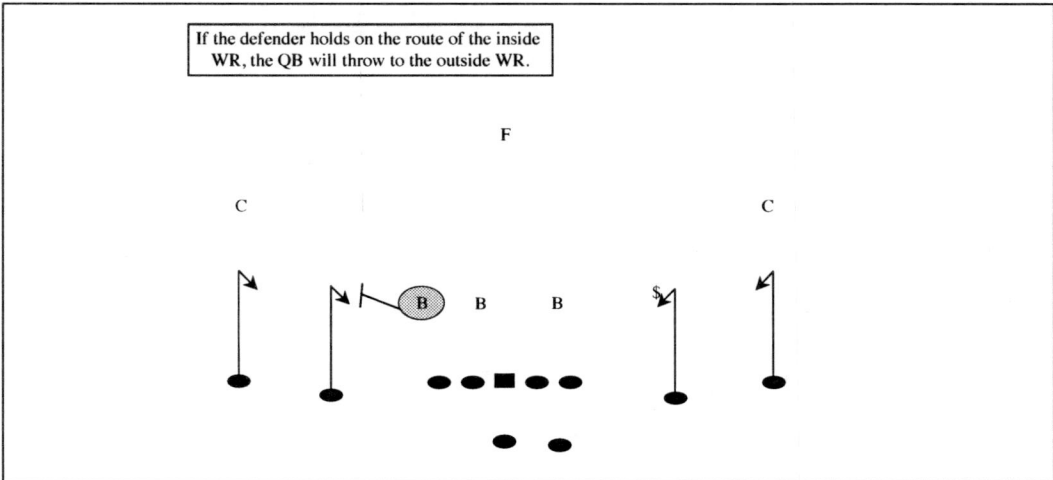

Figure 1-4. Quarterback reads the wall technique by the #2 defender.

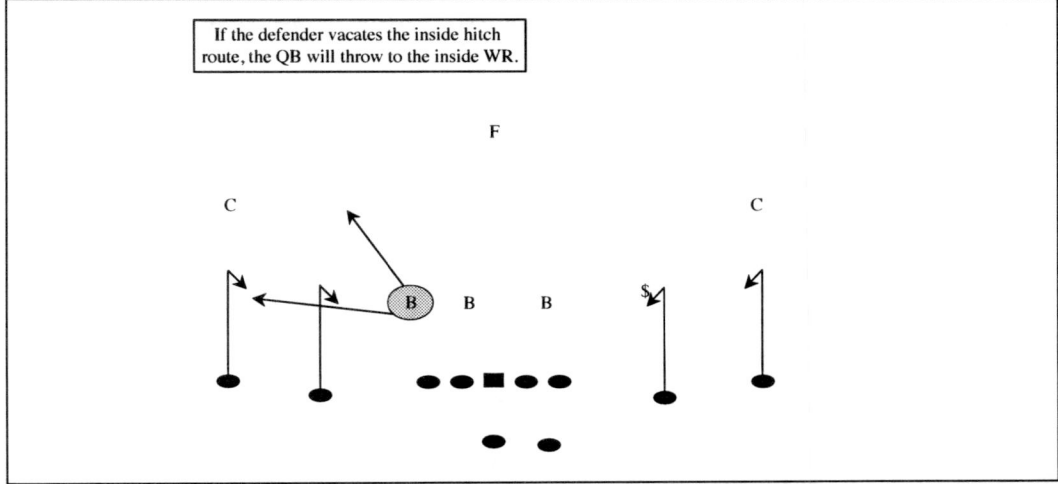

Figure 1-5. Quarterback reads the uncovered technique by the #2 defender.

Each receiver will run a hitch route. The hitch route technique is to drive four hard steps and take two buzz or control steps. After the receiver gets to the top of his route, he will get his hands up and snap his head back to the quarterback.

The offensive line will all take a quick set, which entails the linemen popping up into their pass-protection stance and taking two backpedal steps. The linemen will then stop their momentum to be ready to make a strong wall for pass protection. The technique of the offensive line will not change on any of the quick-pass routes, so pass protection will be limited to this chapter.

The hitch route can be run out of several different formations within the spread offense, including 2 x 2 sets, 3 x 1 sets, 3 x 2 sets, and 4 x 1 sets.

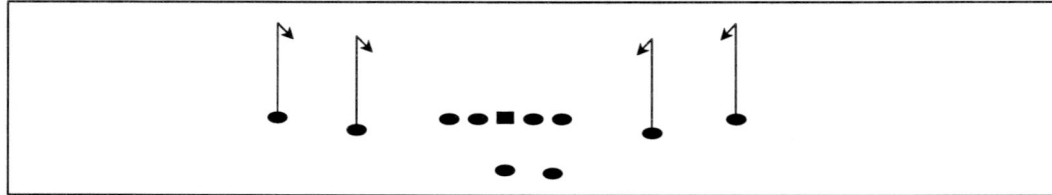

Figure 1-6. Hitch route in a 2 x 2 set

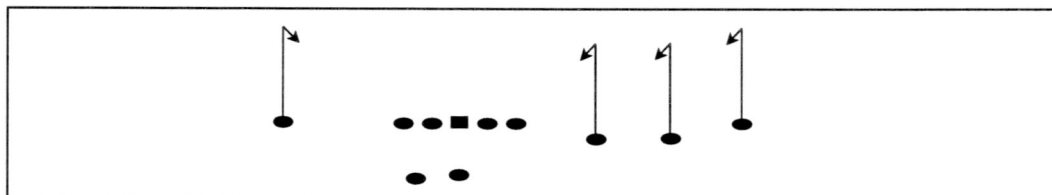

Figure 1-7. Hitch route in a 3 x 1 set

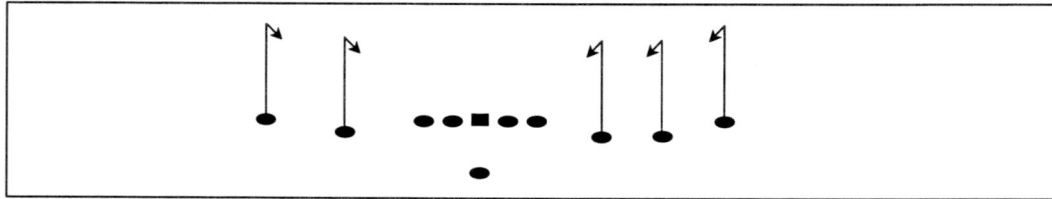

Figure 1-8. Hitch route in a 3 x 2 set

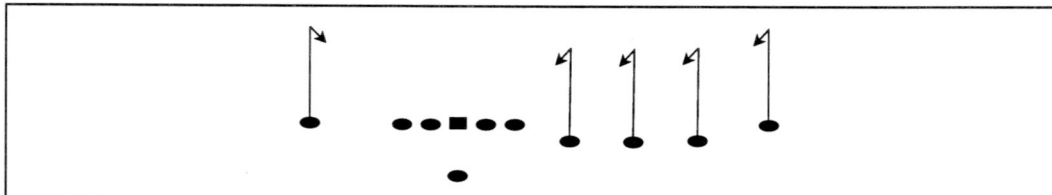

Figure 1-9. Hitch route in a 4 x 1 set

Play #2: The Hitch-and-Go Route

Several tags can be used with the hitch route. The first tag for the hitch route is the go tag. The go tag is a double-move tag that is given to assigned players. Usually, the best positions to execute this tag are the outside receivers. However, the go tag can also be used for inside receivers.

The technique of the tagged receiver is to initially run the normal hitch route. When the receiver gets to the top of his route, he will turn his head and shoulders to the quarterback and raise his hands to catch a pass. He would like to avoid contact with the defender as he turns back upfield. The receiver will take the best angle for release, either a spin to the sideline or a shuffle slide to avoid contact.

The quarterback will pick a side of the defense, catch the snap, and pump fake to the receiver lined up to the side he picked. The quarterback's next step is critical to the success of the play. After his pump fake, he will set his feet and throw the ball. It's important for the quarterback to set his feet and throw the ball quickly. A common error of the quarterback is to take a three-step drop after the pump fake. A three-step drop makes for a longer throw and gives the defense more time to react to the double move.

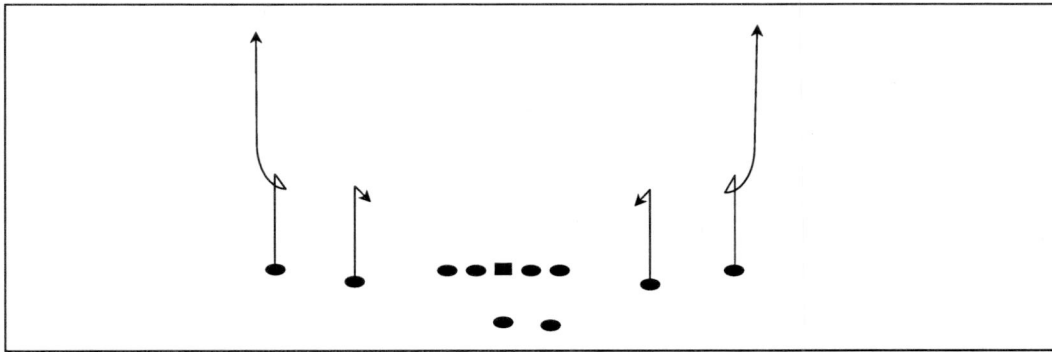

Figure 1-10. Hitch-and-go route in a 2 x 2 set

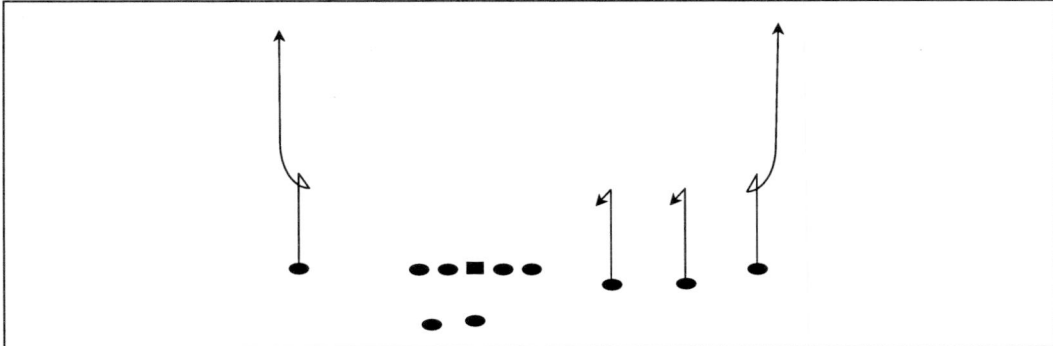

Figure 1-11. Hitch-and-go route in a 3 x 1 set

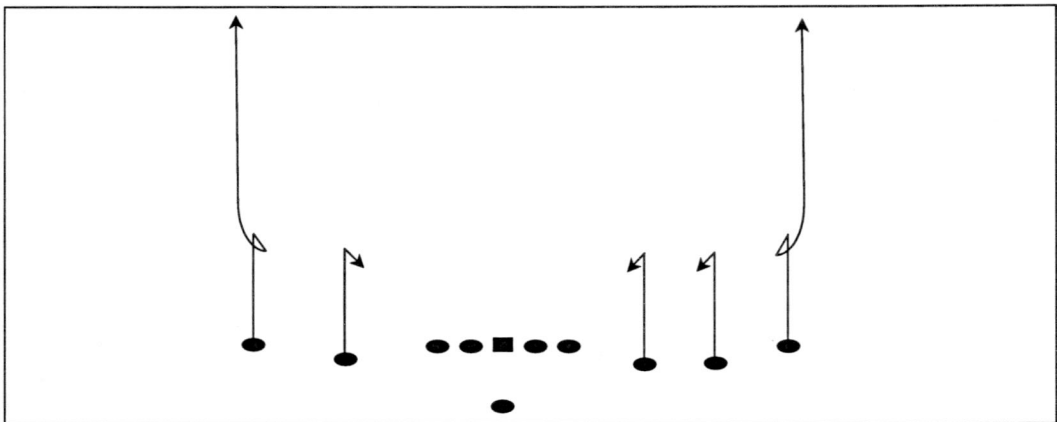
Figure 1-12. Hitch-and-go route in a 3 x 2 set

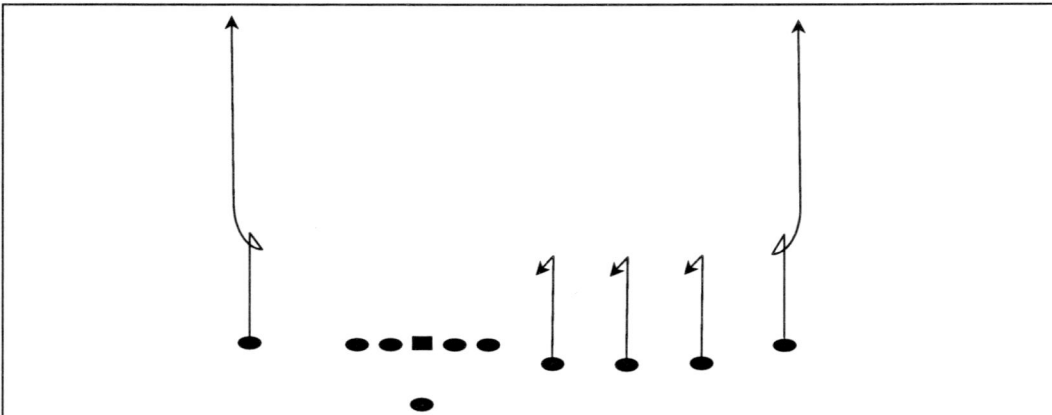
Figure 1-13. Hitch-and-go route in a 4 x 1 set

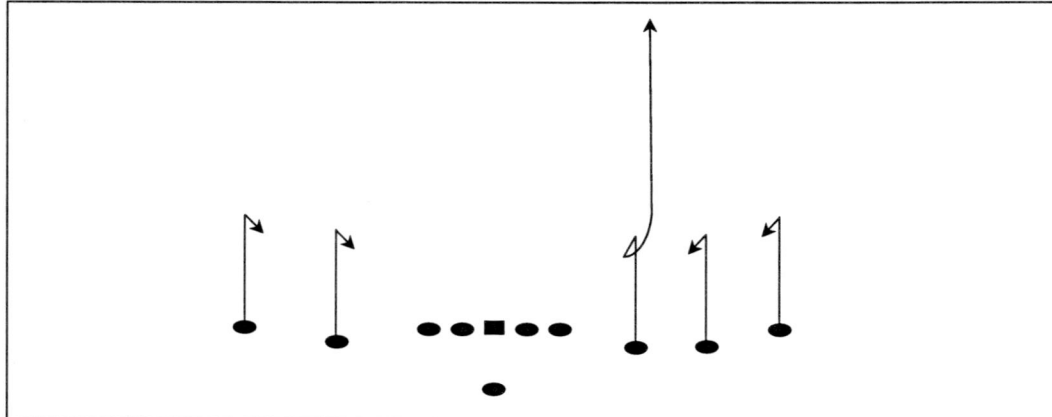
Figure 1-14. Hitch-and-go route to a single receiver in a 3 x 2 set

Play #3: The Hitch Route With a Corner Tag

The corner tag is used primarily versus teams that consistently play man-to-man or cover 2 zone. This play is used for a single receiver and has proven to be most successful when used with an inside receiver in a 3 x 1 set.

The corner tag is given to a specific receiver, and the tag tells the receiver to make a corner-route cut at seven yards deep. He will then angle his route at 20 yards deep, if he gets to the sideline. Against man-to-man defense, the tagged receiver needs to beat the defender to the outside before making the corner cut.

On the corner tag, versus man-to-man defense, the quarterback will read the defender over the tagged receiver. He wants to throw the receiver open to the sideline. Versus cover 2 zone defense, the quarterback will read the #1 defender. If the #1 defender hangs on the hitch route by the outside receiver, the quarterback will throw the corner route. If the #1 defender backpedals at the snap and continues to gain depth, the quarterback will throw the hitch route to the outside receiver.

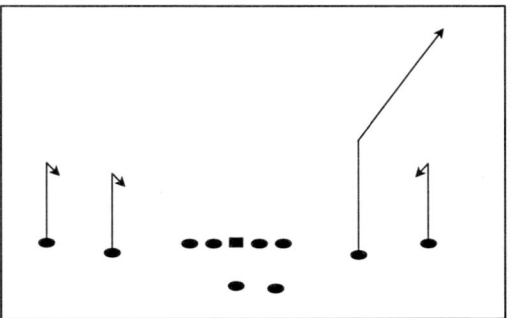

Figure 1-15. Hitch route with a corner tag in a 2 x 2 set

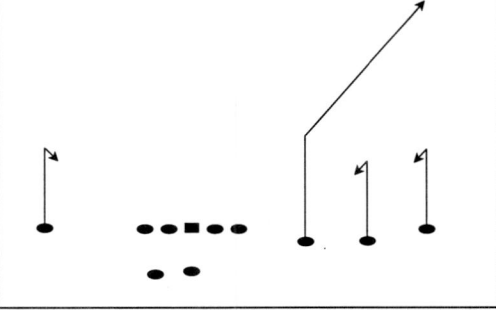

Figure 1-16. Hitch route with a corner tag in a 3 x 1 set

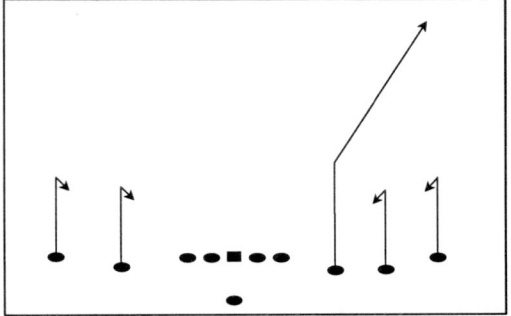

Figure 1-17. Hitch route with a corner tag in a 3 x 2 set

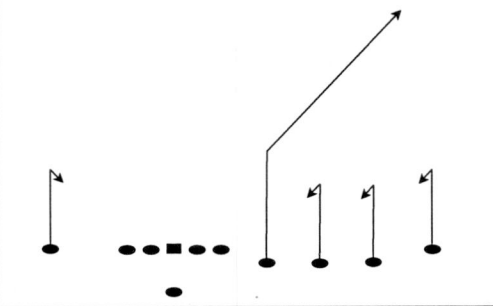

Figure 1-18. Hitch route with a corner tag in a 4 x 1 set

Play #4: The Hitch Route With a Post Tag

The post tag is used primarily versus teams that play man-to-man defense with no safety help. In this manner, the tag is best applied to an inside receiver. The tag can also be used for an outside receiver versus a cover 4 deep zone defense.

On this route, the tagged receiver will push his route to seven yards deep and then break at a 45-degree angle to the middle of the field. If the receiver is playing versus man-to-man defense, he will need to beat the defender inside before making the post cut. If the player tagged is an outside receiver (versus cover 4 deep zone), he will need to take his post route up the hash and beat the safety on top.

The quarterback will read the defender over the tagged receiver versus man-to-man defense. If the defense is playing cover 4 deep zone, the quarterback will read the safety to the side of the tagged receiver. If the safety gains depth to stay on top of the post route, the quarterback will throw to the hitch route. If the safety holds on the hitch route, the quarterback will throw to the outside receiver on the post route.

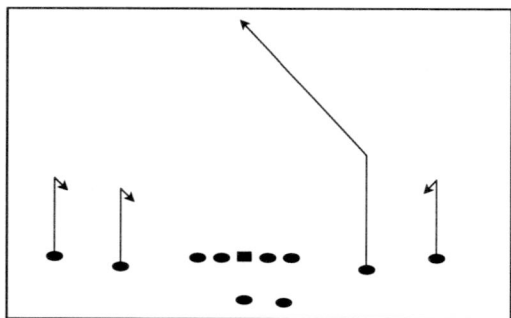

Figure 1-19. Hitch route with a post tag in a 2 x 2 set

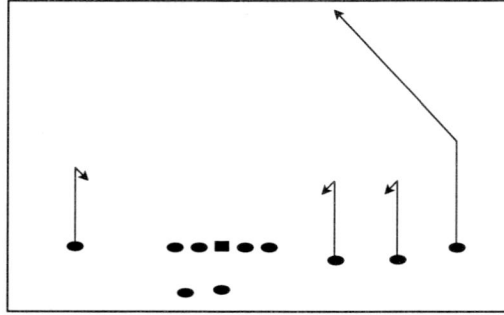

Figure 1-20. Hitch route with a post tag in a 3 x 1 set

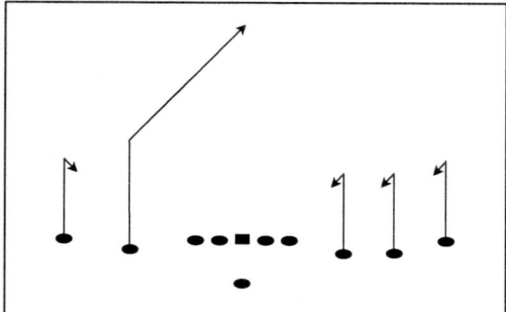

Figure 1-21. Hitch route with a post tag in a 3 x 2 set

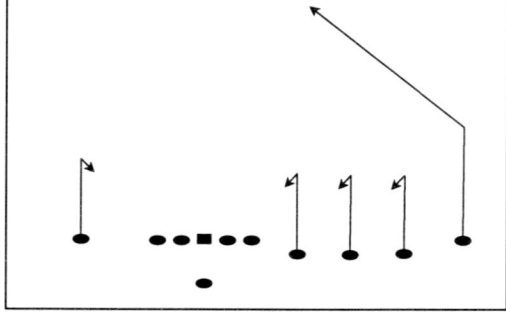

Figure 1-22. Hitch route with a post tag in a 4 x 1 set

Play #5: The Hitch Route With an Inside Seam Tag

The seam tag is used versus cover 3 zone teams, cover 4 zone teams, and man-to-man defensive teams when the #1 defenders are playing too deep in their coverage to defend the hitch route by the outside receiver.

The seam tag tells the inside receivers to run a seam route, landmarking the hash marks to their respective side. In a 3 x 1 set, both inside receivers will run vertical routes, with the outside receiver landmarking the near hash and the inside receiver landmarking the opposite hash. The outside receivers run the same hitch routes, as their cuts are unaffected by the seam tag. The outside receivers should expect the ball on the seam tag, as they become the primary receiver to their side of the formation.

When the seam tag is called, it is expected that the hitch route to the outside receiver will be an easy completion, so the pre-snap read for the quarterback is the depth of the #1 defender. Once the ball has been snapped, the quarterback will then read the #2 defender. If the #2 defender can get under the hitch route by the outside receiver before the quarterback can get the ball to the hitch route, the quarterback has to throw to the seam route. If the #2 defender doesn't work to get under the hitch route by the outside receiver, the quarterback will then throw to the outside receiver on the hitch route.

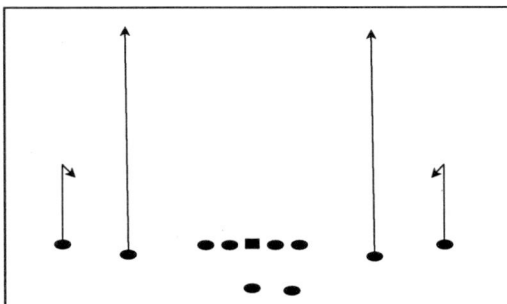

Figure 1-23. Hitch route with a seam tag in a 2 x 2 set

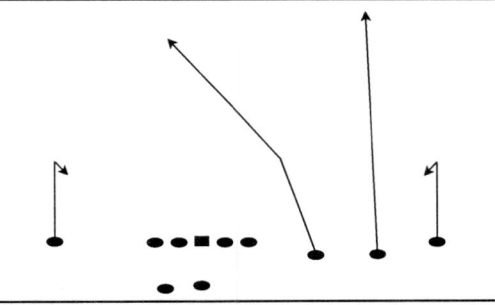

Figure 1-24. Hitch route with a seam tag in a 3 x 1 set

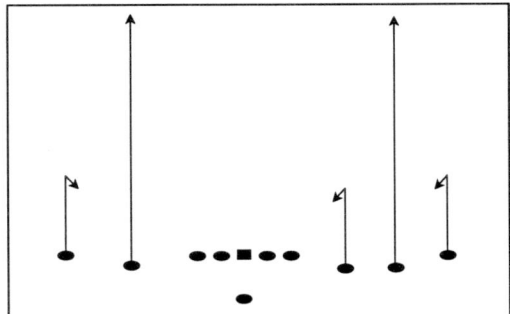

Figure 1-25. Hitch route with a seam tag in a 3 x 2 set

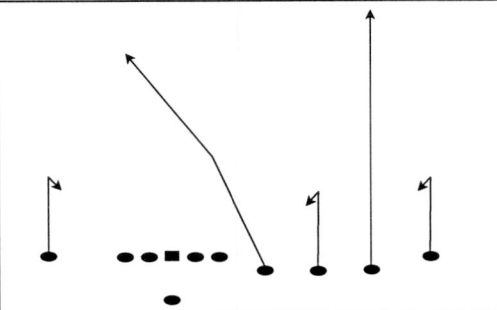

Figure 1-26. Hitch route with a seam tag in a 4 x 1 set

Play #6: The Hitch Route Out of a Bunch Set

A typical way to align in bunch is to have the receivers set the bunch at the normal width of the #2 receiver. This alignment sets the bunch 8 to 12 yards from the offensive tackle. The bunch alignment puts two, three, or four receivers in close proximity to one another. A typical base rule is to have one yard of distance from receiver to receiver, widthwise and depthwise. A traditional three-man bunch set looks like an upside-down V.

Lining up in a bunch set is another way to run the hitch route. This alignment creates one more adjustment for the defense. The defense also has to work on recognizing another formation.

When running the hitch route out of the bunch set, the receivers only need to remember their landmarks for their regular hitch route. They want to maximize space on this route, so the inside receiver will release inside, the middle receiver will release straight up the field, and the outside receiver will release outside and work toward the numbers to set up.

The quarterback will read this route inside-out.

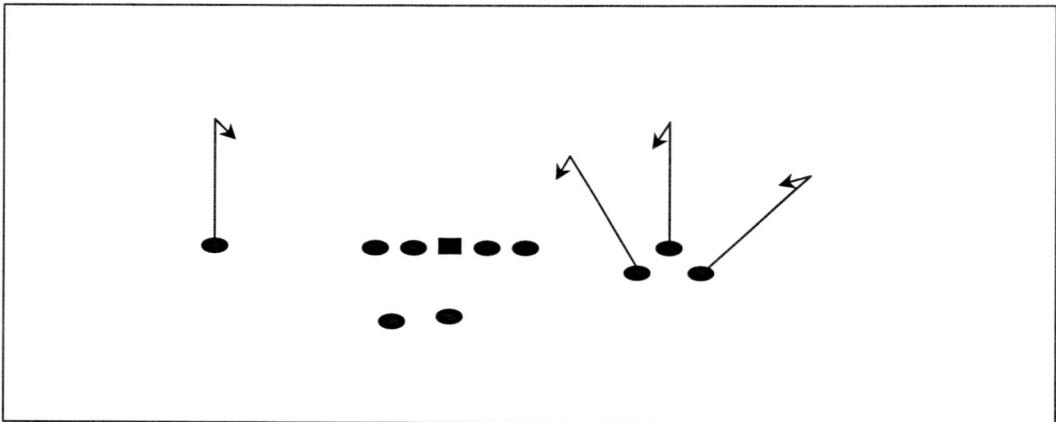

Figure 1-27. Hitch route out of a 3 x 1 bunch set

2

Slant Routes

Introduction

Like many of the quick-passing routes, the quarterback will pick a side of the formation to which he will throw the ball. His decision is based on finding the shortest throw that is the most open. He makes this decision pre-snap. The quarterback will then read the #2 defender post-snap.

Play #7: The Slant Route

The slant route has become a very good way to attack traditional defenses. It has also proven to be a good route versus man or zone defenses.

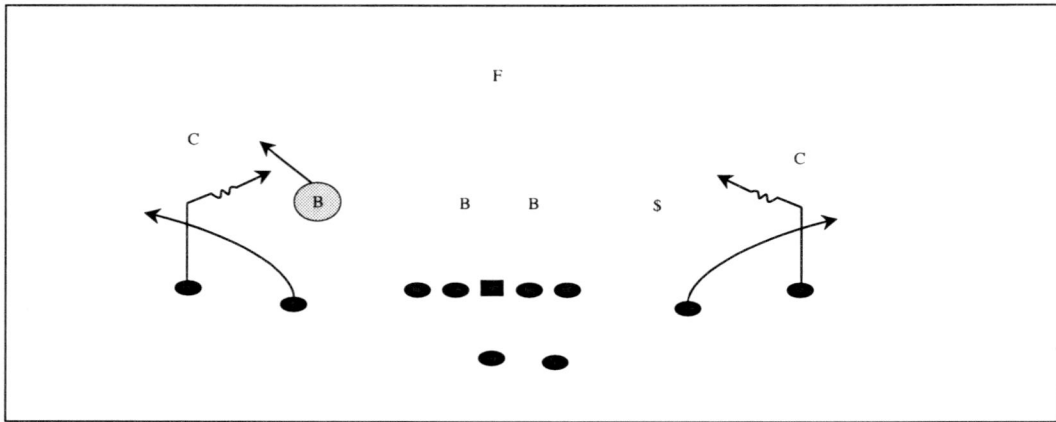

Figure 2-1. Quarterback reads the #2 defender and should throw to the shoot route.

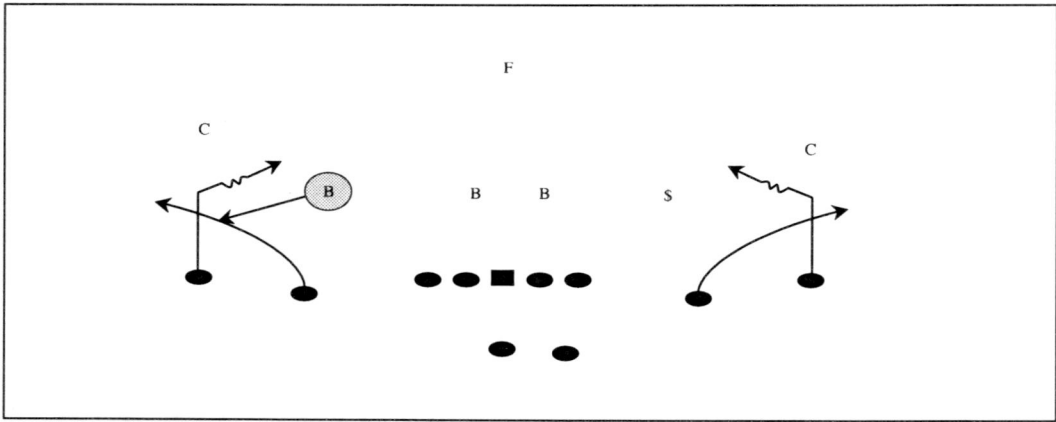

Figure 2-2. Quarterback reads the #2 defender and should throw the ball to the slant-sit route.

After the ball is snapped, the quarterback will read the #2 defender to the side of the formation that gives him the best opportunity for a completion. He wants to make the defender wrong. If the defender backpedals or holds his pre-snap alignment, the quarterback will throw the ball to the inside receiver on the shoot route. If the defender drives downhill on the shoot route of the #2 receiver, the quarterback will pause momentarily and then throw to the outside receiver on the slant-sit route.

The outside receivers will each run a slant-sit route. The slant-sit route technique is to drive four hard steps and then break inside at a 45-degree angle. The receiver's landmark is one step inside the #2 defender. If the opponent is playing man-to-man defense, the outside receiver will keep moving on his route. If the opponent is playing zone defense, the receiver will settle and stay open as long as possible.

The inside receivers will each run a shoot route, which is to drive one step forward, then bend to the outside and accelerate to the sideline. He will need to look over his outside shoulder after his third step. His route should gradually build up to a depth of five yards.

The slant route can be run out of several different formations within the spread offense, including 2 x 2 sets, 3 x 1 sets, 3 x 2 sets, and 4 x 1 sets. When in 3 x 1 or 3 x 2 sets, a good rule is to have the middle receiver run a seam route, as shown in Figures 2-4 and 2-5. When lined up in a 4 x 1 set, the best route to have the inside receiver run is a four-step slant route and keep pushing vertically, as shown in Figure 2-6.

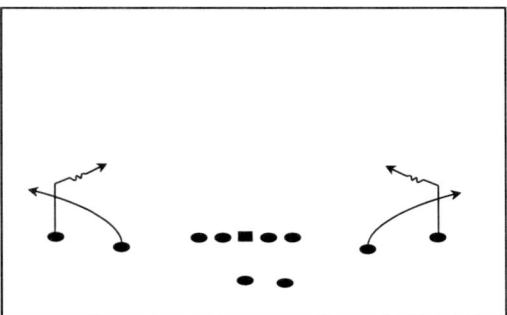

Figure 2-3. Slant route in a 2 x 2 set

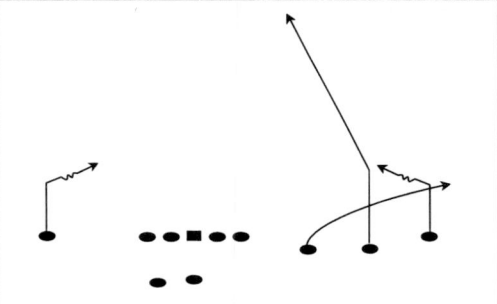

Figure 2-4. Slant route in a 3 x 1 set

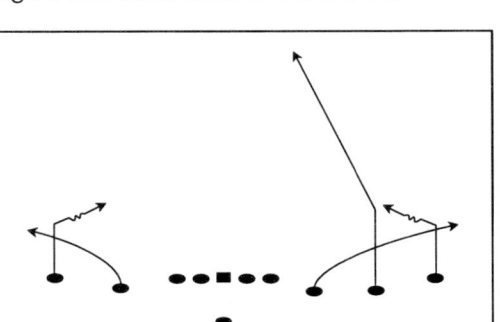

Figure 2-5. Slant route in a 3 x 2 set

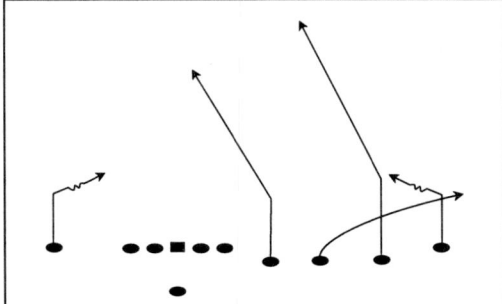

Figure 2-6. Slant route in a 4 x 1 set

Play #8: The Double-Slant Route Tag

Several tags can be used with the slant route. The first tag for the slant route is the double-slant tag. The double-slant route puts all receivers on slant routes.

The technique of the inside receivers is to drive four steps and break inside. After one step inside, the receiver should then run straight up the field.

The quarterback will pick a side of the defense and read the #2 defender, just like the regular slant route. If the defender carries the route of the inside receiver, by running with him, the quarterback will throw to the outside receiver. If the #2 defender allows the inside receiver to get inside of him, or if he releases the receiver and moves to the flat, the quarterback will throw to the inside receiver. The double-slant tag is good way to attack man-to-man or cover 2 defenses.

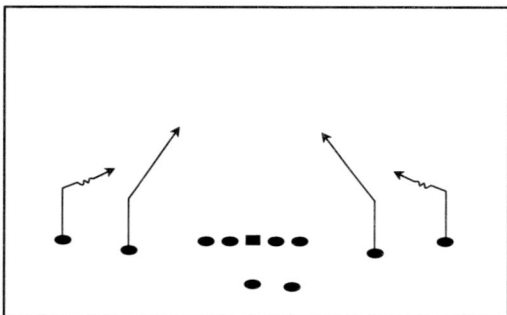

Figure 2-7. Double-slant route in a 2 x 2 set

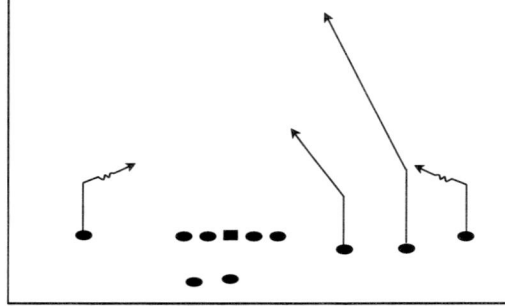

Figure 2-8. Double-slant route in a 3 x 1 set

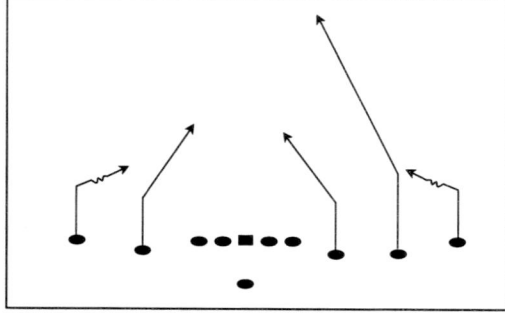

Figure 2-9. Double-slant route in a 3 x 2 set

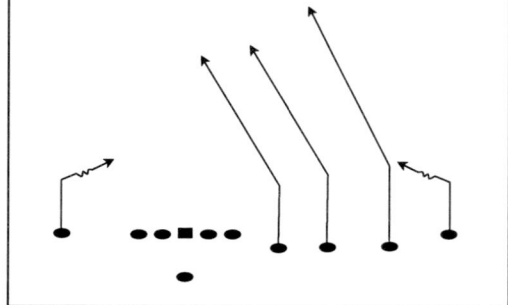

Figure 2-10. Double-slant route in a 4 x 1 set

Play #9: The Wheel-Route Tag

The wheel tag is used primarily versus teams that consistently play man-to-man, but it can also be used versus zone teams that use their cornerbacks to help defend on quick routes. The wheel tag is used for the inside receiver. His technique will be to sell the shoot route for five steps and then turn the route up the sideline.

The quarterback will pick a side of the defense, catch the snap, and pump fake to the receiver lined up to the side he picked. The quarterback's footwork is again critical to the success of the play. After his pump fake, he will set his feet and throw the ball. It's important for the quarterback to set his feet and throw the ball quickly. A common error of the quarterback is to take a three-step drop after the pump fake. A three-step drop makes for a longer throw and gives the defense more time to react to the double move.

On the wheel tag, versus man-to-man defense, the quarterback will read the defender over the inside receiver. If the defense has covered the wheel, the quarterback can come back down to the slant-sit route.

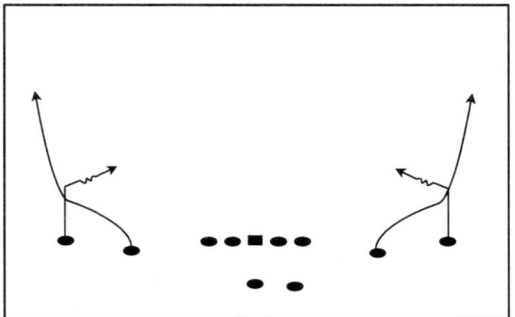

Figure 2-11. Slant route with a wheel tag in a 2 x 2 set

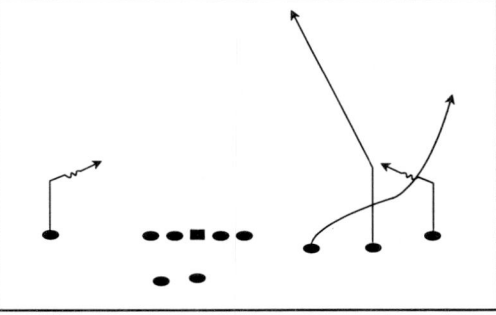

Figure 2-12. Slant route with a wheel tag in a 3 x 1 set

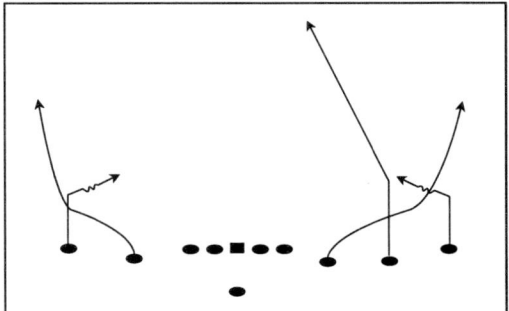

Figure 2-13. Slant route with a wheel tag in a 3 x 2 set

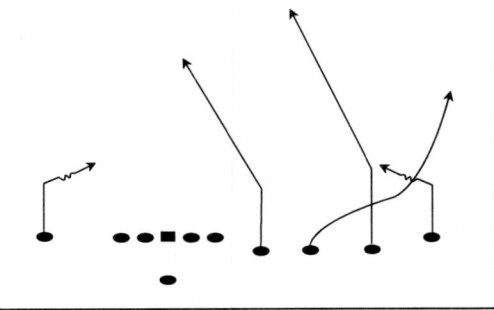

Figure 2-14. Slant route with a wheel tag in a 4 x 1 set

Play #10: The Slant Route With a Switch Tag

The switch tag tells the #1 and #2 receivers to exchange routes. In 2 x 2 sets, this would put the outside receiver on an out route and the inside receiver on a slant-sit route, as shown in Figure 2-15.

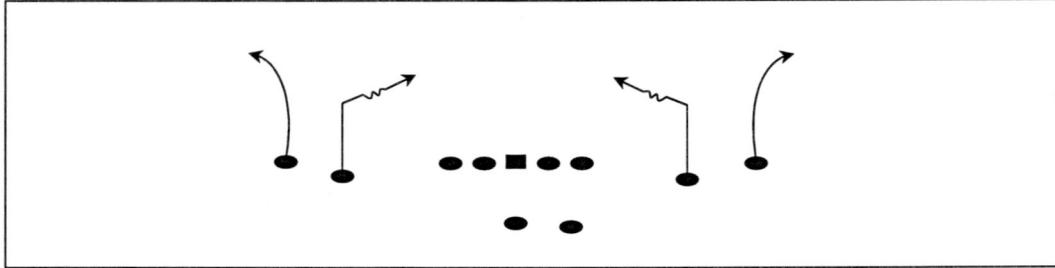

Figure 2-15. Slant route with a switch tag in a 2 x 2 set

The switch tag can be used to give the quarterback a quick and easy throw to the outside receiver in a 2 x 2 set, or it can give him a quick read of the #2 defender in 3 x 1 or 3 x 2 sets. The switch tag is a good choice versus a cover 4.

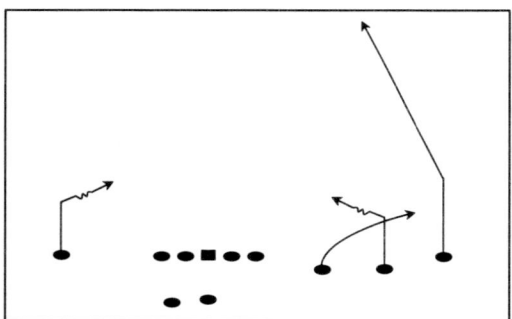

Figure 2-16. Slant route with a switch tag in a 3 x 1 set

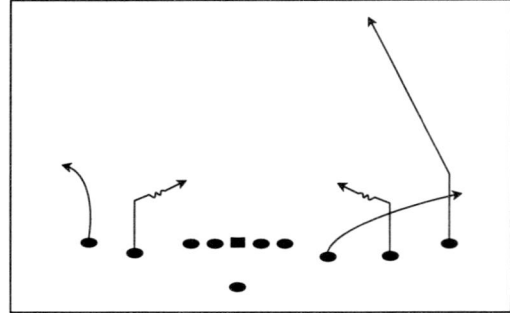

Figure 2-17. Slant route with a switch tag in a 3 x 2 set

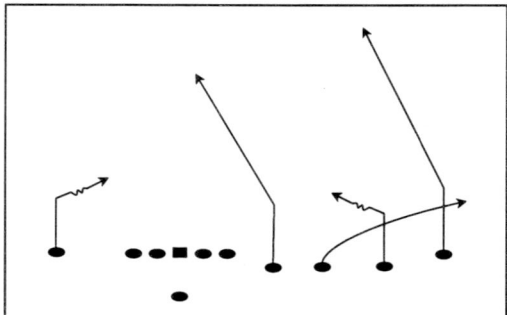

Figure 2-18. Slant route with a switch tag in a 4 x 1 set

Play #11: The Slant Route With a Swap Tag

The swap tag tells the #2 and #3 receivers to exchange routes. A swap tag in a 3 x 1 or a 3 x 2 set to the three-receiver side would put the inside receiver on a seam route and the middle receiver on a shoot route.

The swap call doesn't change anything for the quarterback. He will still read the #2 defender, and he will read the reaction of the #2 defender as he would in the base-slant route. The tag does make the read quicker for the quarterback, and it helps keep the #3 defender away from the read.

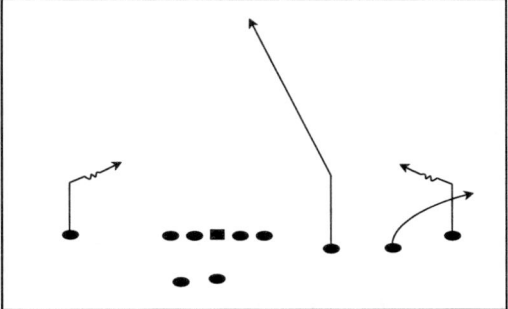

Figure 2-19. Slant route with a swap tag in a 3 x 1 set

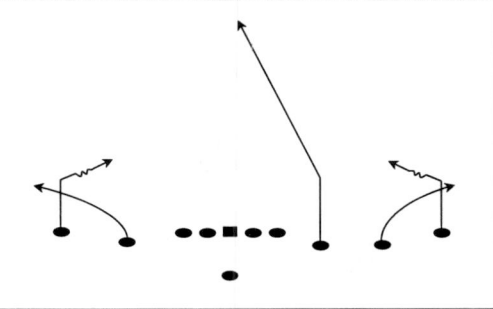

Figure 2-20. Slant route with a swap tag in a 3 x 2 set

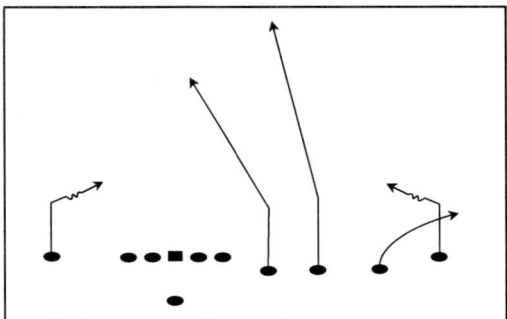

Figure 2-21. Slant route with a swap tag in a 4 x 1 set

Play #12: The Slant Route With a Bubble Tag

The bubble tag tells the receiver that has the shoot route to run a bubble route instead. All other cuts on the route are the same as the base-slant route.

The bubble tag is read by the quarterback just like the normal slant route. However, it is called more often versus man-to-man defenses in order to get a more open throw for the slant route.

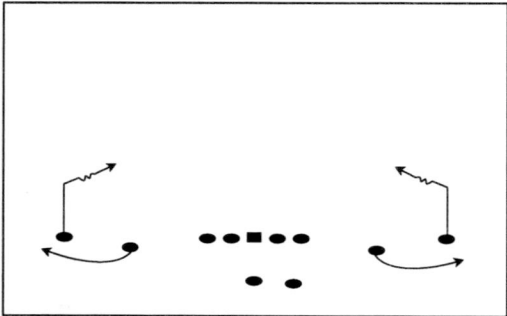

Figure 2-22. Slant route with a bubble tag out of a 2 x 2 set

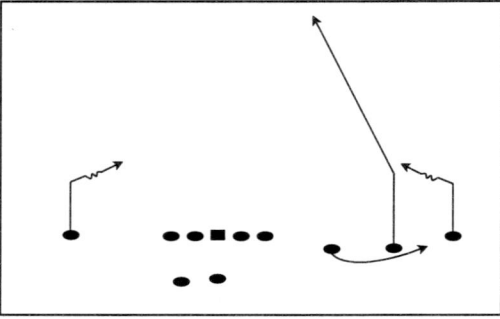

Figure 2-23. Slant route with a bubble tag out of a 3 x 1 set

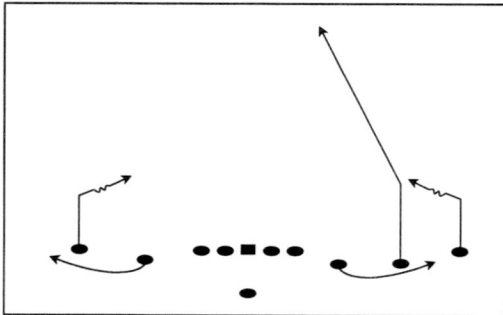

Figure 2-24. Slant route with a bubble tag out of a 3 x 2 set

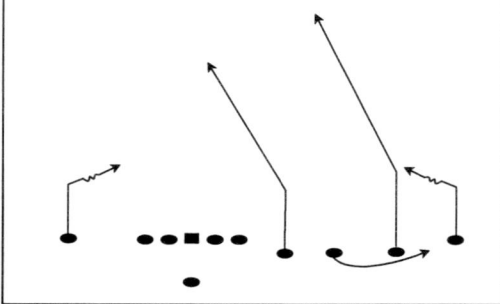

Figure 2-25. Slant route with a bubble tag out of a 4 x 1 set

3

Out Routes

Introduction

Like many of the quick-passing routes, the quarterback will pick a side of the formation to which he will throw the ball. His decision is based on finding the shortest throw that is the most open. He makes this decision pre-snap.

Play #13: The Out Route

The out route has proven to be a very successful route with a high completion percentage. The quarterback will still look for the shortest, most open route before the snap. He will expect to throw the ball to the inside receiver, especially in a 2 x 2 set. If the out route is taken away, the quarterback can redirect to the vertical route by the outside receiver.

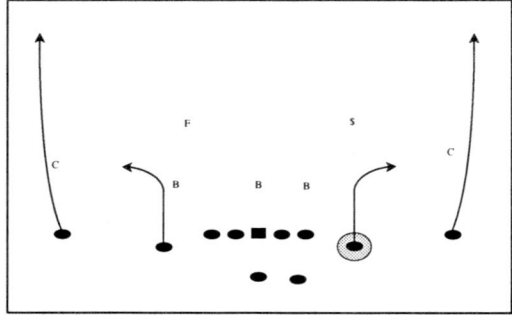

Figure 3-1. Quarterback identifies the easiest completion in a 2 x 2 set.

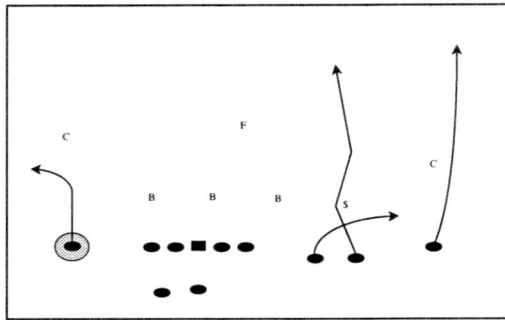

Figure 3-2. Quarterback identifies the easiest completion in a 3 x 1 set.

The outside receivers will release outside and go vertical. The only time they should get the ball on this play will be versus a cover 2 zone. When playing against a cover 2 zone, the outside receivers need to start to coast on their route at 12 to 15 yards in order to give the quarterback the best angle to get the ball to them.

In a 2 x 2 set, the inside receivers will run a four-step speed out. They will drive three hard steps, and on the fourth step, they will take a 45-degree step to the outside. Their fifth step should be parallel to the line of scrimmage. The inside receivers should expect the ball right out of their break. When playing against man-to-man defense, the receivers will each make a stick cut after leaning against the defender. This is a mirrored route in all 2 x 2 sets.

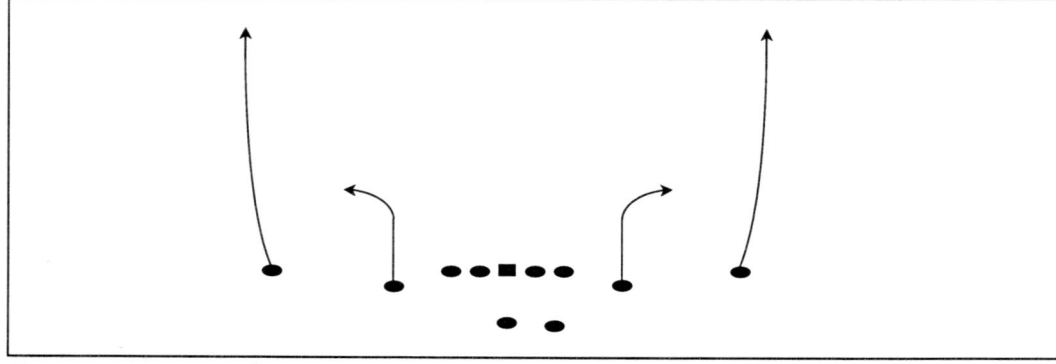

Figure 3-3. Out route in a 2 x 2 set

In a 3 x 1, 3 x 2, or 4 x 1 set, the routes by the inside receivers change. To the three-receiver side, the middle receiver will run a rub-vertical route. His technique is to angle inside, to rub the first defender inside of him, and then to release downfield, attempting to gain his original alignment width before he gets to 10 yards. The inside receiver will run the same route he does on the slant route, a shoot. On the backside, the single receiver will run the four-step speed out. The #4 receiver will run the four-step slant as shown in Figure 3-6.

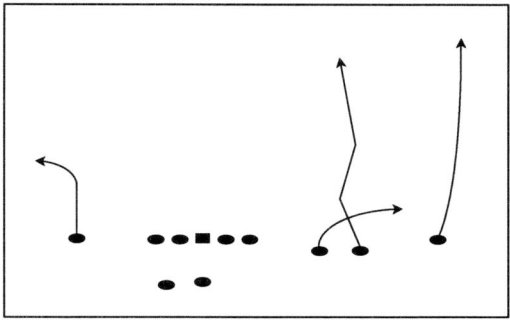

Figure 3-4. Out route in a 3 x 1 set

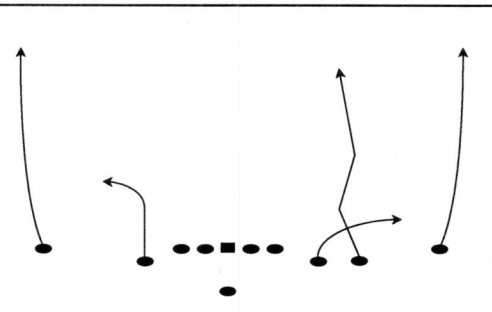

Figure 3-5. Out route in a 3 x 2 set

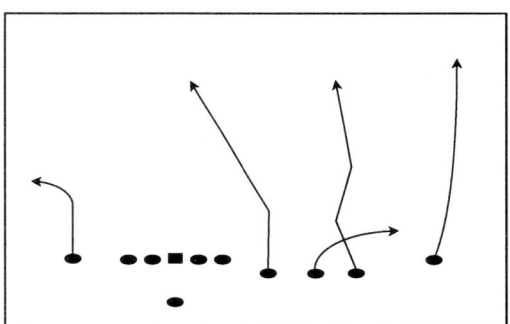

Figure 3-6. Out route in a 4 x 1 set

The out route can be run out of several different formations within the spread offense, including 2 x 2 sets, 3 x 1 sets, 3 x 2 sets, and 4 x 1 sets. The route can be used to attack any coverage faced.

Play #14: The Double-Out Route Tag

On the double out, the quarterback will pick a side and read the route outside in. All receivers run the four-step speed-out route. This route is good to attack man-to-man defenses as well as a cover 3 zone or a cover 4 zone.

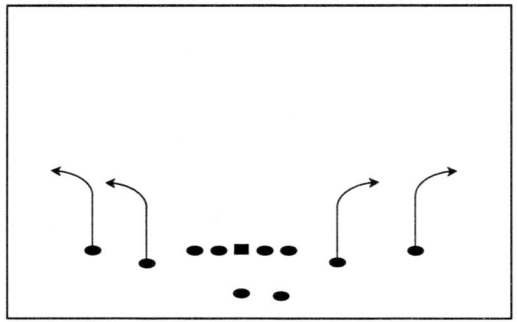

Figure 3-7. Double out route in a 2 x 2 set

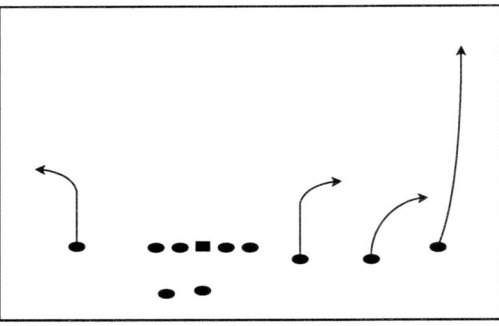

Figure 3-8. Double out route in a 3 x 1 set

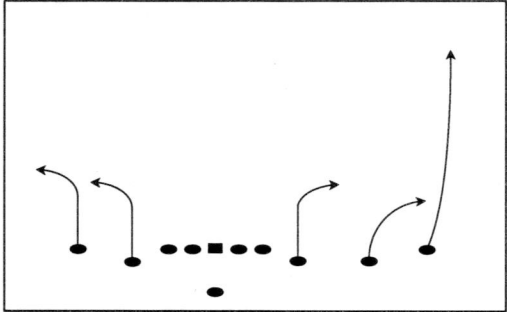

Figure 3-9. Double out route in a 3 x 2 set

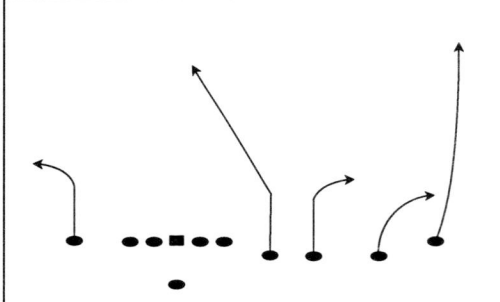

Figure 3-10. Double out route in a 4 x 1 set

Play #15: The Out Route With a Curl Tag

The curl tag is good for attacking a team that is driving hard on the out routes. The tag is also good for attacking man-to-man teams on the three-receiver side, as it provides a natural rub.

The curl tag tells the first receiver lined up outside of the out route to run a curl. The curl route is preceded by a rub. Many times defenders get confused as receivers cross paths and leave one receiver uncovered. The first receiver inside the curl tag will adjust his route from a four-step speed out, to a shoot route.

On the curl tag, the quarterback will read the defender over the receiver that will run the shoot route. If the quarterback can complete the shoot route, he will throw there. If the defense jumps the shoot route, the quarterback will redirect to the curl route.

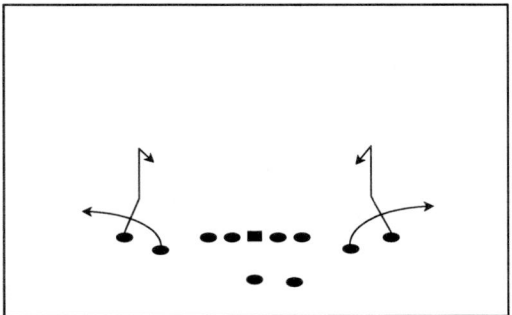

Figure 3-11. Out route with a curl tag in a 2 x 2 set

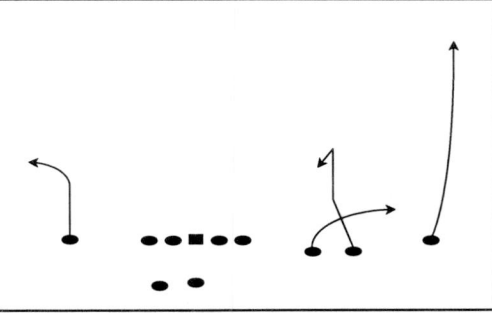

Figure 3-12. Out route with a curl tag in a 3 x 1 set

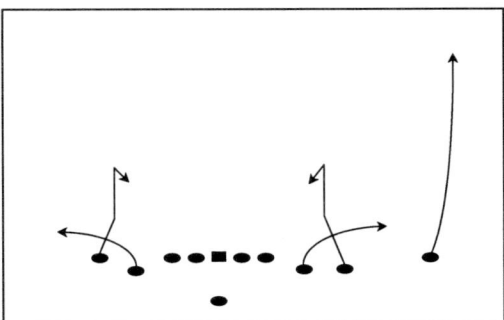

Figure 3-13. Out route with a curl tag in a 3 x 2 set

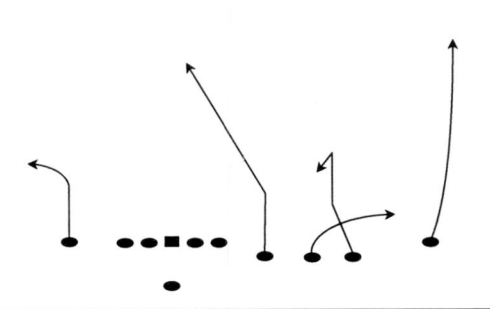

Figure 3-14. Out route with a curl tag in a 4 x 1 set

Play #16: The Out Route With a Switch Tag

The switch tag is used primarily versus man-to-man defenses, but it is also good for attacking a cover 2 zone as well as a cover 4 zone. The switch tag exchanges the routes of the #1 and the #2 receivers. The one rule for receivers to remember on this tag is to exchange the landmark of the route, not just the cut.

The outside receiver will shrink his alignment and run the four-step speed out route. The inside receiver will run a corner route. His break will be at seven yards, and he will aim 25 yards deep at the sideline. The quarterback will read the #1 defender, and he will think outside in on this route.

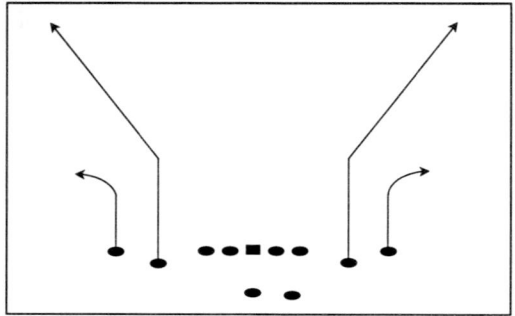

Figure 3-15. Out route with a switch tag in a 2 x 2 set

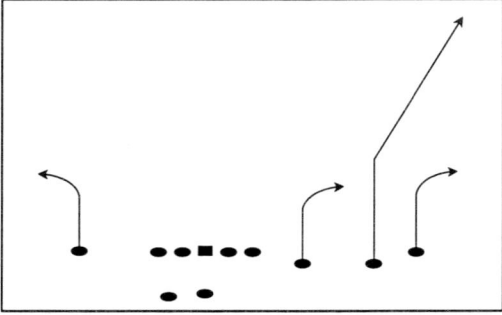

Figure 3-16. Out route with a switch tag in a 3 x 1 set

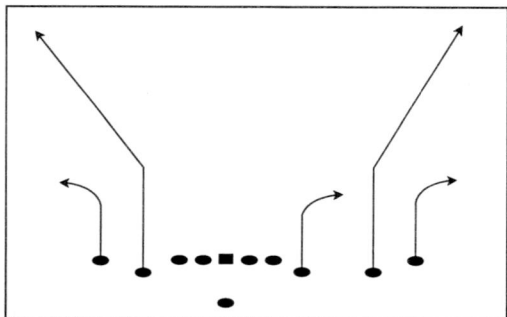

Figure 3-17. Out route with a switch tag in a 3 x 2 set

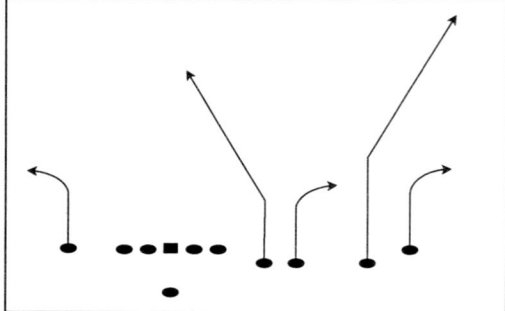

Figure 3-18. Out route with a switch tag in a 4 x 1 set

Play #17: The Out Route With a Switch-Seam Tag

The switch-seam tag is used to hold the safety away from the read of the quarterback. The route can be used just like the switch tag, but the seam makes it safer for the quarterback to attack the #1 defender.

The inside receiver will run a seam route on this tag. All other receiver techniques are identical to the switch tag.

The quarterback will read the switch seam tag just like the switch tag. He will read the #1 defender and think outside in.

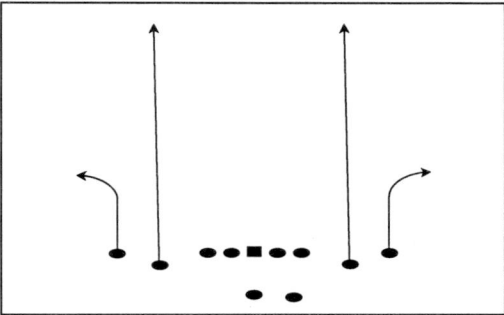

Figure 3-19. Out route with a switch-seam tag in a 2 x 2 set

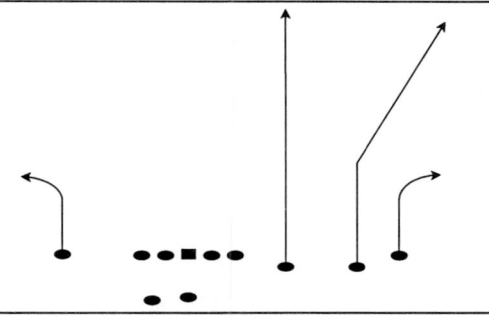

Figure 3-20. Out route with a switch-seam tag in a 3 x 1 set

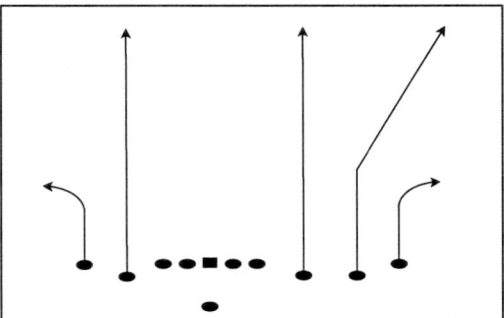

Figure 3-21. Out route with a switch-seam tag in a 3 x 2 set

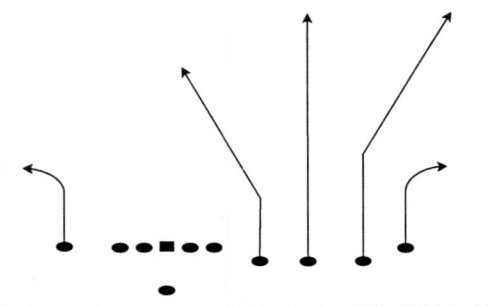

Figure 3-22. Out route with a switch-seam tag in a 4 x 1 set

Play #18: The Out Route in a Bunch Set

Lining up in a bunch set is another way to run the out route. When running the out route out of the bunch set, the receivers only need to remember their landmarks for their regular out route. The quarterback will read the defender over the shoot route. The out route can also be given a curl tag from a bunch set.

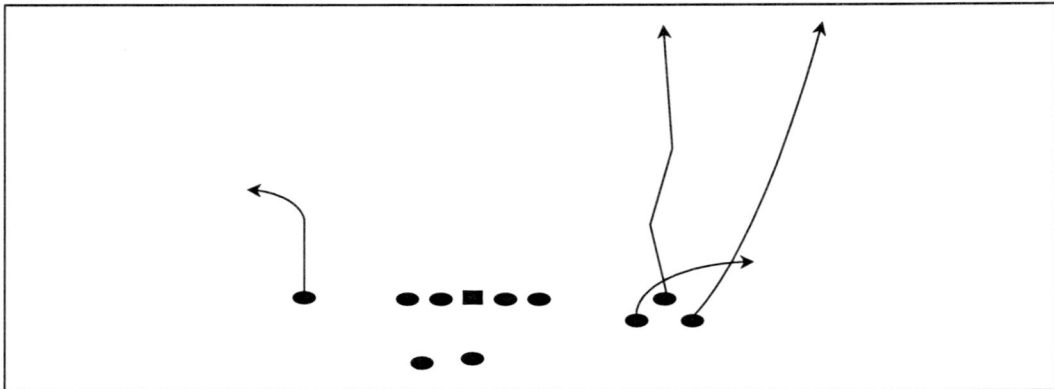

Figure 3-23. Out route in a 3 x 1 bunch set

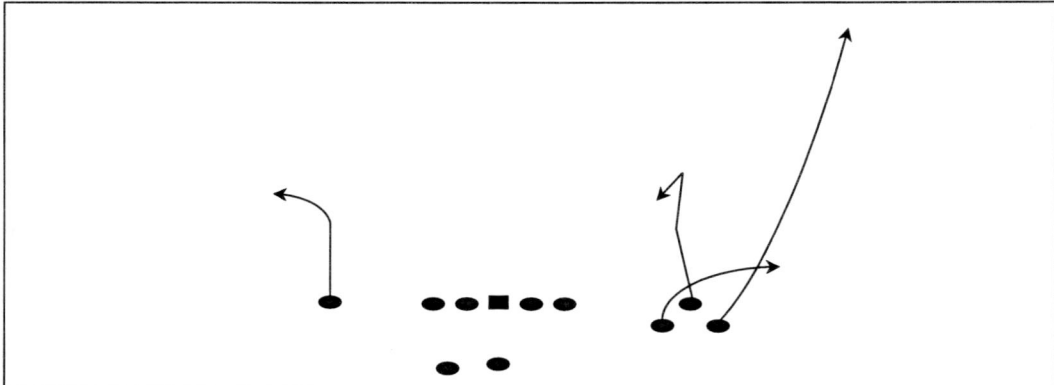

Figure 3-24. Out route with a curl tag in a 3 x 1 bunch set

4

Under Routes

Introduction

As with all quick routes, the quarterback will pick a side of the formation to which he will throw the ball. His decision is based on finding the shortest throw that is the most open. He makes this decision pre-snap.

Play #19: The Under Route

The under route is a non-traditional way to attack the #2 defender. It has proven to be a very efficient route versus man or zone defenses. If the quarterback is disciplined in his read of the #2 defender, it makes the offense "right" every time.

After the ball is snapped, the quarterback will read the #2 defender to the side of the formation that gives him the best opportunity for a completion. He wants to make the defender wrong. If the defender backpedals or holds his pre-snap alignment, the quarterback will throw the ball to the inside receiver on the shoot route. If the defender drives downhill on the shoot route of the #2 receiver, or works for width, the quarterback will pause momentarily and then throw to the outside receiver on the under route.

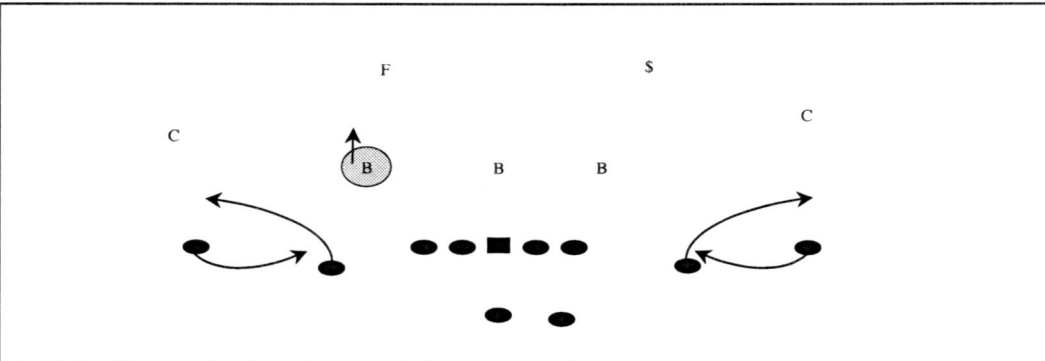

Figure 4-1. The quarterback reads the #2 defender and should throw to the rub-shoot route.

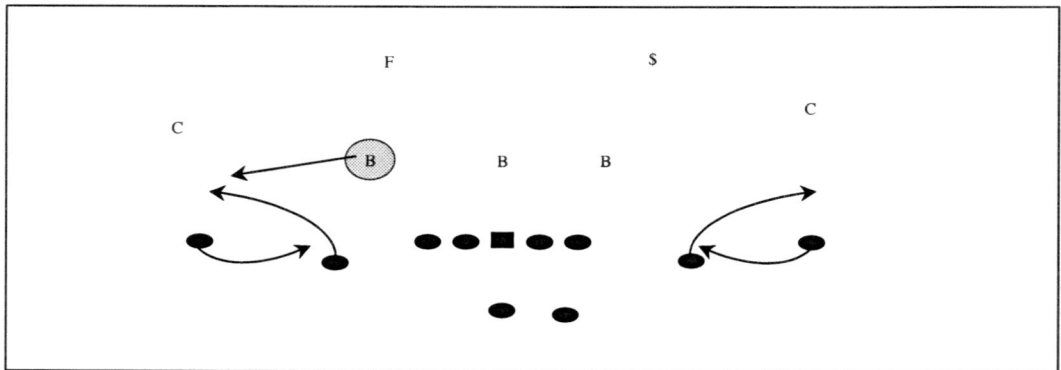

Figure 4-2. The quarterback reads the #2 defender and should throw the ball to the under route.

The outside receivers will simply open up, come inside, and start to work up the field when they reach the feet of the next receiver inside them. The inside receivers will run a rub-shoot route, which is to drive one step forward, then bend to the outside and accelerate to the sideline. The receiver needs to try to run through the defender covering the flat zone. The receiver needs to look over his outside shoulder after his third step. His route should gradually build up to a depth of five yards.

This route is a mirrored route, with modifications for three and four-receiver sides of the formation, as shown in Figures 4-4, 4-5, and 4-6. On a three-receiver side, the inside receiver runs a seam route. On a four-receiver side, the inside receiver runs a four-step slant, and the next receiver out still has the seam route. The under route can be run out of several different formations within the spread offense, including 2 x 2 sets, 3 x 1 sets, 3 x 2 sets, and 4 x 1 sets.

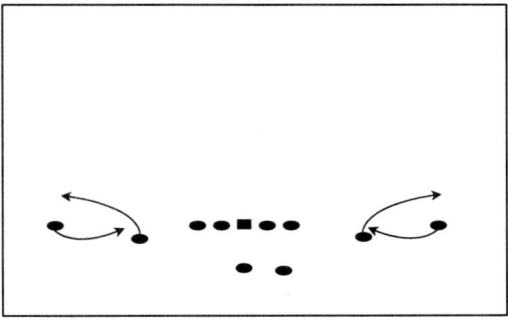

Figure 4-3. Under route in a 2 x 2 set

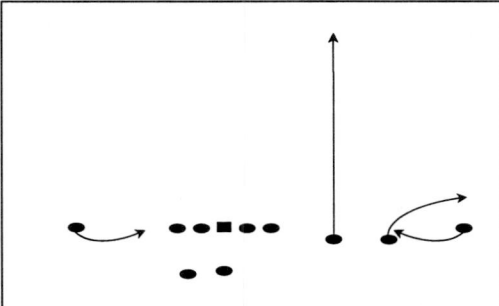

Figure 4-4. Under route in a 3 x 1 set

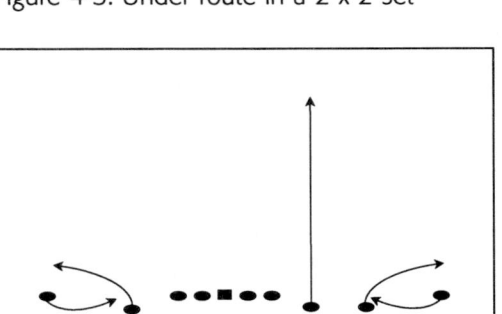

Figure 4-5. Under route in a 3 x 2 set

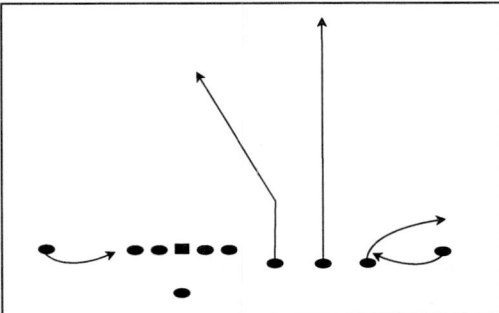

Figure 4-6. Under route in a 4 x 1 set

Play #20: The Under Route With a Follow Tag

The follow tag is used to attack teams that employ man-to-man defenses. It is especially good for attacking man-to-man defenses that bracket or switch when receivers cross each other's paths.

The follow tag only adjusts the receiver running the rub-shoot. This receiver will still run his rub-shoot, but after his fifth step, he will pivot and return back to the inside, following the under route. This route will look like a pick-and-roll in basketball.

The quarterback will initially read this like the regular under route. When he sees both routes covered, he will pause for a second and then trigger the ball to the receiver running the follow route.

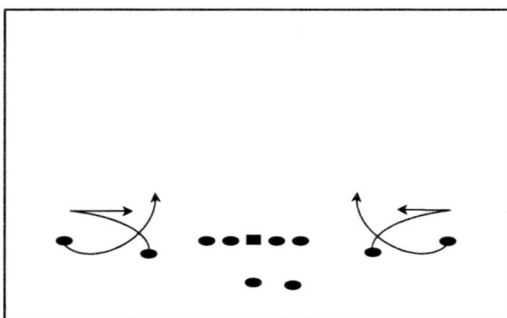

Figure 4-7. Under route with a follow tag in a 2 x 2 set

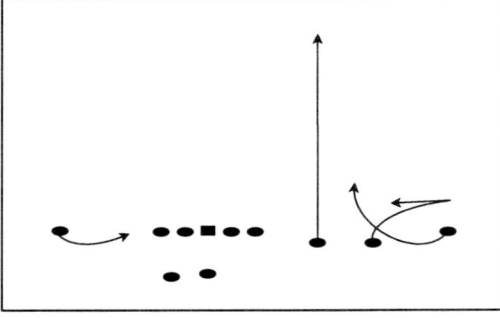

Figure 4-8. Under route with a follow tag in a 3 x 1 set

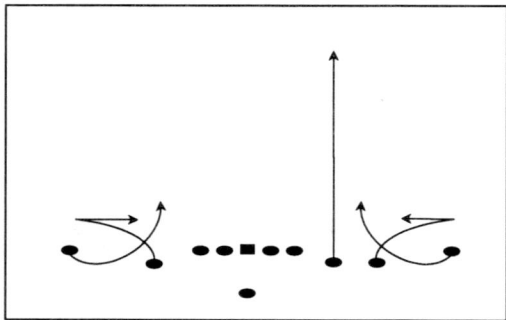

Figure 4-9. Under route with a follow tag in a 3 x 2 set

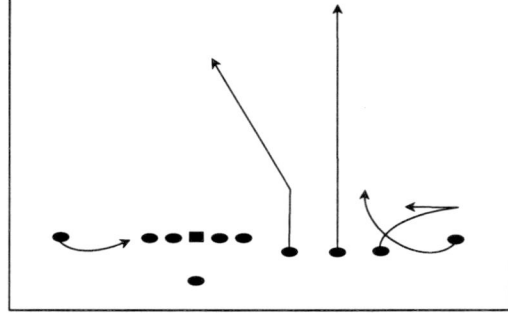

Figure 4-10. Under route with a follow tag in a 4 x 1 set

Play #21: The Under Route With a Wheel Tag

The wheel tag is best to run from a three-receiver side of a formation. It is used to attack man-to-man or cover 2 zone defenses. This route is called versus cover 2 zone when the #1 defender is staying close to the line of scrimmage and covering the rub-shoot route.

The wheel tag tells the receiver that is running the rub-shoot to turn the shoot up the sideline, just like the wheel tag in the slant route. The wheel runner needs to avoid contact as he turns up the field.

The quarterback will read the defender over the rub-shoot first and then the #1 defender. If the quarterback can throw the ball to the under, he will. If he is covered, then he will throw to the wheel route.

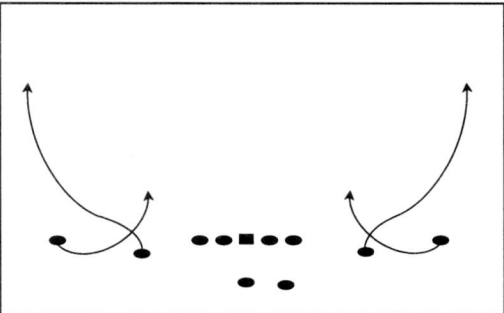

Figure 4-11. Under route with a wheel tag in a 2 x 2 set

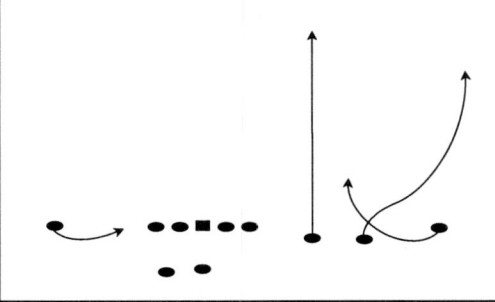

Figure 4-12. Under route with a wheel tag in a 3 x 1 set

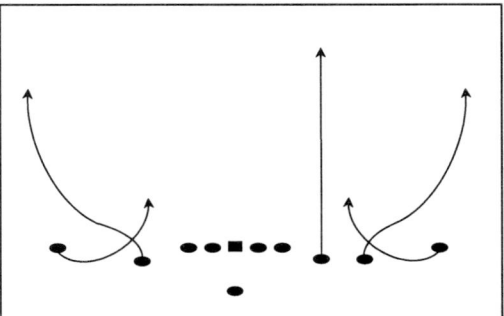

Figure 4-13. Under route with a wheel tag in a 3 x 2 set

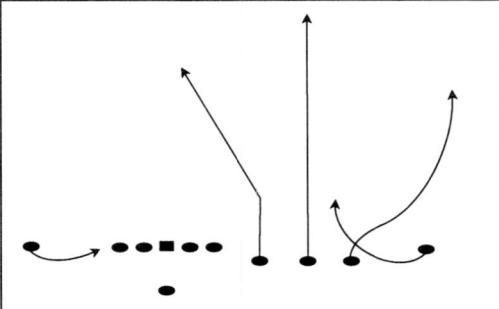

Figure 4-14. Under route with a wheel tag in a 4 x 1 set

Play #22: The Under Route With a Switch Tag

The switch tag is used primarily versus teams that play cover 4 zone defense. The switch tag tells the #1 and #2 receivers to exchange routes. This change puts the #1 receiver on the rub-shoot route and the #2 receiver on the under route.

The quarterback will read the defender over the seam route on any three-receiver side of the formation. If this defender backpedals at all, the quarterback will throw to the under route. If the defender does anything else, the quarterback will throw to the seam. In any two-receiver side of the formation, the quarterback can throw to the outside receiver on the rub-shoot route, reading the #1 defender.

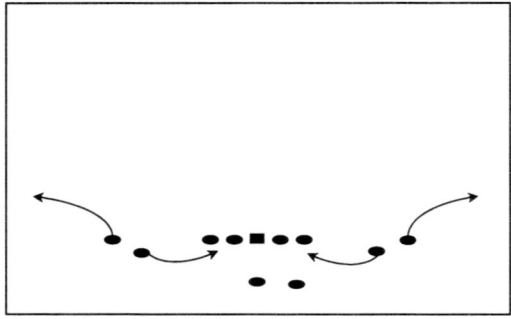

Figure 4-15. Under route with a switch tag in a 2 x 2 set

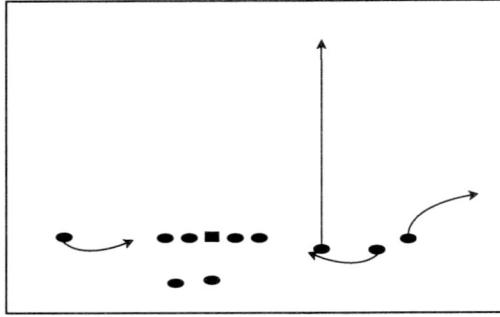

Figure 4-16. Under route with a switch tag in a 3 x 1 set

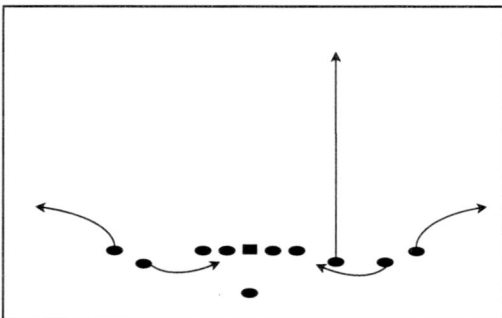

Figure 4-17. Under route with a switch tag in a 3 x 2 set

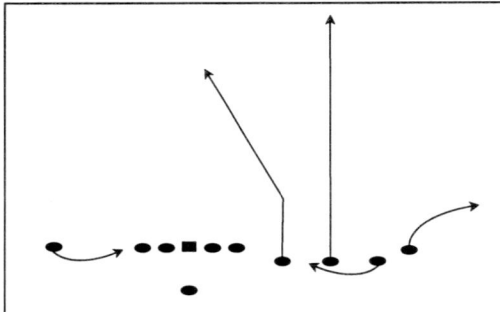

Figure 4-18. Under route with a switch tag in a 4 x 1 set

Play #23: The Under Route With a Swap Tag

The swap tag is a good change-up to the base under route. It attacks the recognition of the defense after the snap. The swap tag tells the #2 and #3 receivers to exchange routes. This change puts the #2 receiver on the seam route and the #3 receiver on the rub-shoot route. The quarterback read is identical to the base under route. The only difference is that the read happens a little slower, as the rub-shoot route is farther away from the under.

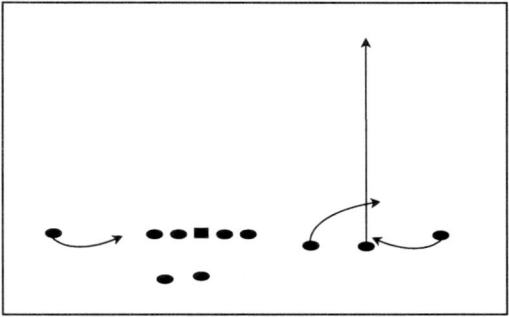

Figure 4-19. Under route with a swap tag in a 3 x 1 set

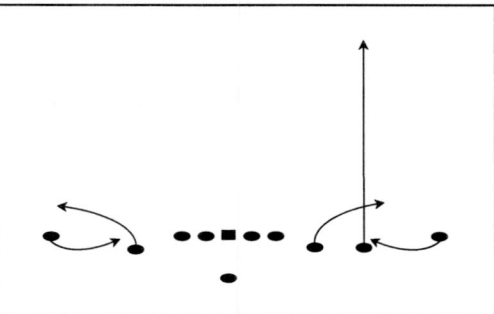

Figure 4-20. Under route with a swap tag in a 3 x 2 set

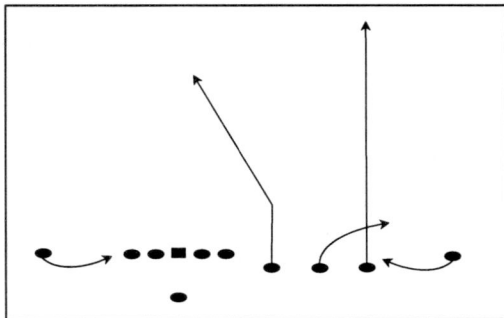

Figure 4-21. Under route with a swap tag in a 4 x 1 set

Play #24: The Under Route With a Corner Tag

The corner tag allows the offense to read the #1 defender. It is a good adjustment to a team that is able to cover the under and the rub-shoot with their #1 and #2 defenders.

The only adjustment for the receivers is the seam route. The tag tells this receiver to run a corner route. He will push vertically for seven yards and then break to the corner, aiming 25 yards deep at the sideline.

The read for the quarterback is to read the #1 defender. If he is holding to cover the rub-shoot route, he is leaving the corner route open. If he backpedals at the snap, then the quarterback has to throw to the rub-shoot route. The quarterback will read this route inside out.

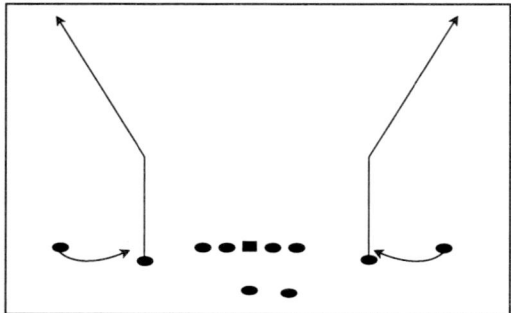

Figure 4-22. Under route with a corner tag in a 2 x 2 set

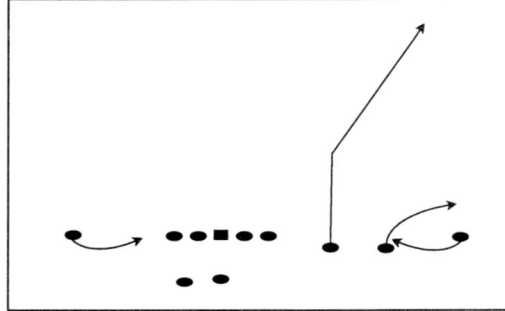

Figure 4-23. Under route with a corner tag in a 3 x 1 set

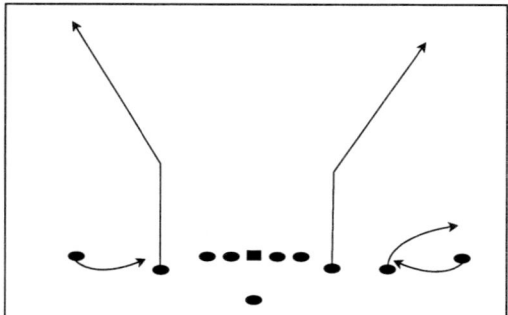

Figure 4-24. Under route with a corner tag in a 3 x 2 set

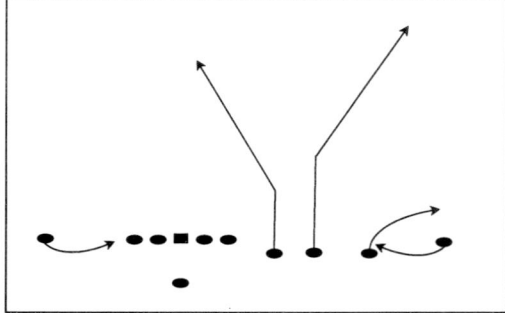

Figure 4-25. Under route with a corner tag in a 4 x 1 set

Play #25: The Under Route With an Individual Tag

On the individually-tagged route, the tagged receiver runs the under route, and the receivers inside of the tagged receiver run the rub-shoot and seam routes. The receiver outside the tagged receiver runs a vertical route.

The quarterback will read the defender over the receiver running the rub-shoot. If that defender gets width at the snap, the quarterback will throw to the under route. If he doesn't, the quarterback will throw to the rub-shoot route.

This route is good for attacking a defense that has a really good corner, but whose interior pass defenders aren't as strong. This route is also good for attacking man-to-man defenses.

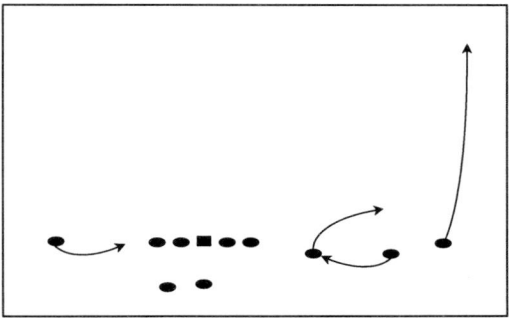

Figure 4-26. Individually tagged under route in a 3 x 1 set

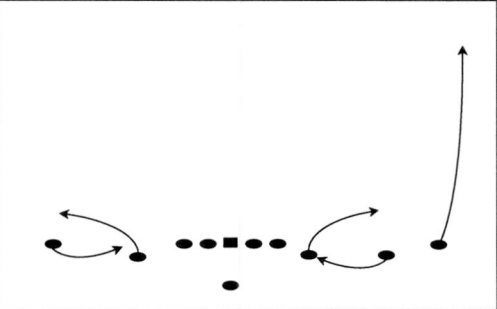

Figure 4-27. Individually tagged under route in a 3 x 2 set

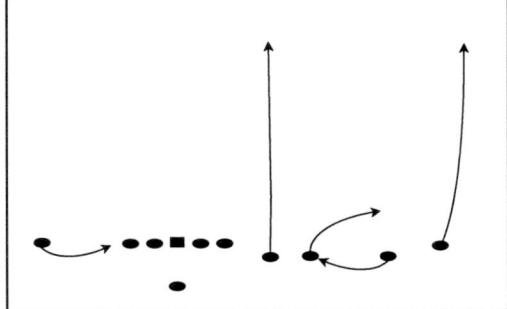

Figure 4-28. Individually tagged under route in a 4 x 1 set

5

In Routes

Introduction

Like many of the quick-passing routes, the quarterback will pick a side of the formation to which he will throw the ball. His decision is based on finding the shortest throw that is the most open. He makes this decision pre-snap.

Play #26: The In Route

The in route has become a very good way to attack cover 2 zone and man-to-man defenses. Like the other quick-pass routes, the quarterback will pick a side to read and stay with that side. After the ball is snapped, the quarterback will read the #2 defender to the side of the formation that gives him the best opportunity for a completion. He wants to make the defender wrong. If the defender sits or gains width, the quarterback will throw the ball to the inside receiver on the slant route. If the defender backpedals, the quarterback will pause momentarily and then throw to the outside receiver on the in route.

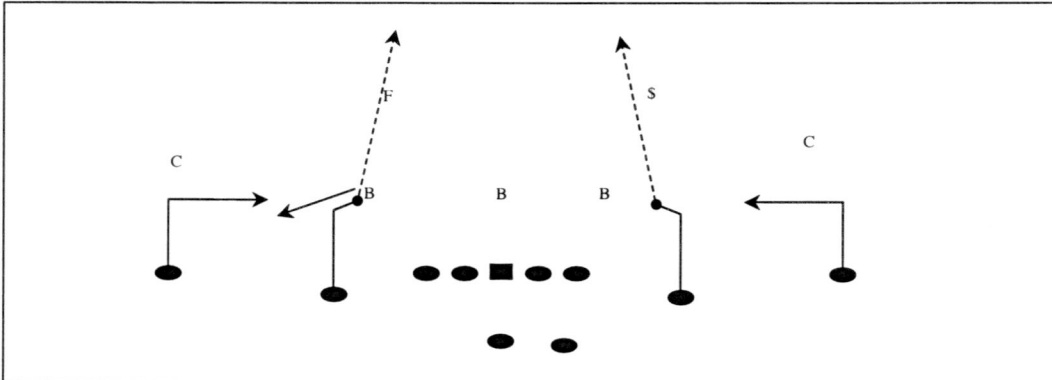

Figure 5-1. The quarterback reads the #2 defender and should throw to the slant route.

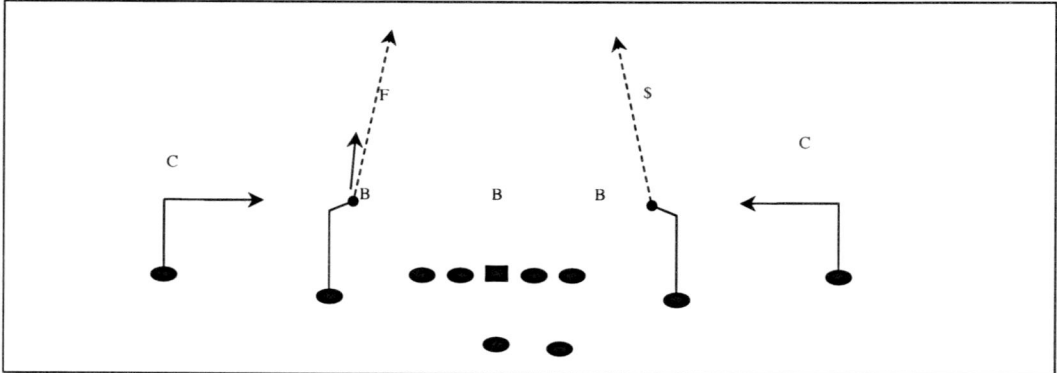

Figure 5-2. The quarterback reads the #2 defender and should throw the ball to the in route.

The inside receivers run a four-step slant route. The route will look more like a seam route versus man-to-man defenses. Versus zone defenses, it will look like the slant-sit route used by the outside receiver on the slant package. The outside receivers will run a four-step in route. When the receiver gets to his fourth step, he will plant and drive inside, parallel to the line of scrimmage.

The in route is mirrored in any 2 x 2 set, as seen in Figure 5-3. When the in route is used in 3 x 1 or 3 x 2 sets, a good rule is to have the inside receivers landmark the hash marks to balance out their spacing. The in route can be run out of several different formations within the spread offense, including 2 x 2 sets, 3 x 1 sets, and 3 x 2 sets.

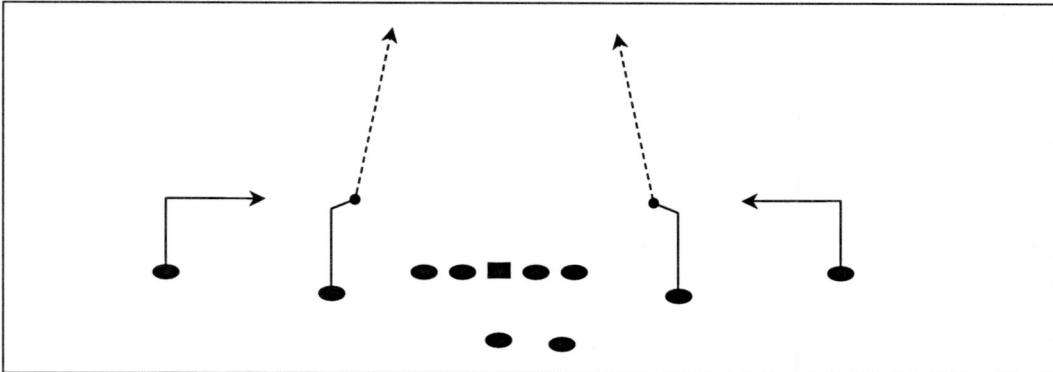

Figure 5-3. In route in a 2 x 2 set

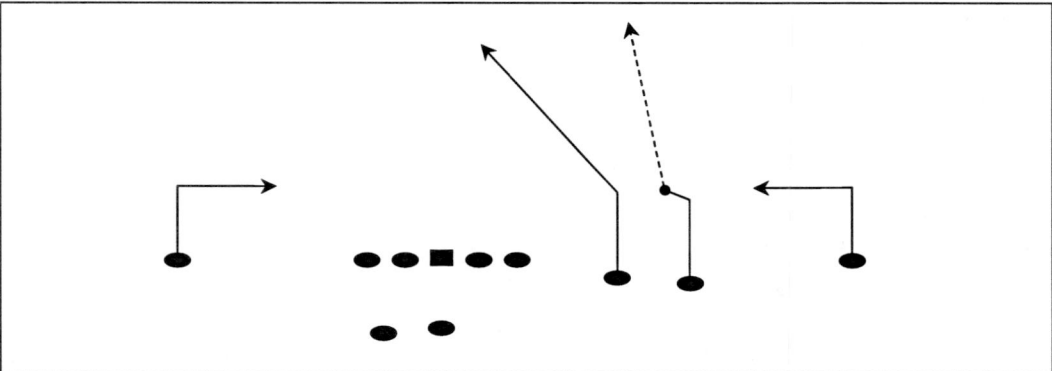

Figure 5-4. In route in a 3 x 1 set

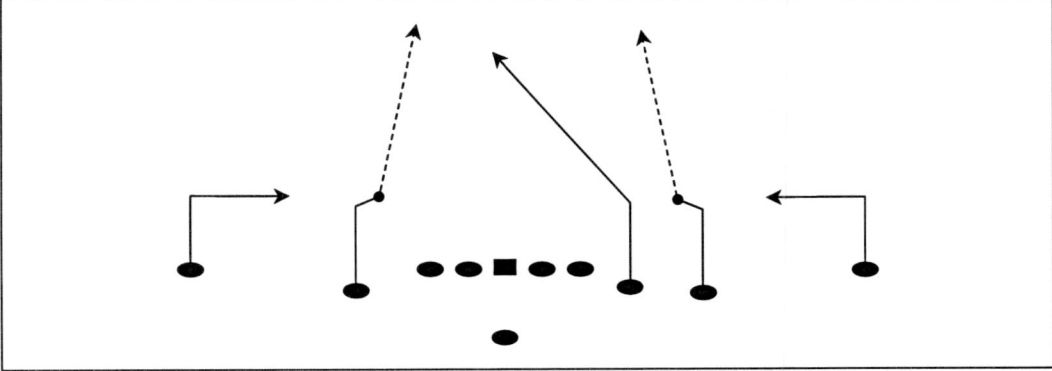

Figure 5-5. In route in a 3 x 2 set

Play #27: The Under Route With a Corner Tag

The corner tag is a great way to attack man-to-man defenses as well as cover 2 zone defenses. This route has proven to be a good red zone and goal line route.

The corner tag tells each of the inside receivers to run a corner route and make his break at seven yards deep. The receivers will then aim their route to be 25 yards deep on the sideline. Against man-to-man defenses, the tagged receiver needs to beat the defender to the outside before making the corner cut.

On the corner tag, versus man-to-man defense, the quarterback will read the defender over the tagged receiver. He will throw the ball to a spot that is midway between the two nearest defenders. This throw will be within five yards of the sideline. Versus cover 2 zone defense, the quarterback will read the #1 defender. If the #1 defender drives on the in route by the outside receiver, the quarterback will throw the corner route. If the #1 defender backpedals at the snap and continues to gain depth, the quarterback will throw the in route to the outside receiver.

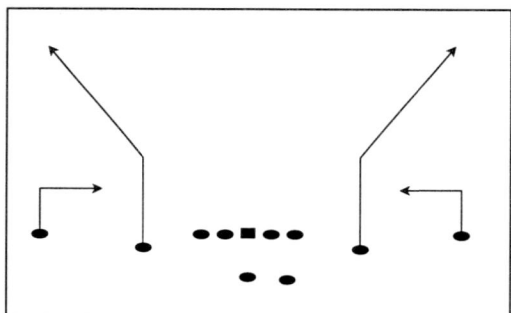

Figure 5-6. In route with a corner tag in a 2 x 2 set

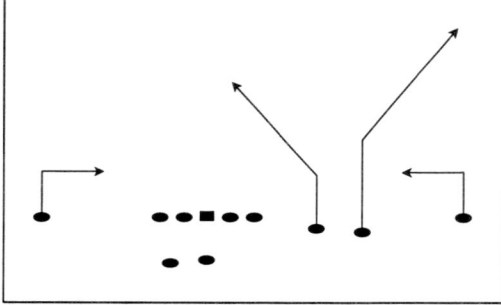

Figure 5-7. In route with a corner tag in a 3 x 1 set

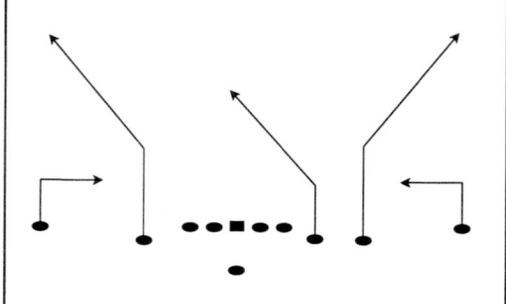

Figure 5-8. In route with a corner tag in a 3 x 2 set

Play #28: The In Route With a Seam Tag

The seam tag is used versus cover 3 zone teams, cover 4 zone teams, and man-to-man defensive teams when the #1 defenders are playing too deep in their coverage to defend the in route by the outside receiver. This route is used just like the seam tag in the hitch package.

The seam tag tells the inside receivers to run a seam route, landmarking the hash marks to their respective sides. In a 3 x 1 set, both inside receivers will run vertical routes, with the #2 receiver landmarking the near hash and the inside receiver landmarking the opposite hash. The outside receivers run the same in routes, as their cuts are unaffected by the seam tag. The outside receivers should expect the ball on the seam tag, as they become the primary receiver to their side of the formation.

When the seam tag is called, it is expected that the in route to the outside receiver will be an easy completion, so the pre-snap read for the quarterback is the depth of the #1 defender. Once the ball has been snapped, the quarterback will then read the #2 defender. If the #2 defender can get under the in route by the outside receiver before the quarterback can get the ball to the in route, the quarterback has to throw to the seam route. If the #2 defender doesn't work to get under the in route by the outside receiver, the quarterback will then throw to the outside receiver on the in route.

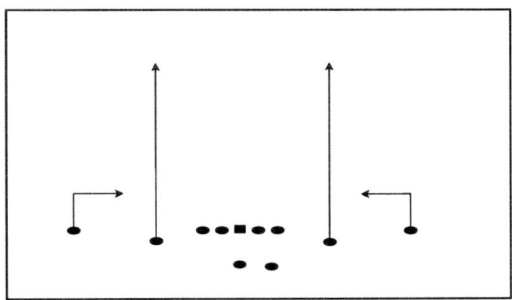

Figure 5-9. In route with a seam tag in a 2 x 2 set

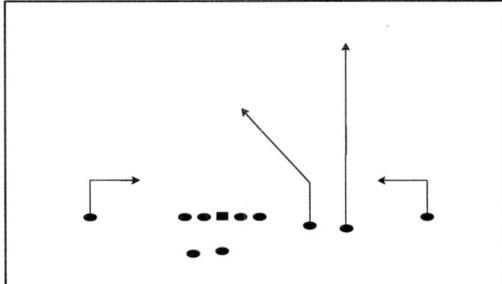

Figure 5-10. In route with a seam tag in a 3 x 1 set

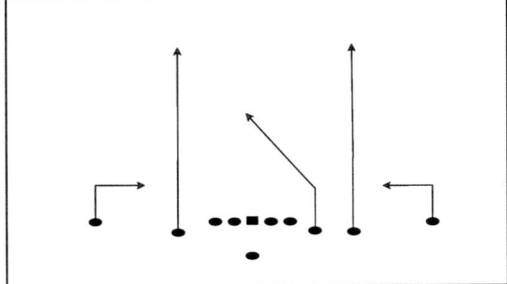

Figure 5-11. In route with a seam tag in a 3 x 2 set

Play #29: The In Route With a Dig Tag

The dig tag is used primarily versus teams that play cover 4 zone or cover 2 zone defenses. On this route, the #2 receiver will adjust his route to a dig route at ten yards deep. The receiver will drive vertically to ten yards and then break flat and to the inside. If there are three receivers on a side of a formation, the #3 receiver will landmark the opposite hash mark. The quarterback will read this tag just like the basic in route. The only difference is that this tag gives him the opportunity to throw to the inside receiver a second later.

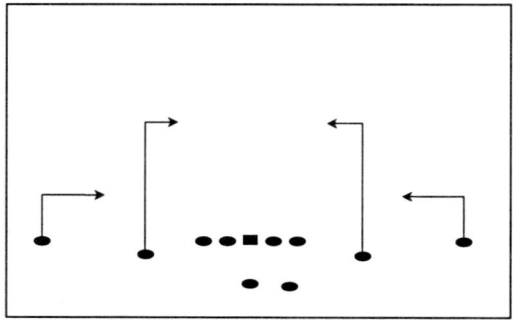

Figure 5-12. In route with a dig tag in a 2 x 2 set

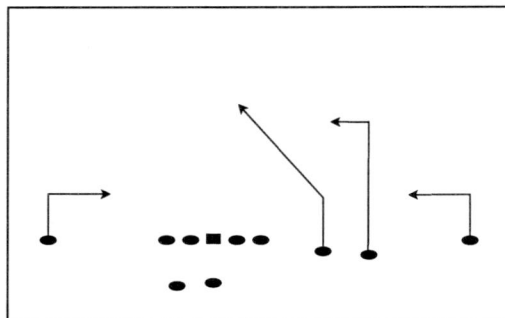

Figure 5-13. In route with a dig tag in a 3 x 1 set

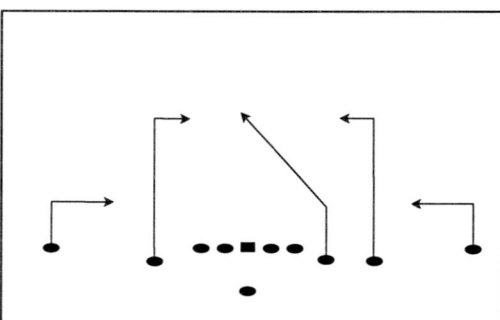

Figure 5-14. In route with a dig tag in a 3 x 2 set

6

Spacing Routes

Introduction

The spacing route gives the play caller the ability to call any quick route to a single receiver. It also has the backside receivers run slower developing routes to which the quarterback can throw if the single-receiver route is covered.

The backside receivers will run modified hitch routes to maximize the space between each other and to slow down their route completion to time up for the quarterback. The outside receiver will run his normal hitch route, but he will angle his route outside. He will want to finish his route five yards from the sideline. The #2 receiver will run his hitch route to 10 yards directly up the field. The #3 receiver will run his hitch route inside. He would like to hook up five yards deep in front of the near offensive tackle. If there is a fourth receiver, he will run the four-step slant.

The quarterback's completion percentage will be greatly increased by identifying the defense before the snap. Recognizing the defense will help him anticipate to which side of the formation the football should go. See Figures 6-1 and 6-2.

After the ball is snapped, the quarterback will look to the single receiver first every time. If the single receiver is open, the quarterback will deliver the football on time. If the single receiver is covered, the quarterback will pivot, open up to the backside, and identify his receivers, working inside out. He will deliver the football to the first open receiver that he identifies.

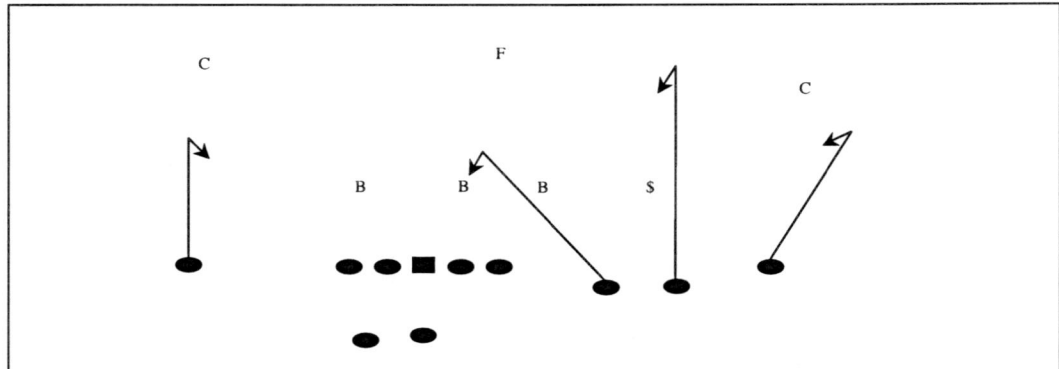

Figure 6-1. The defense is overrotated to the trips side.

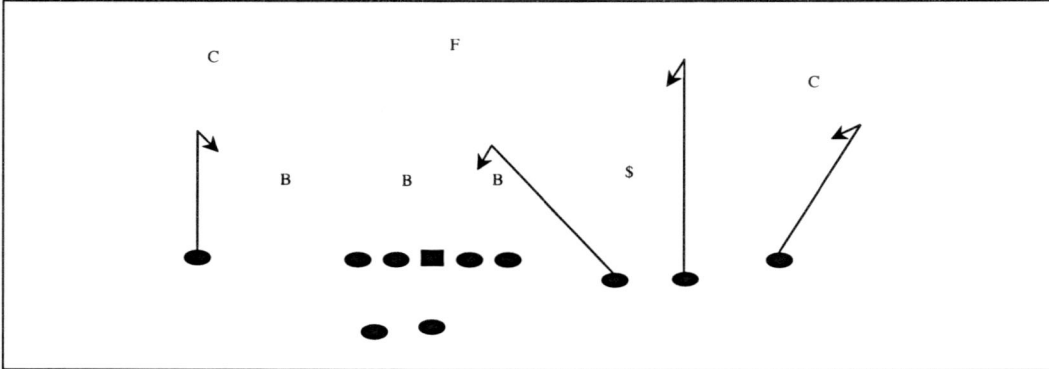

Figure 6-2. The defense is in a 2-on-1 advantage with the single receiver.

Play #30: The Hitch Route With Backside Spacing Routes

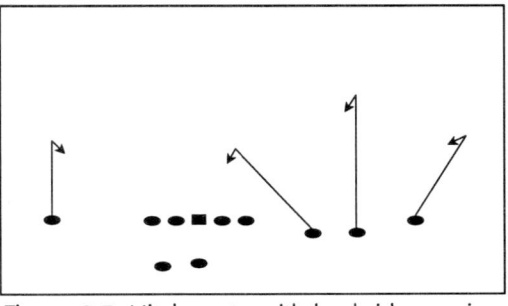 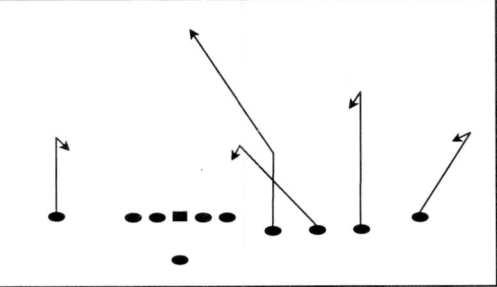

Figure 6-3. Hitch route with backside spacing routes in a 3 x 1 set

Figure 6-4. Hitch route with backside spacing routes in a 4 x 1 set

Play #31: The Out Route With Backside Spacing Routes

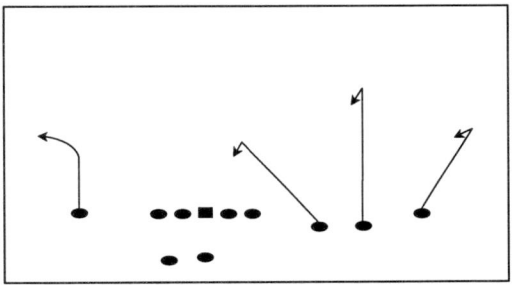 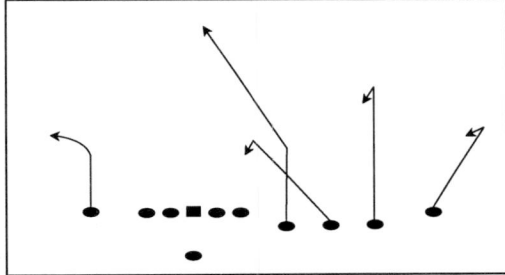

Figure 6-5. Out route with backside spacing routes in a 3 x 1 set

Figure 6-6. Out route with backside spacing routes in a 4 x 1 set

Play #32: The Slant Route With Backside Spacing Routes

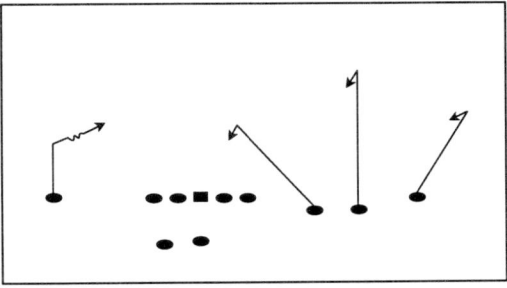 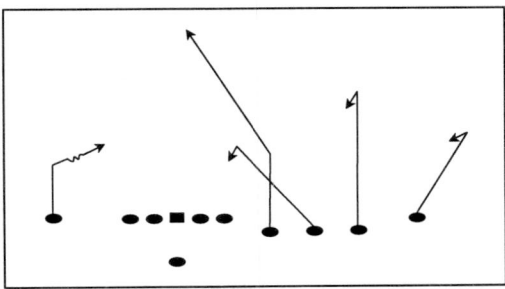

Figure 6-7. Slant route with backside spacing routes in a 3 x 1 set

Figure 6-8. Slant route with backside spacing routes in a 4 x 1 set

Play #33: The Go Route With Backside Spacing Routes

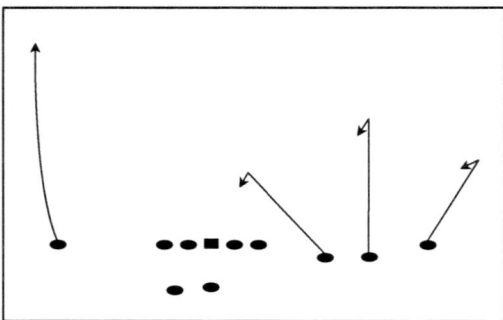

Figure 6-9. Go route with backside spacing routes in a 3 x 1 set

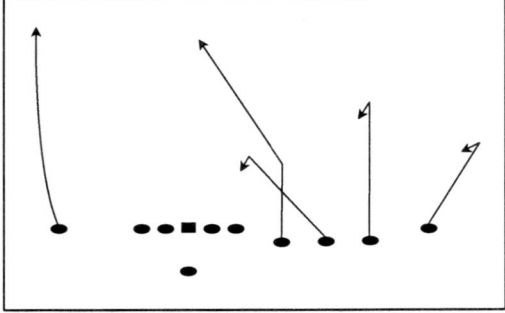

Figure 6-10. Go route with backside spacing routes in a 4 x 1 set

7

Split Calls to Attack Coverage

Introduction

The split call allows you to attack different anticipated coverages by the opponent. If an upcoming opponent plays man-to-man coverage 75% of the time and plays cover 3 zone the rest of the time, the split call will allow you to call one quick route to the left side that could beat man-to-man defense and call another quick route to the right side to beat cover 3 zone.

Play #34: The Hitch Route Packaged With the Out Route

Figures 7-1 through 7-5 show different ways to use the hitch package with the out package. After the quarterback picks a side, the reads will remain the same as if the route was called to both sides. The hitch route package is a good cover 3 or cover 4 beater. The out route package is typically used to attack man-to-man or cover 2 zone.

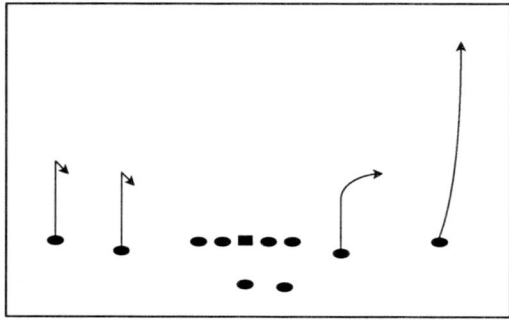

Figure 7-1. Hitch route and out route in a 2 x 2 set

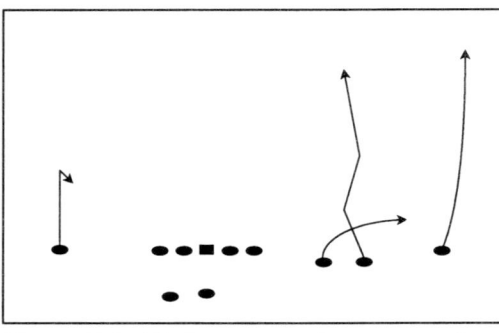

Figure 7-2. Hitch route and out route in a 3 x 1 set

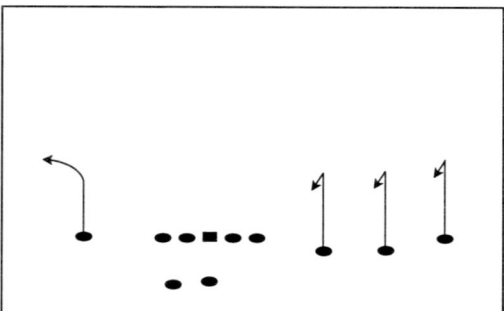

Figure 7-3. Hitch route and out route in a 3 x 1 set

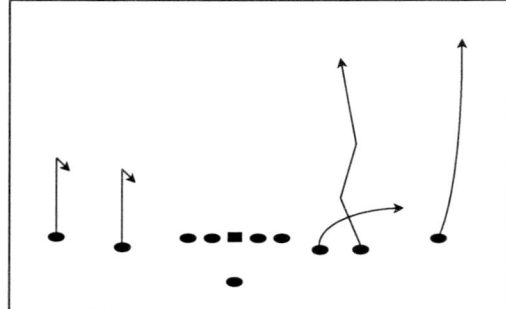

Figure 7-4. Hitch route and out route in a 3 x 2 set

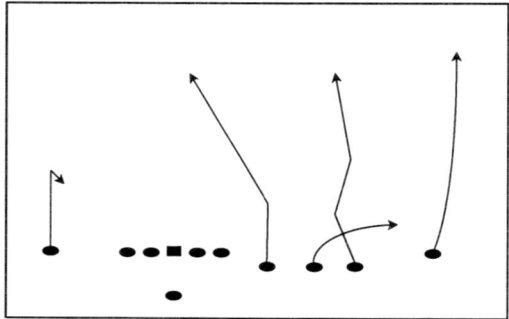

Figure 7-5. Hitch route and out route in a 4 x 1 set

Play #35: The Hitch Route Packaged With the In Route

Figures 7-6 through 7-10 show different ways to use the hitch package with the in package. After the quarterback picks a side, the reads will remain the same as if the route was called to both sides. The hitch route package is a good cover 3 or cover 4 beater. The in route package is typically used to attack man-to-man or cover 2 zone.

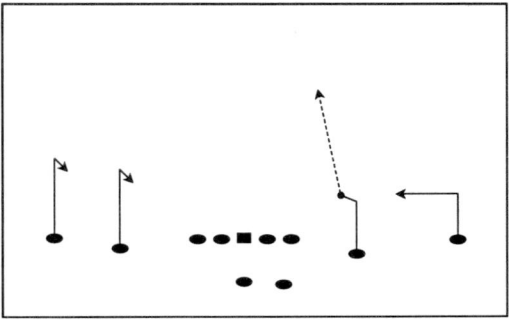

Figure 7-6. Hitch route and in route in a 2 x 2 set

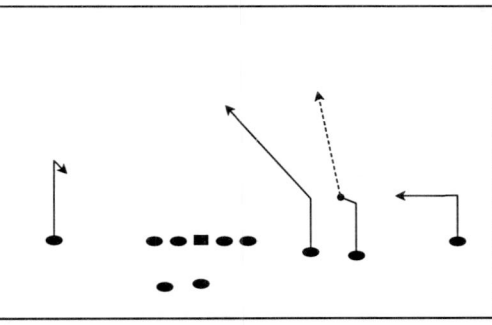

Figure 7-7. Hitch route and in route in a 3 x 1 set

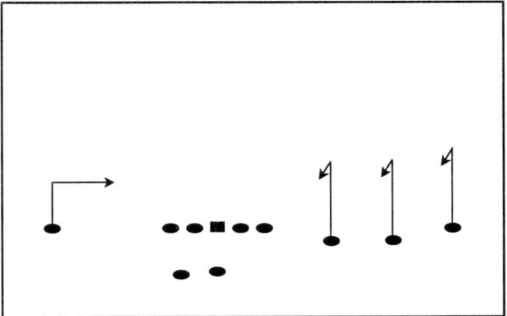

Figure 7-8. Hitch route and in route in a 3 x 1 set

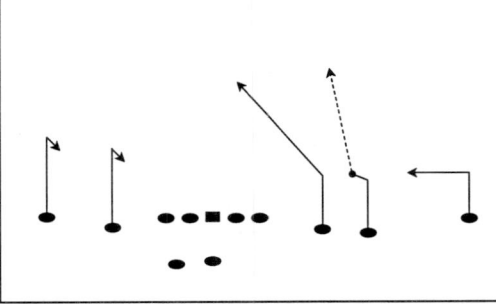

Figure 7-9. Hitch route and in route in a 3 x 2 set

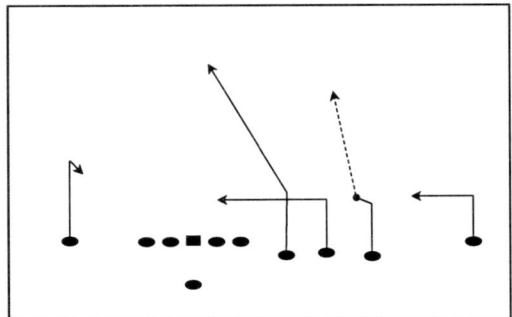

Figure 7-10. Hitch route and in route in a 4 x 1 set

Play #36: The Out Route Packaged With the Under Route

Figures 7-11 through 7-14 show different ways to use the out package with the under package. After the quarterback picks a side, the reads will remain the same as if the route was called to both sides. The out route package is typically used to attack man-to-man or cover 2 zone. The under route package is a good cover 3 or cover 4 beater.

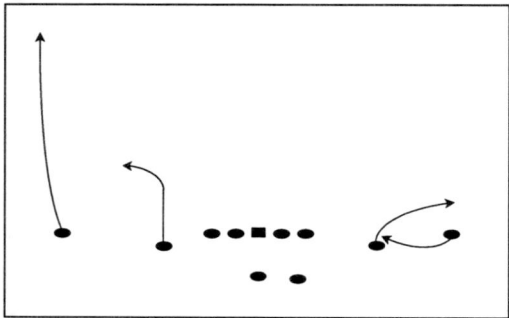

Figure 7-11. Out route and under route in a 2 x 2 set

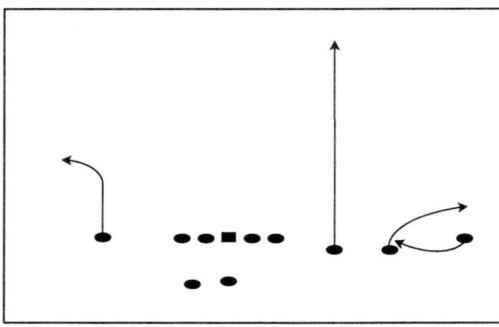

Figure 7-12. Out route and under route in a 3 x 1 set

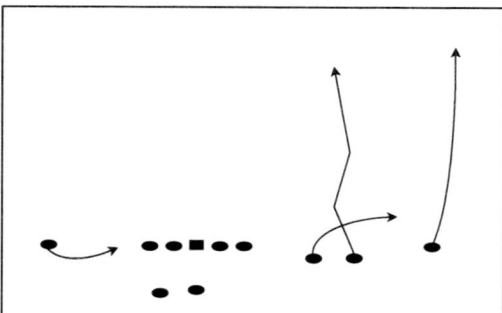

Figure 7-13. Out route and under route in a 3 x 2 set

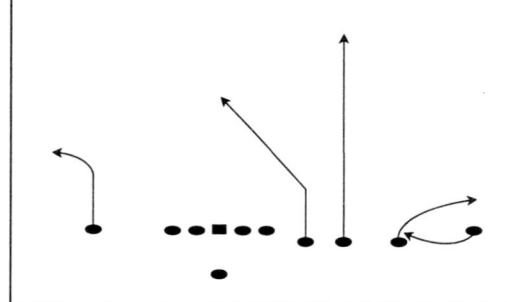

Figure 7-14. Out route and under route in a 4 x 1 set

Play #37: The Slant Route Packaged With the Out Route

Figures 7-15 through 7-19 show different ways to use the slant package with the out package. After the quarterback picks a side, the reads will remain the same as if the route was called to both sides. The slant route package is a good cover 3 or cover 4 beater. The out route package is typically used to attack man-to-man or cover 2 zone.

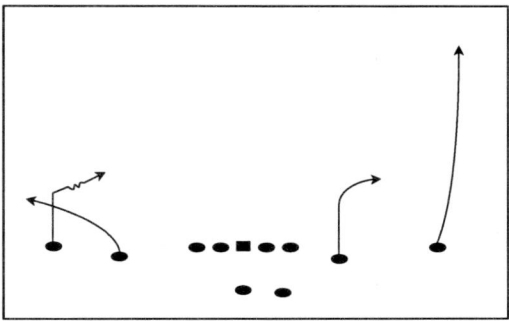

Figure 7-15. Slant route and out route in a 2 x 2 set

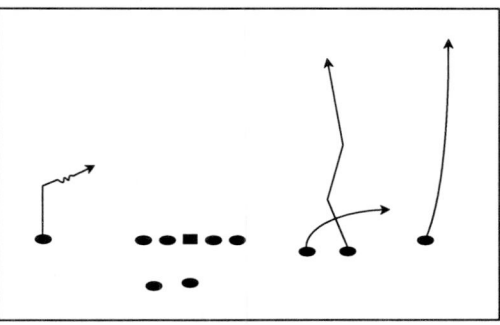

Figure 7-16. Slant route and out route in a 3 x 1 set

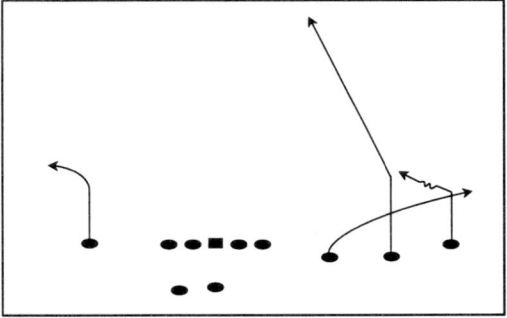

Figure 7-17. Slant route and out route in a 3 x 1 set

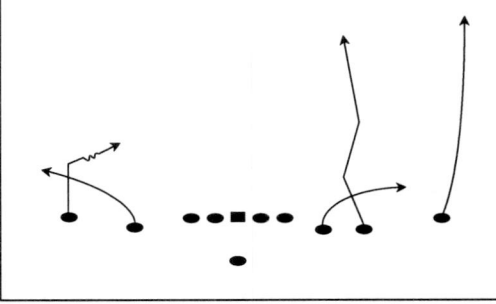

Figure 7-18. Slant route and out route in a 3 x 2 set

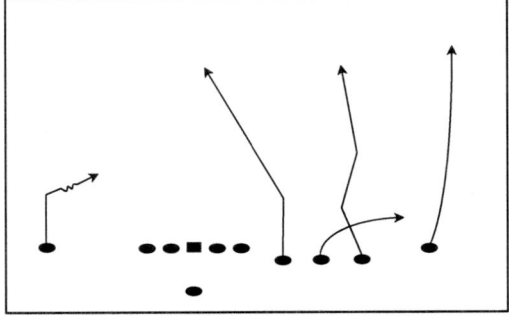

Figure 7-19. Slant route and out route in a 4 x 1 set

Section 2
The Dropback Passing Game

8

Curl Routes

Introduction

The quarterback will need to identify the #3 defender to the strongside of the formation because the #3 defender is the quarterback's first read on the curl play.

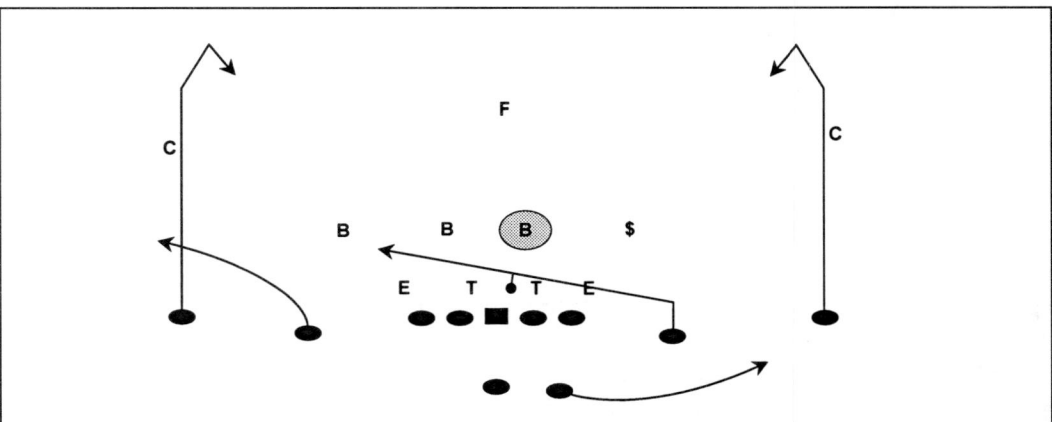

Figure 8-1. Finding the #3 defender

Play #38: The Curl Route

The curl route is one of the oldest and most effective ways to attack cover 3 zone defenses.

The offensive linemen will all take a dropback pass set, which entails the linemen popping up into their pass-protection stance and taking four backpedal steps. The linemen will then stop their momentum to be ready to make a strong wall for pass protection. The technique of the offensive line will not change on any of the dropback pass routes, so pass protection will be limited to this chapter.

On the curl route, the quarterback will read the #3 defender to the strongside of the formation. If the defender walls out the drag route of the strongside inside receiver, the quarterback will move his eyes to the #2 defender and throw to the open receiver based on the movement of the #2 defender. Figure 8-2 shows the wall technique of the #3 defender.

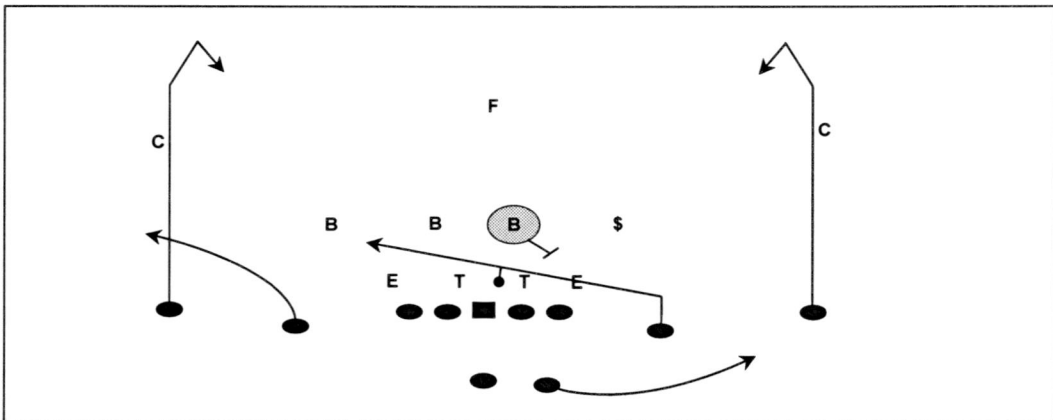

Figure 8-2. Quarterback reading the wall technique of the #3 defender

If the #3 defender reacts to play man-to-man defense on the running back, the quarterback should let the #3 defender clear and then throw to the drag route. Figure 8-3 shows the #3 defender chasing the running back in man-to-man coverage.

The quarterback is also looking for the #3 defender to drop to his curl zone quickly, without trying to collision the drag route. Figure 8-4 shows the #3 defender dropping quickly into zone coverage.

The last reaction the #3 defender can give the quarterback is to blitz the quarterback. In this case, the quarterback will throw to the drag route immediately. Figure 8-5 shows the #3 defender blitzing.

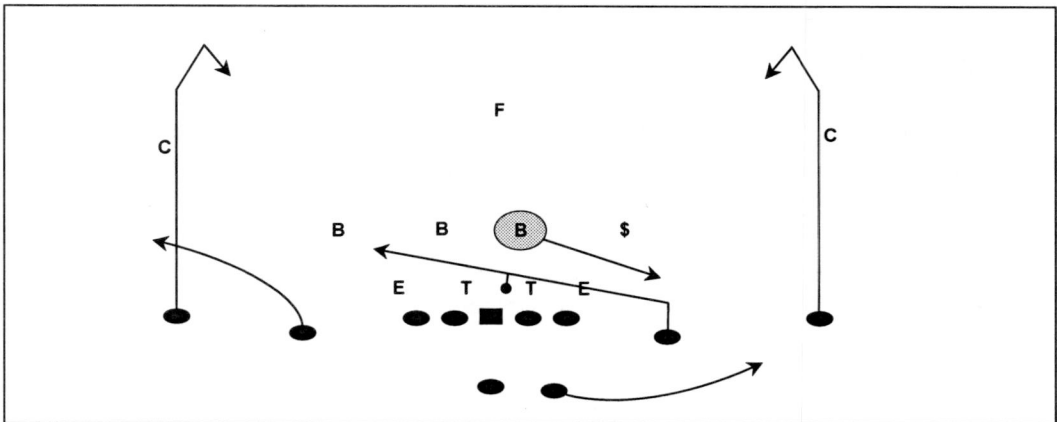

Figure 8-3. Quarterback reading the man-to-man technique of the #3 defender on the back

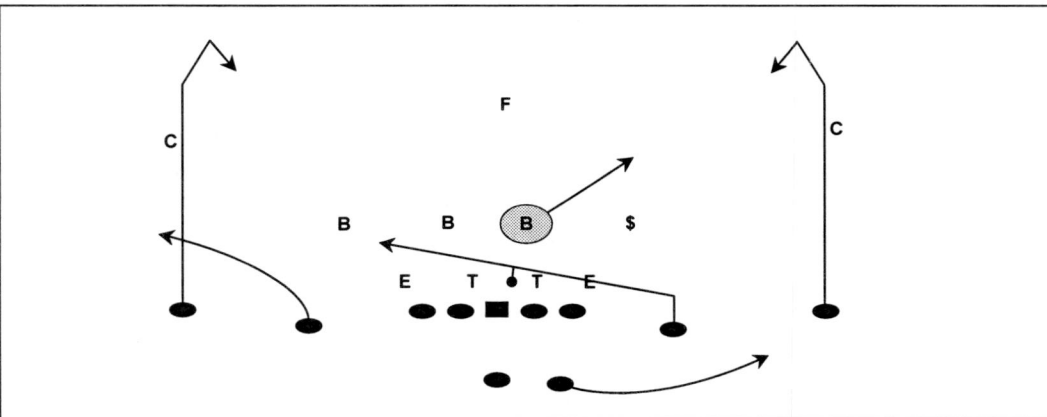

Figure 8-4. Quarterback reading the drop technique of the #3 defender

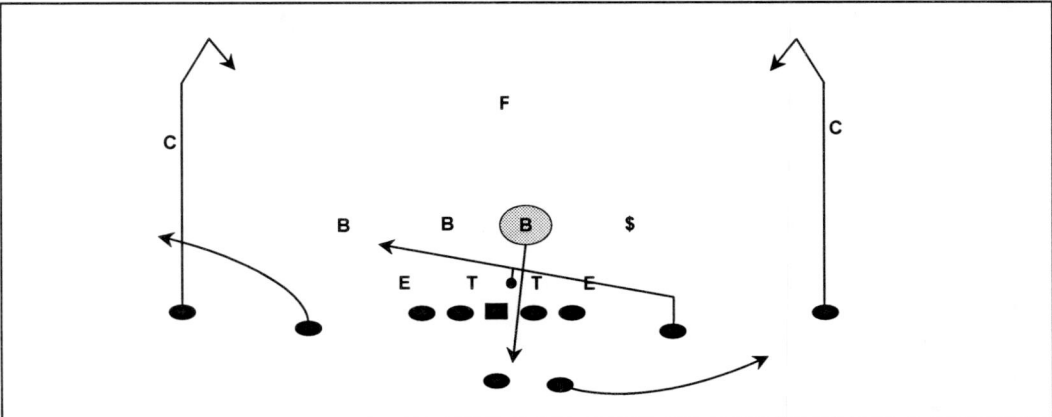

Figure 8-5. Quarterback reading the blitz of the #3 defender

A good rule for the quarterback is to throw the ball to the drag route every time, unless the #3 defender walls the drag route.

If aligned in the backfield, the running back will run a swing route, looking back for the football over his inside shoulder after his third step,. He will follow receiver rules if he is lined up as a receiver.

The outside receivers run post-curl routes, and they will break to the post at eight yards and curl at 12 yards. The outside receivers need to run their routes while keeping their eyes on the #2 defender. If the #2 defender drops for width, the curl route will be more inside. If the #2 defender drops for more depth, the curl route will stay more outside.

The strongside inside receiver will run the drag route. His technique will be to take two steps vertical and then break flat inside. He will need to look for the ball right off of his break. If it's man-to-man defense, he will keep running his route. If it's zone defense, he will settle in the first open area to which he comes, in between the tackles.

The weakside inside receiver will run a shoot route, just like in the slant route package. This route is the same route the #2 receiver will run on any three- or four-receiver sides of the formation. If there is a #4 receiver, he will run a four-step slant route.

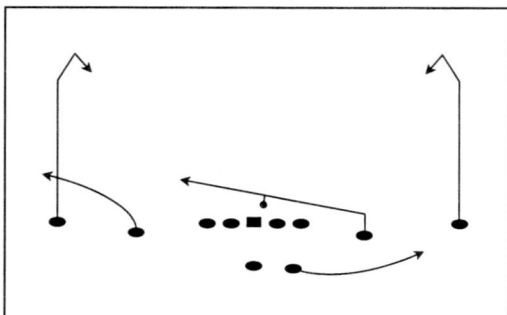

Figure 8-6. Curl route in a 2 x 2 set

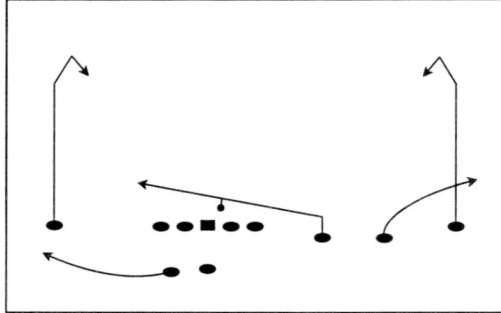

Figure 8-7. Curl route in a 3 x 1 set

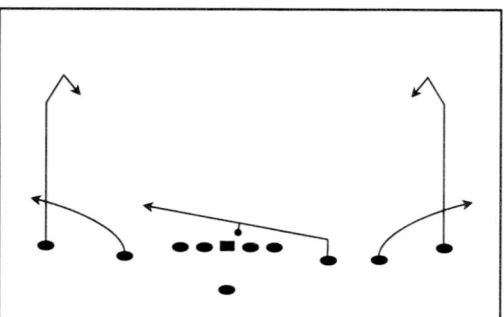

Figure 8-8. Curl route in a 3 x 2 set

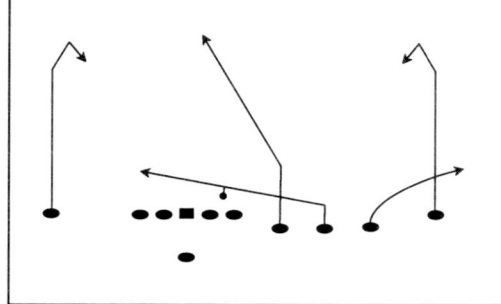

Figure 8-9. Curl route in a 4 x 1 set

Play #39: The All-Curl Route

The all-curl route is a good tag for defeating man-to-man coverage. It is also good to use when in a third-and-long situation. The quarterback will pick a receiver and throw to that receiver on his break. The running back will be in protection if lined up in the backfield. He will run a curl route if lined up as a receiver.

The receivers all run curl routes, but instead of running post-curl routes, they will run stick-curl routes at 10 yards. The stick-curl route technique is to drive vertically up the field, selling a vertical route, stick the top of his route, and turn back to the quarterback, with his hands up. The receiver will possibly need to come back down his stem to catch the football.

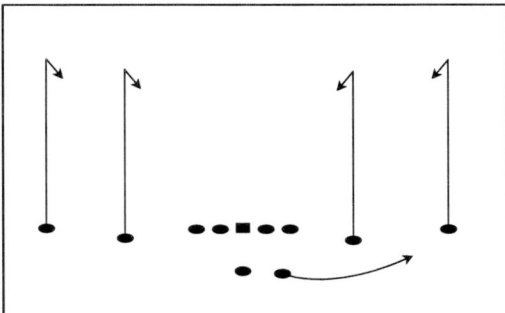

Figure 8-10. All-curl route in a 2 x 2 set

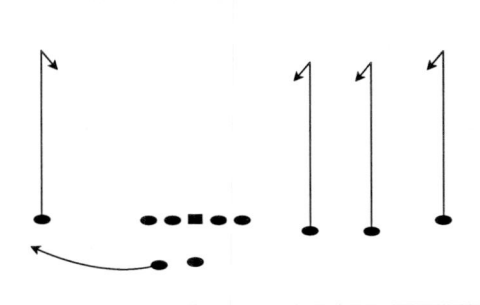

Figure 8-11. All-curl route in a 3 x 1 set

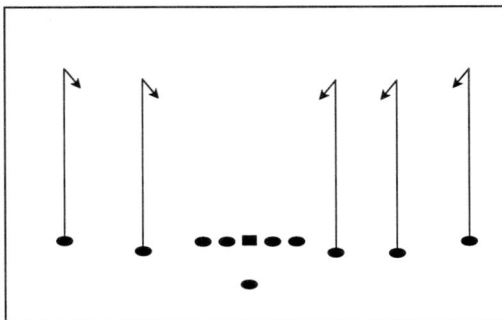

Figure 8-12. All-curl route in a 3 x 2 set

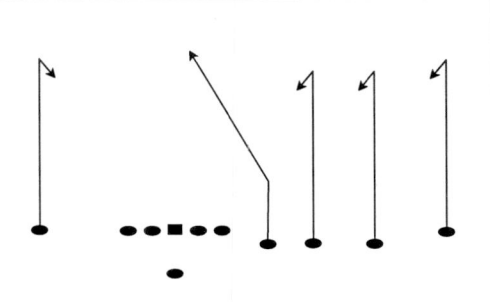

Figure 8-13. All-curl route in a 4 x 1 set

Play #40: The Curl Route With a Corner Tag

The corner tag is good for attacking man-to-man coverage as well as zone coverage. The corner route is a good man defense beater. The curl and the shoot routes are good zone beaters. The corner tag is only applied to a three-receiver side of the formation.

The quarterback will now read the #2 defender for the curl or shoot route. If the shoot route is covered by the #2 defender and the curl route is covered by the #1 defender, the quarterback will throw the football to the corner route.

The running back will run a swing route, looking back for the football over his inside shoulder after his third step. If lined up as a receiver, the running back will follow receiver rules.

The outside receivers run post-curl routes, and they will break to the post at 8 yards and curl at 12 yards, just like the normal curl route. The strongside inside receiver will run a corner route. He will push vertically to 10 yards, dip his shoulder to the post, and break to the corner, aiming 25 yards deep at the sideline. The #2 receiver will run a shoot route. If there is a #4 receiver, he will run a four-step slant route.

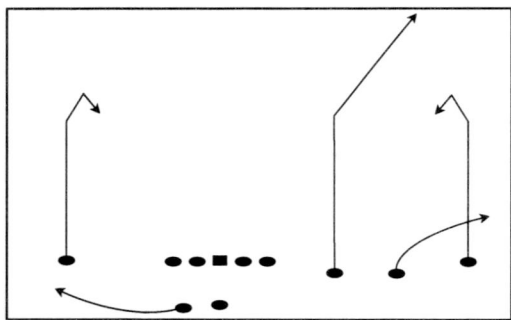

Figure 8-14. Curl route with a corner tag in a 3 x 1 set

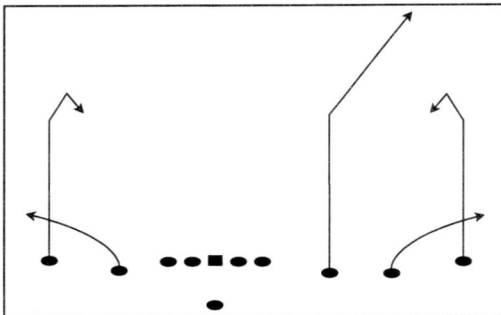

Figure 8-15. Curl route with a corner tag in a 3 x 2 set

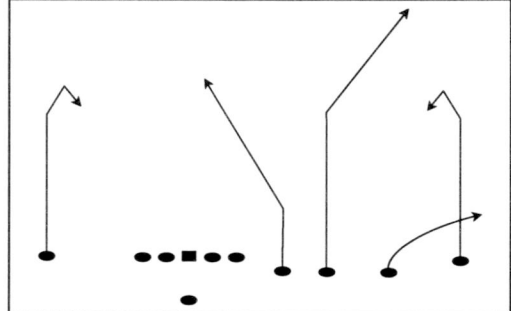

Figure 8-16. Curl route with a corner tag in a 4 x 1 set

Play #41: The Curl Route With a Switch Tag

The switch tag tells the #1 and #2 receivers to exchange routes. This change will put the #1 receiver on the shoot route and the #2 receiver on the post-curl route. All other responsibilities on the curl route remain the same, including the quarterback's read.

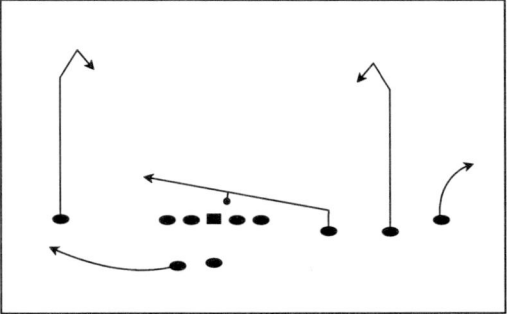

Figure 8-17. Curl route with a switch tag in a 3 x 1 set

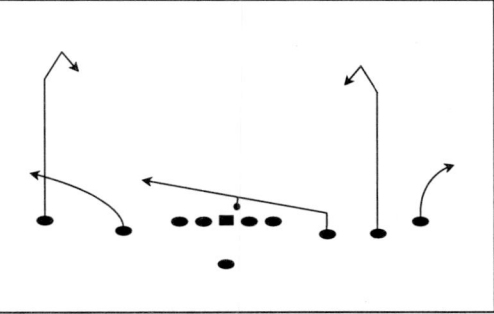

Figure 8-18. Curl route with a switch tag in a 3 x 2 set

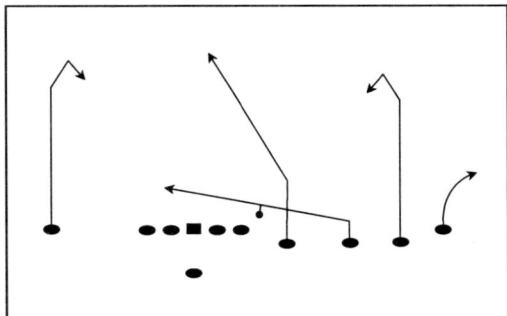

Figure 8-19. Curl route with a switch tag in a 4 x 1 set

Play #42: The Curl Route With a Swap Tag

The swap tag tells the #2 and #3 receivers to exchange routes, putting the #2 receiver on the drag route and the #3 receiver on the shoot route. This change creates a rub for the drag route, which is good versus man-to-man defenses. All other responsibilities on the curl route remain the same, including the quarterback's read.

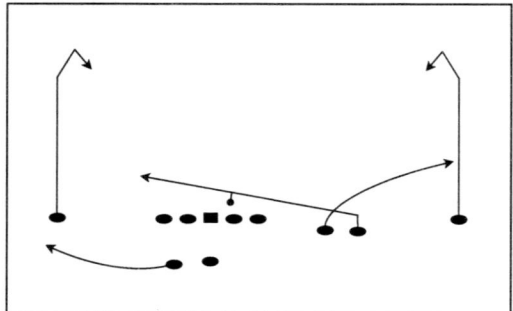

Figure 8-20. Curl route with a swap tag in a 3 x 1 set

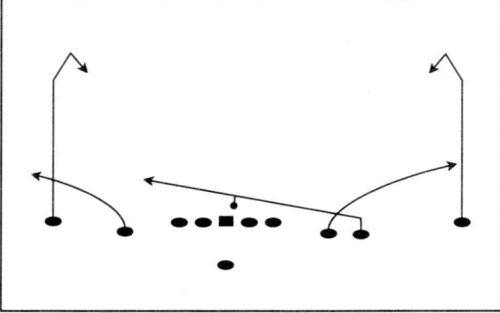

Figure 8-21. Curl route with a swap tag in a 3 x 2 set

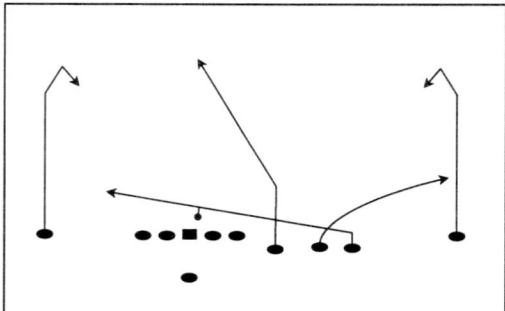

Figure 8-22. Curl route with a swap tag in a 4 x 1 set

9

Smash Routes

Introduction

The quarterback will need to identify the #1 defender as well as the basic coverage family. The hitch route is a good option versus cover 3 and cover 4 zones. The corner route is a good option versus cover 2 zone and man-to-man coverage.

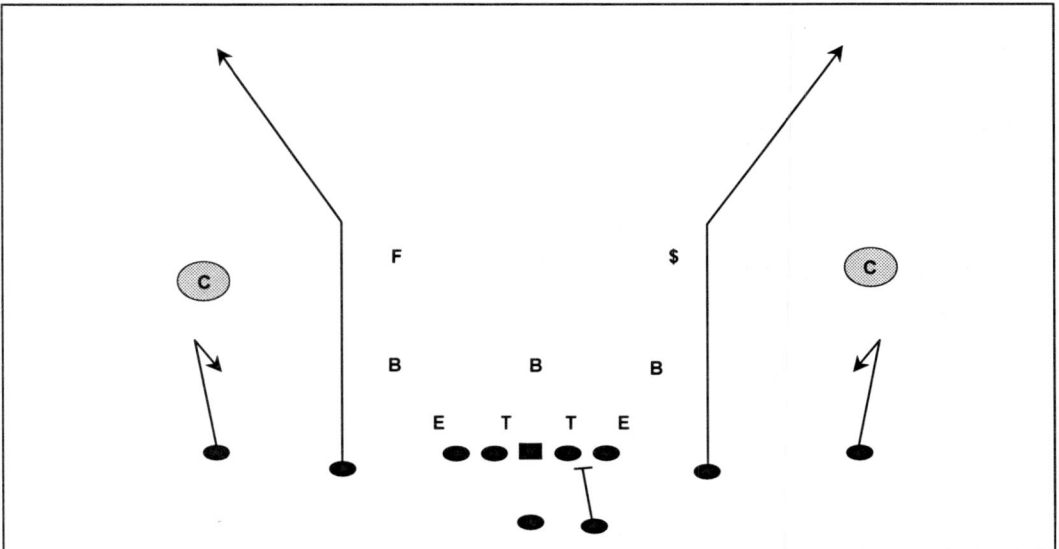

Figure 9-1. Pre-snap identification of the #1 defender in a cover 2 defense

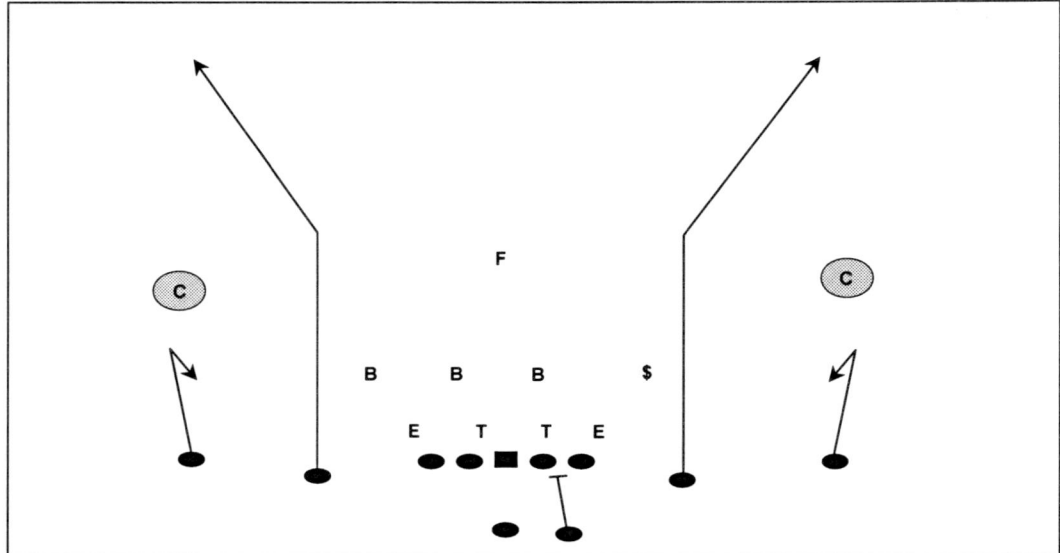

Figure 9-2. Pre-snap identification of the #1 defender in a cover 3 defense

Play #43: The Smash Route

The smash route is a good way to attack multiple defenses, including man-to-man, cover 2, cover 3, and cover 4 zone defenses.

The quarterback will need to pick a side of the defense to attack and stay with that side. He will read the #1 defender. If the defender backpedals at the snap, the quarterback will throw the football to the #1 receiver on the hitch route. If the #1 defender doesn't move or moves toward the line of scrimmage, the quarterback will throw the football to the corner route.

The running back will be in protection if he is aligned in the backfield. He will follow receiver rules if he is lined up as a receiver.

The outside receivers will run a hitch route. The hitch route technique is to drive four hard steps and take two buzz or control steps. After the receiver gets to the top of his route, he will get his hands up and snap his head back to the quarterback.

The inside receivers will run a corner route. Their technique is to push vertically to 10 yards, dip their shoulders to the post, and break to the corner, aiming 25 yards deep at the sideline.

In any three- or four-receiver side of the formation, the #2 receiver runs the corner route, the #3 receiver runs a seam route, and the #4 receiver runs a four-step slant route.

The smash route can be run out of several different formations within the spread offense, including 2 x 2 sets, 3 x 1 sets, 3 x 2 sets, and 4 x 1 sets.

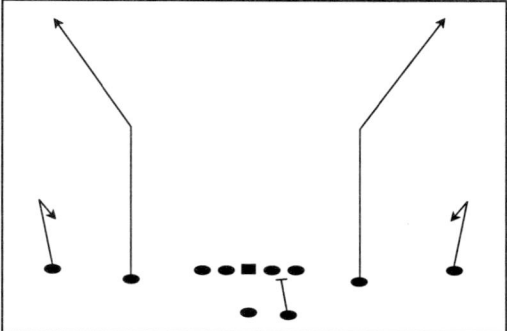

Figure 9-3. Smash route in a 2 x 2 set

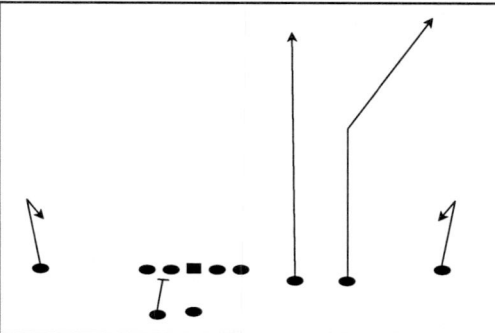

Figure 9-4. Smash route in a 3 x 1 set

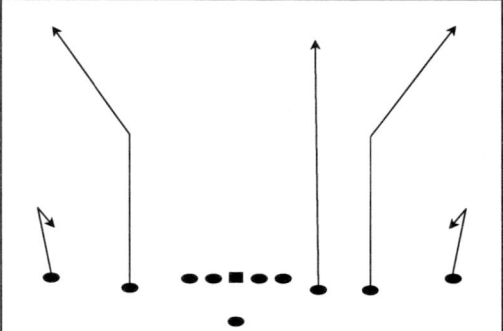

Figure 9-5. Smash route in a 3 x 2 set

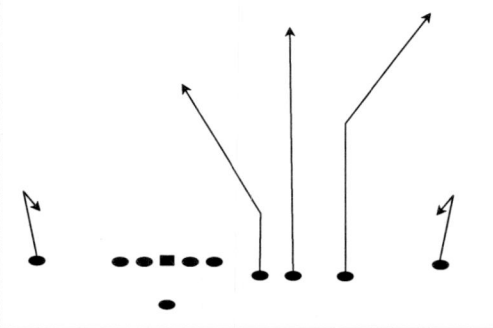

Figure 9-6. Smash route in a 4 x 1 set

Play #44: The Smash Route With a Curl Tag

The curl tag gives the quarterback the option of throwing at a stationary receiver at a depth of 8 to 10 yards. The curl tag is also a good tag to use versus a team that mixes up coverages. The curl tag makes for a good cover 3 zone beater, and the smash side is good for beating cover 2 and man-to-man defenses.

The quarterback has the choice to throw to the tagged receiver, if the defense allows, or he can stay on his normal read. The only change on the route is the tagged receiver. He will run a 10-yard stick-curl route.

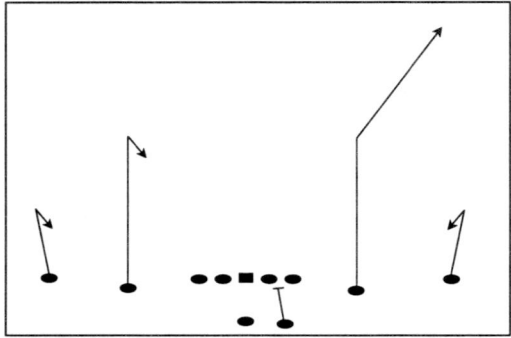

Figure 9-7. Smash route with a curl tag in a 2 x 2 set

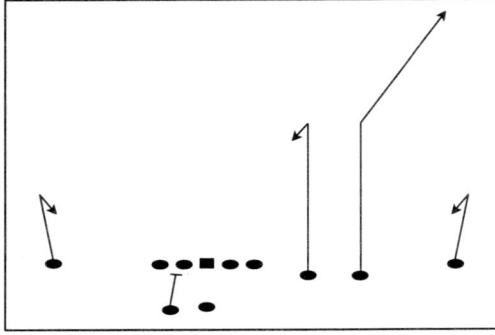

Figure 9-8. Smash route with a curl tag in a 3 x 1 set

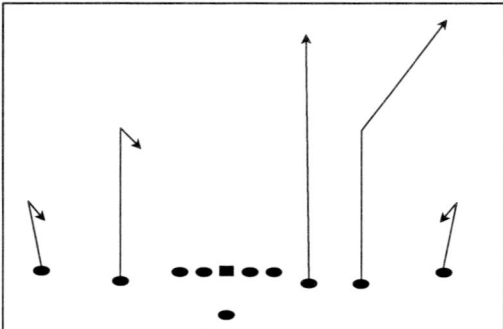

Figure 9-9. Smash route with a curl tag in a 3 x 2 set

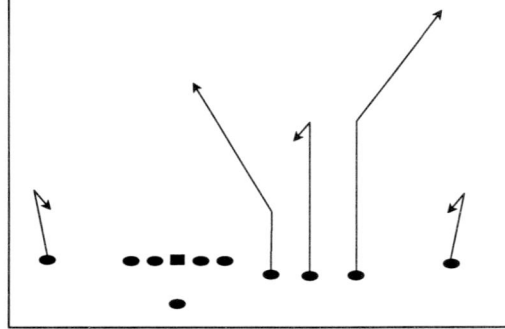

Figure 9-10. Smash route with a curl tag in a 4 x 1 set

Play #45: The Smash Route With a Whip Tag

The whip tag is used to attack man-to-man defenses. Some teams use the whip route by the outside receiver on the smash route package as their default route instead of the hitch route.

The read stays the same for the quarterback.

The only change on the whip tag is the outside receiver. Instead of running the hitch route, he will run a whip route. The technique is to drive inside at a 45-degree angle for five steps. If the defense allows the receiver inside, he will sit inside. If the defense chases the receiver inside or keeps inside leverage, the receiver will continue inside until he receives eye contact from the quarterback. He will then pivot back to the outside and accelerate away from the defense.

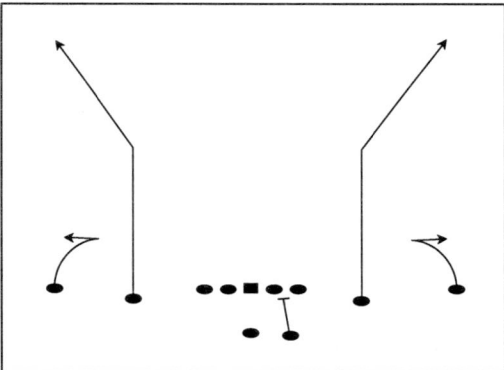

Figure 9-11. Smash route with a whip tag in a 2 x 2 set

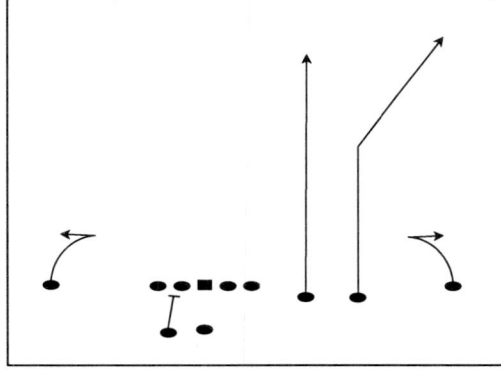

Figure 9-12. Smash route with a whip tag in a 3 x 1 set

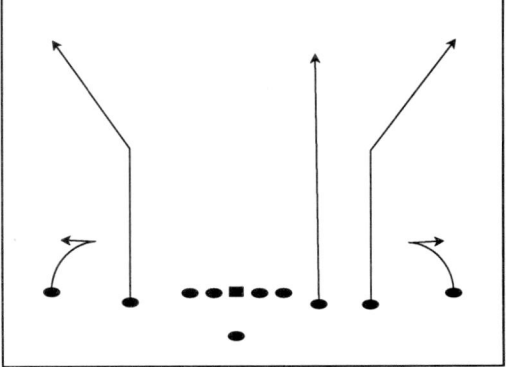

Figure 9-13. Smash route with a whip tag in a 3 x 2 set

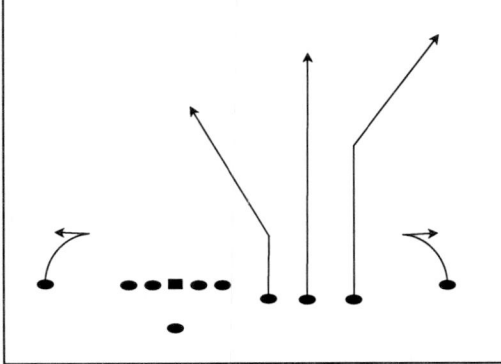

Figure 9-14. Smash route with a whip tag in a 4 x 1 set

Play #46: The Smash Route With a Post Tag

The post tag is a good way to attack defenses that leave the middle of the field open by playing cover 2 or cover 4 zones.

The quarterback will try to throw the post route in a 2 x 2 set, without a viable option to work to next in his progression. In three- or four-receiver sides of a formation, the quarterback can look at the post route and then progress to the corner route and down to the hitch route.

On this route, the tagged receiver will push his route to 10 yards deep and then break at a 45-degree angle to the middle of the field. If the receiver is playing versus man-to-man defense, he will need to beat the defender inside before making the post cut. All other routes remain the same on the post tag.

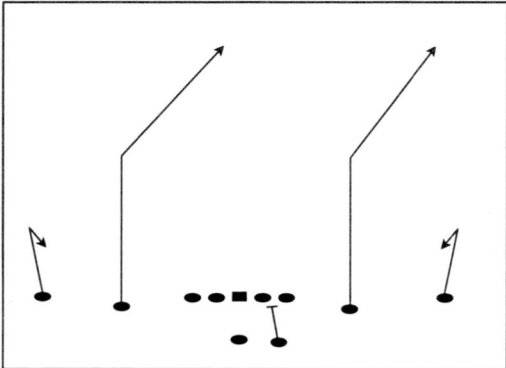

Figure 9-15. Smash route with a post tag in a 2 x 2 set

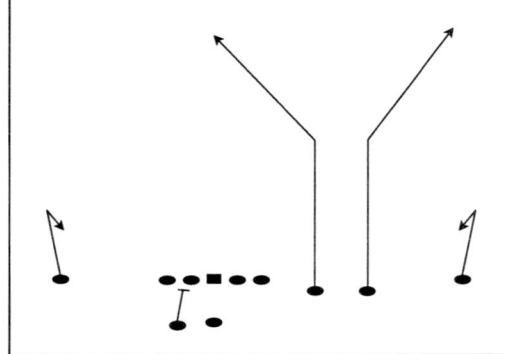

Figure 9-16. Smash route with a post tag in a 3 x 1 set

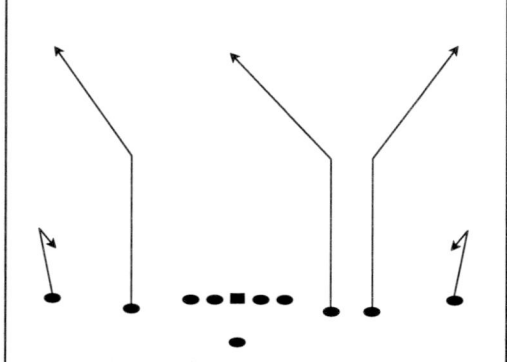

Figure 9-17. Smash route with a post tag in a 3 x 2 set

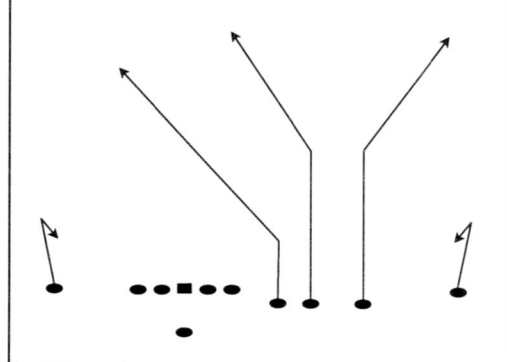

Figure 9-18. Smash route with a post tag in a 4 x 1 set

Play #47: The Smash Route With a Swap Tag

The swap tag exchanges the routes of the #2 and the #3 receivers. This change is a good way to hide the corner route from the #1 defender, especially when attacking cover 2 zone defenses.

The quarterback will read the swap tag just like the base smash route. He will still read the #1 defender.

The swap tag will put the #2 receiver on the seam route and the #3 receiver on the corner route. The #3 receiver will work a slower tempo, letting the #2 receiver clear. Then he will make his corner cut. All other routes remain consistent with the base smash route package.

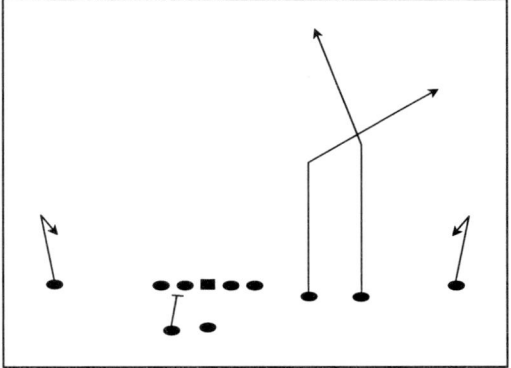

Figure 9-19. Smash route with a swap tag in a 3 x 1 set

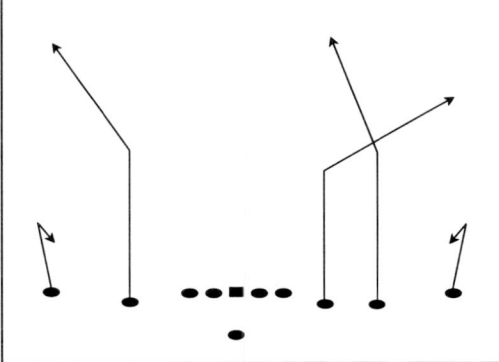

Figure 9-20. Smash route with a swap tag in a 3 x 2 set

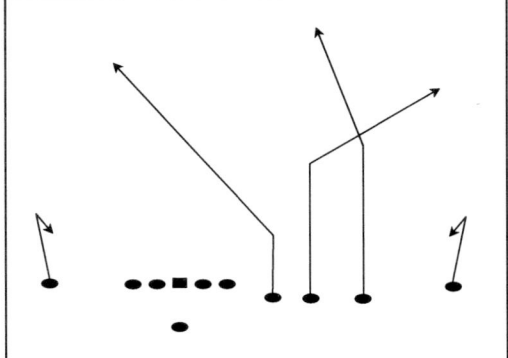

Figure 9-21. Smash route with a swap tag in a 4 x 1 set

10

Vertical Routes

Introduction

The quarterback will need to identify his read key on the vertical route. His read will be the free safety, if there is one. If there is not a free safety, the quarterback will read the hash safety on the strongside of the formation.

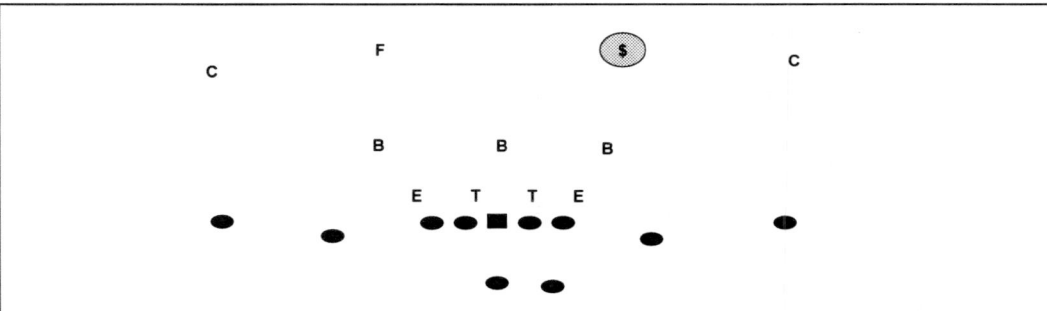

Figure 10-1. Pre-snap identification of the read key versus a cover 2 defense

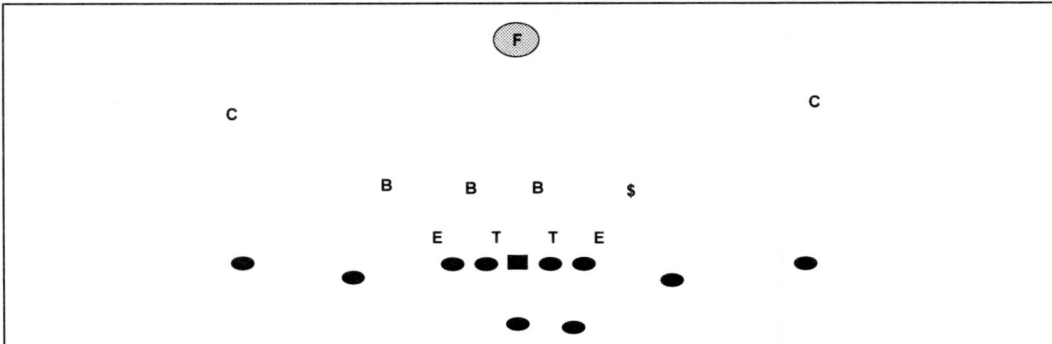

Figure 10-2. Pre-snap identification of the read key versus a cover 3 defense

Play #48: The Vertical Route

The vertical route is a great way to put a scare into the defense and is worth attempting early in the game, even if it is not successful. The defense will recognize that one play could very well be worth six points.

With a safety in the middle of the field, the quarterback will try to influence the safety to move to one hash or the other. If he can move the safety with his eyes, by looking at the inside receiver on one side, the quarterback will throw to the opposite inside receiver. If the quarterback can't move the safety, he will attempt to throw to the nearest inside receiver, or the receiver with the best leverage on the free safety.

When the defense is playing with two safeties, the quarterback will then make a progression read on the route. In a 2 x 2 set, he will look from the strongside inside receiver on the seam-read route, to the outside receiver on the go-read route, then to the running back on the shoot route. If the formation is a 3 x 1 set, the quarterback will then make a progression read from the inside to the outside and then down to the back.

The running back will run a shoot route in all formations, looking back for the football over his outside shoulder after his third step.

The outside receivers run a go-read route. They will release vertically down the field, and when they get to seven yards, they will read the defender. If they think they can beat the defender, they will keep working vertically. If they don't think they can get on top of the defender, they will hook up at 12 yards.

The strongside inside receiver will run a seam-read route. If there is a defender on the hash at 10 to 12 yards deep, he will hook up on the hash at 10 yards. If there is not a player on the hash, he will keep running vertically up the hash. In a 3 x 1 set, he will burst to seven yards and then break to the opposite hash. The #2 receiver in a 3 x 1 set will then have the seam-read route. The backside inside receiver will run a seam route with no read in 2 x 2 and 3 x 2 sets.

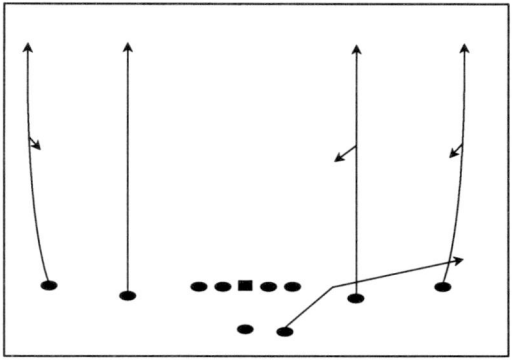

Figure 10-3. Vertical route in a 2 x 2 set

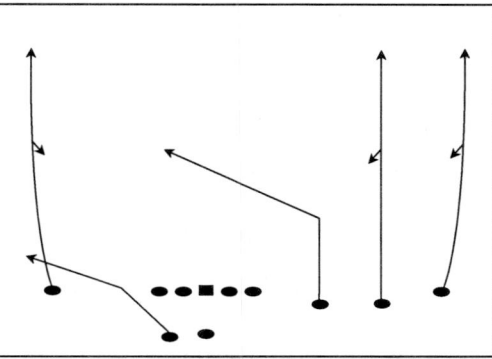

Figure 10-4. Vertical route in a 3 x 1 set

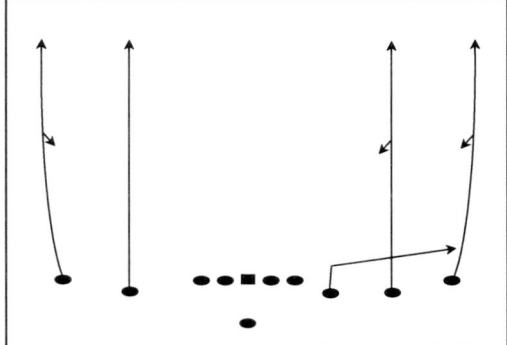

Figure 10-5. Vertical route in a 3 x 2 set

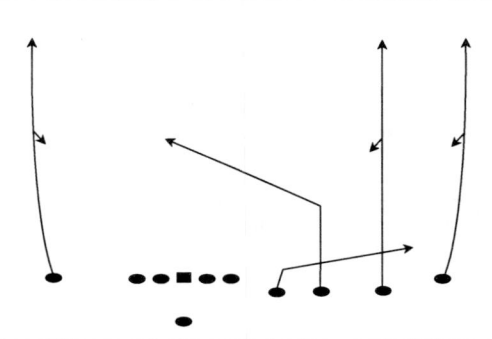

Figure 10-6. Vertical route in a 4 x 1 set

Play #49: The Vertical Route With an Under Tag

The under tag tells the tagged receiver to run a two-step under route. The under tag is a good tag to use versus teams that have their linebackers drop for depth quickly. The quarterback will look at the under first and then work his normal vertical progression. The only route that is adjusted is the tagged receiver. The tagged receiver is an outside receiver; therefore, one of the go-read routes is given up.

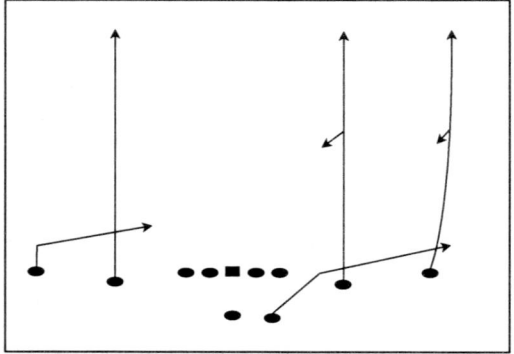

Figure 10-7. Vertical route with an under tag in a 2 x 2 set

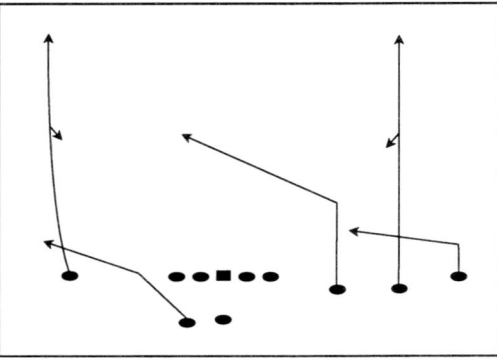

Figure 10-8. Vertical route with an under tag in a 3 x 1 set

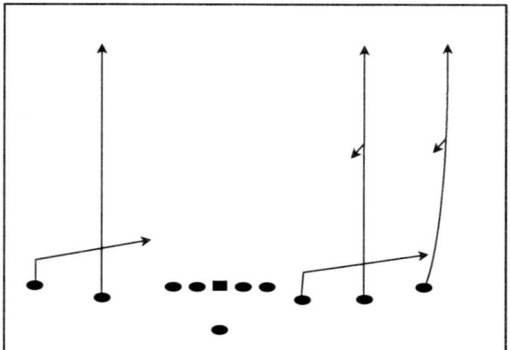

Figure 10-9. Vertical route with an under tag in a 3 x 2 set

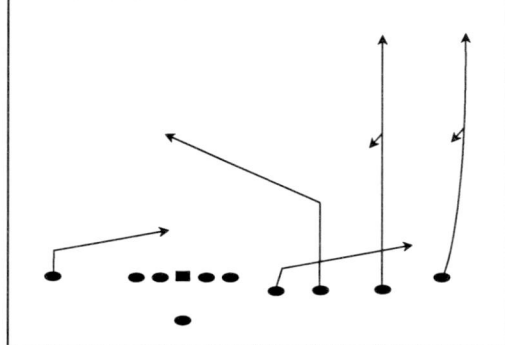

Figure 10-10. Vertical route with an under tag in a 4 x 1 set

Play #50: The Vertical Route With a Post Tag

The post tag is an excellent way to attack teams with two high safeties. The post route can split the safeties. The quarterback will look to the post route first and then work his normal vertical progression. The tagged receiver will run a 10-yard post route. All other routes will remain the same as the base vertical route package.

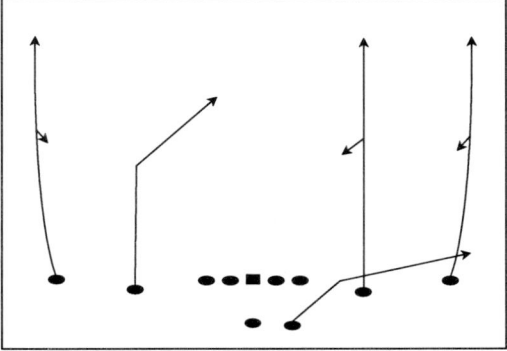

Figure 10-11. Vertical route with a post tag in a 2 x 2 set

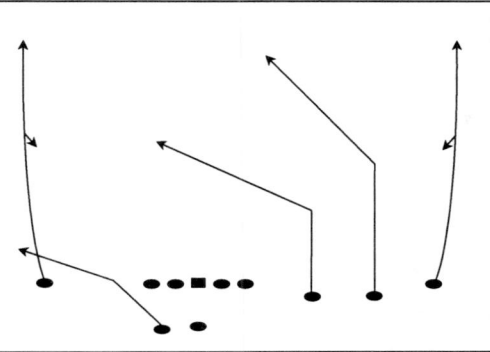

Figure 10-12. Vertical route with a post tag in a 3 x 1 set

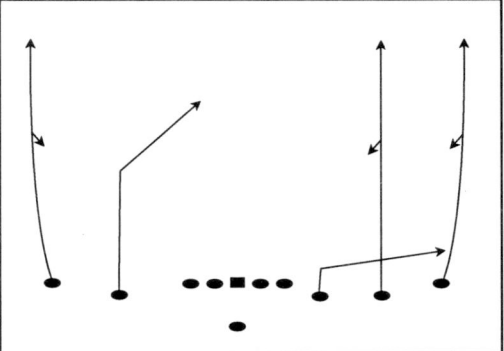

Figure 10-13. Vertical route with a post tag in a 3 x 2 set

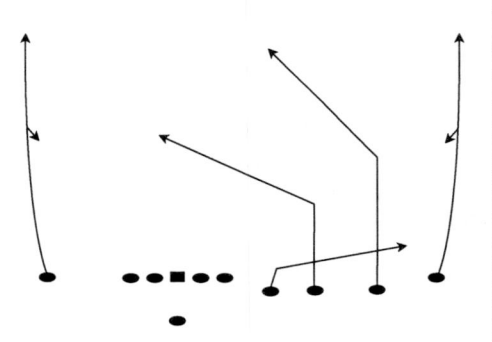

Figure 10-14. Vertical route with a post tag in a 4 x 1 set

Play #51: The Five Vertical Route

The five vertical route is a good way to attack a defense that is playing eight or nine players in pass coverage and not applying any pressure on the quarterback.

The quarterback will read the weakside safety. If he runs with the seam route, the quarterback will throw the football to the running back on the seven-yard post route. If the safety holds and plays the post route, the quarterback will throw the football to the weakside inside receiver on the seam route. If the quarterback cannot get the football to either the post or the seam route, his third option will be the seam-read on the strongside of the formation.

The five vertical tag tells the running back that he will run a seven-yard post route instead of his normal shoot route. All other routes are identical to the basic vertical route package.

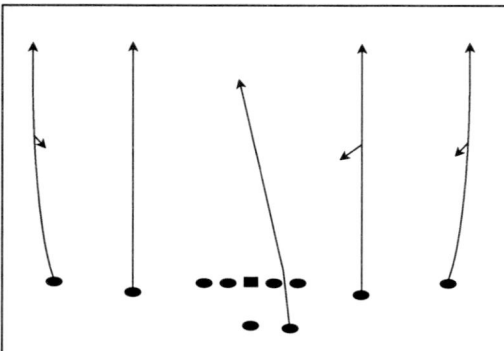

Figure 10-15. Five vertical route in a 2 x 2 set

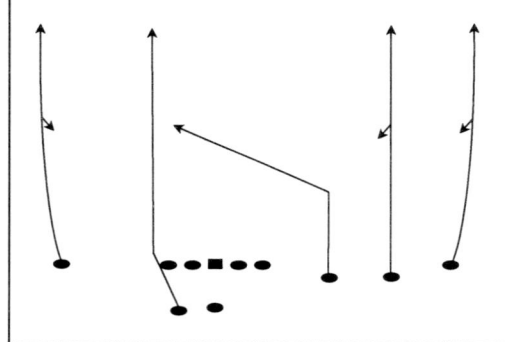

Figure 10-16. Five vertical route in a 3 x 1 set

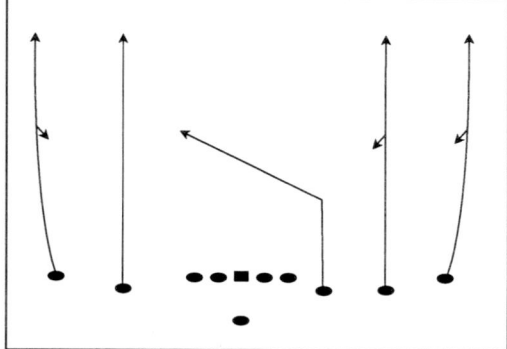

Figure 10-17. Five vertical route in a 3 x 2 set

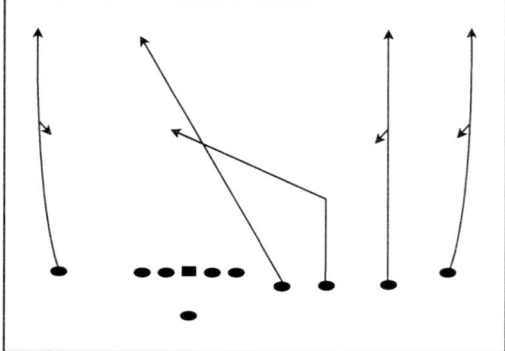

Figure 10-18. Five vertical route in a 4 x 1 set

Play #52: The Vertical Route With a Dig Tag

The dig tag is a good way to high-low the #2 defender.

The quarterback will read the #2 defender to the strongside. If the defender reacts outside to the shoot route, the quarterback will throw the football to the dig route. If the defender backs up, the quarterback will throw the football to the shoot route.

The tagged receiver will run a 10-yard dig route. The next receiver in will run a go route, and he will landmark the numbers painted on the field. If the field is not marked with numbers, then the landmark is seven yards from the sideline. The remaining receivers will run their normal vertical routes.

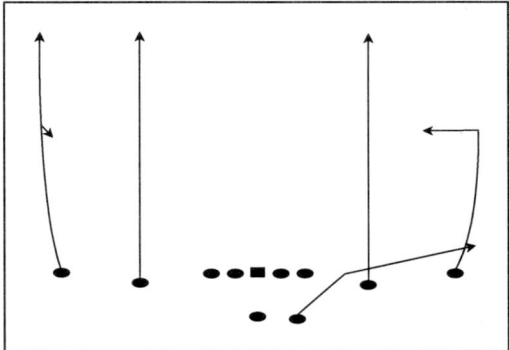

Figure 10-19. Vertical route with a dig tag in a 2 x 2 set

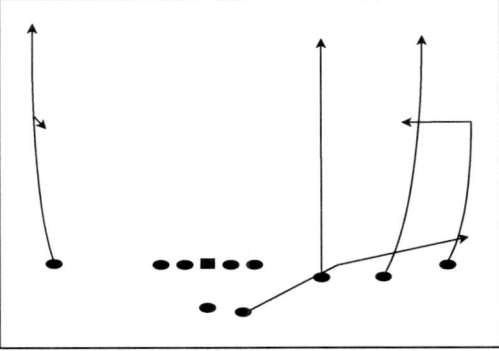

Figure 10-20. Vertical route with a dig tag in a 3 x 1 set

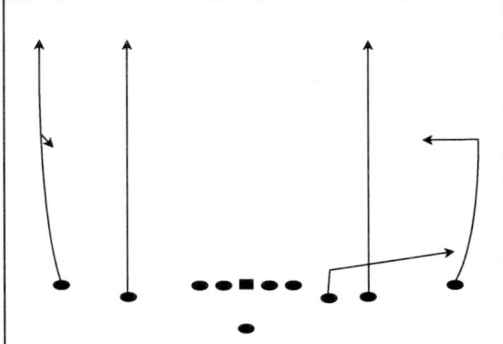

Figure 10-21. Vertical route with a dig tag in a 3 x 2 set

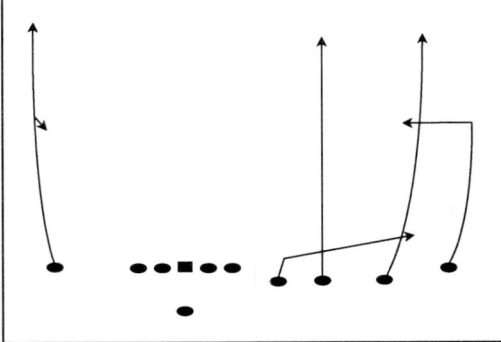

Figure 10-22. Vertical route with a dig tag in a 4 x 1 set

Play #53: The Vertical Route With a Curl Tag

The curl tag is a good way to create a stationary target in a third-and-long situation. A good way to use the play is to tag the receiver that has the seam-read route on the curl. The curl tag tells the receiver to run to 10 yards, plant, and pivot back to the quarterback. The quarterback will look to the curl tag first and then work his normal vertical progression. The remaining receivers will run their normal vertical routes.

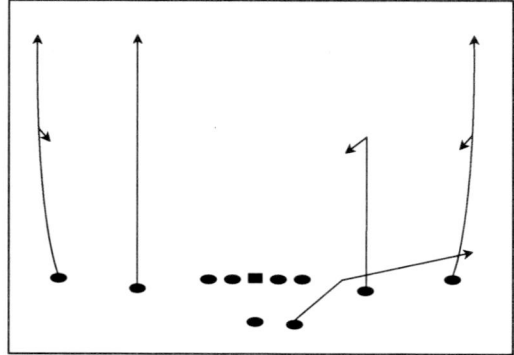

Figure 10-23. Vertical route with a curl tag in a 2 x 2 set

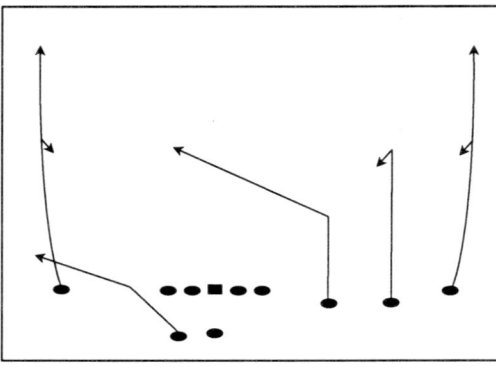

Figure 10-24. Vertical route with a curl tag in a 3 x 1 set

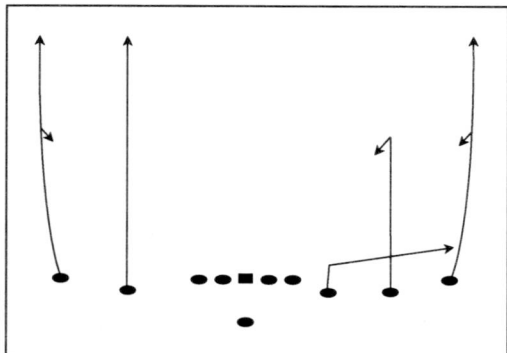

Figure 10-25. Vertical route with a curl tag in a 3 x 2 set

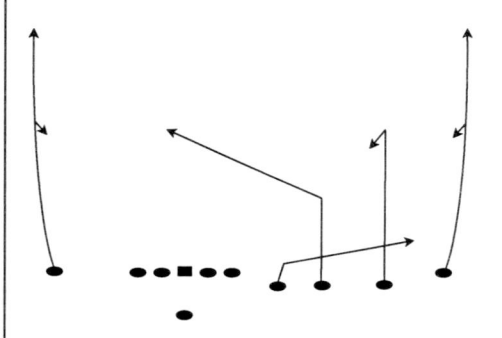

Figure 10-26. Vertical route with a curl tag in a 4 x 1 set

Play #54: The Vertical Route With a Turn Tag

The turn tag is a good way to get a three-receiver flood concept on one side of the field. The tagged receiver will run a 10-yard out route. All other receivers will run their normal vertical routes, with the exception of the playside outside receiver. He can't run a go-read route; therefore, he must convert his route to a go route, with no read. The quarterback will have a progression read from the turn tag to the shoot route, reading the #2 defender.

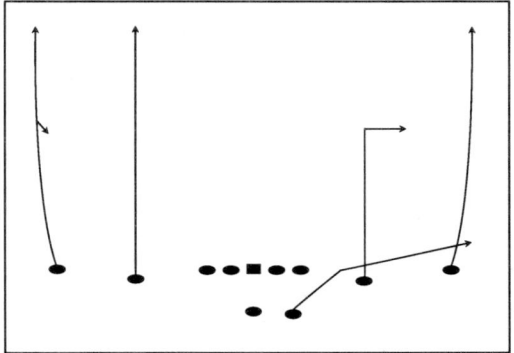

Figure 10-27. Vertical route with a turn tag in a 2 x 2 set

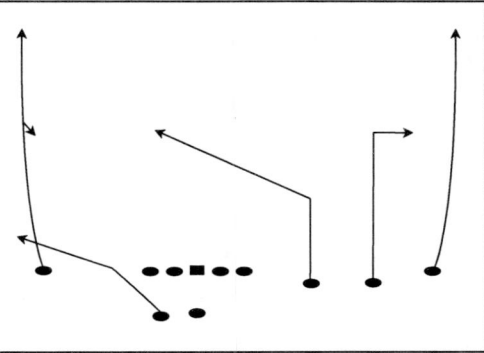

Figure 10-28. Vertical route with a turn tag in a 3 x 1 set

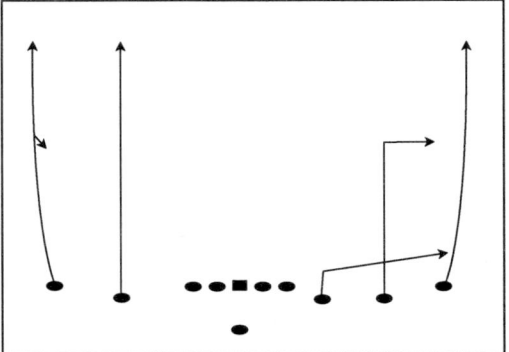

Figure 10-29. Vertical route with a turn tag in a 3 x 2 set

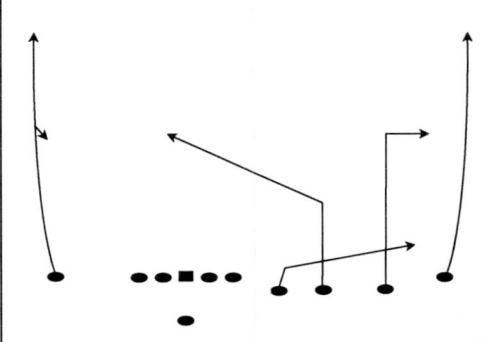

Figure 10-30. Vertical route with a turn tag in a 4 x 1 set

Play #55: The Vertical Route With a Switch Tag

The switch tag tells the #1 and #2 receivers to exchange routes. This change will put the #1 receiver on the seam-read route and the #2 receiver on the go-read route. The switch route can be used for the strongside of the formation, the backside of the formation, or on both sides of the formation. All other responsibilities on this route remain the same, including the quarterback's read.

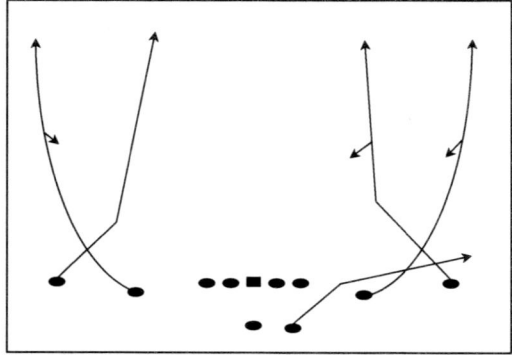

Figure 10-31. Vertical route with a switch tag in a 2 x 2 set

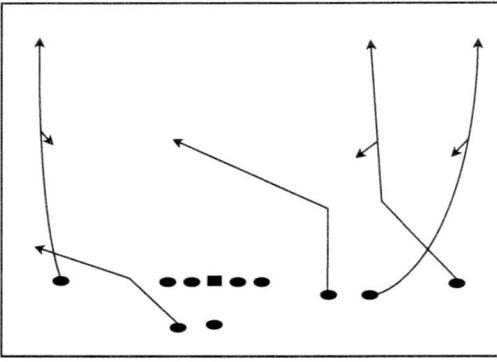

Figure 10-32. Vertical route with a switch tag in a 3 x 1 set

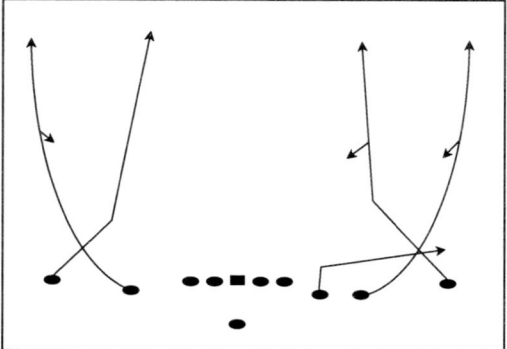

Figure 10-33. Vertical route with a switch tag in a 3 x 2 set

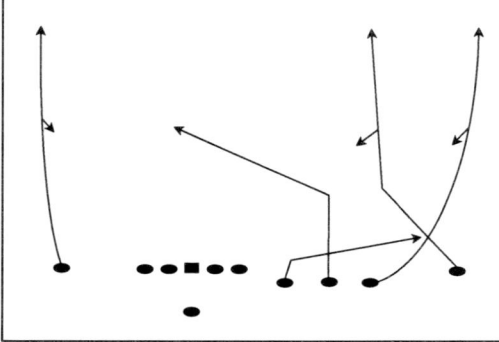

Figure 10-34. Vertical route with a switch tag in a 4 x 1 set

Play #56: The Vertical Route With a Swap Tag

The swap tag tells the #2 and #3 receivers to exchange routes. This change will put the #2 receiver on the seven-yard post route, and the #3 receiver on the seam-read route. This creates a rub for the seam-read route, as the seam-read route will wrap behind the release of the #2 receiver. All other responsibilities on this route remain the same, including the quarterback's read.

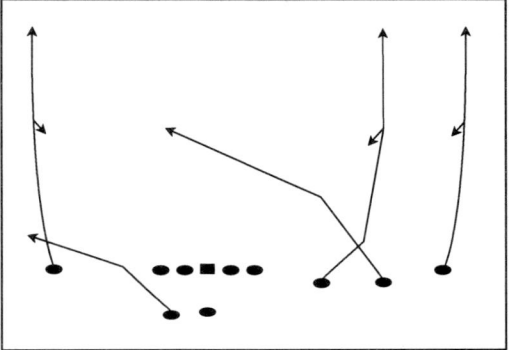

Figure 10-35. Vertical route with a swap tag in a 3 x 1 set

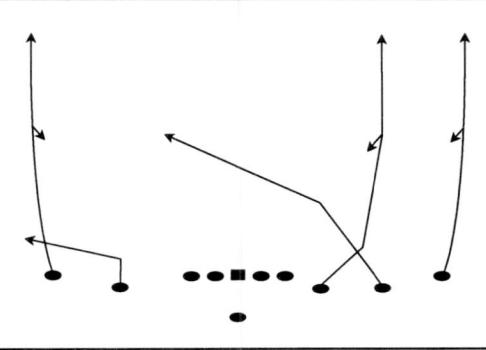

Figure 10-36. Vertical route with a swap tag in a 3 x 2 set

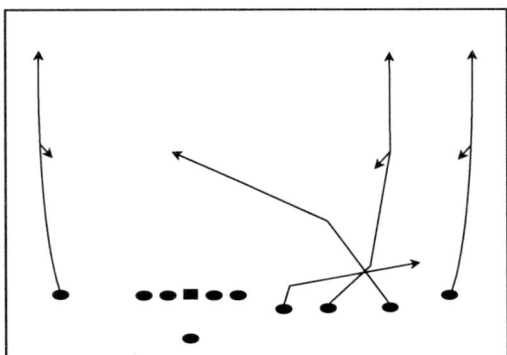

Figure 10-37. Vertical route with a swap tag in a 4 x 1 set

Play #57: The Vertical Route With a Wheel Tag From a Bunch Set

The wheel tag is a good way to get four vertical routes from a bunch set. This route is an excellent way to attack man-to-man coverage.

The quarterback will make a progression read on the route by starting with the seven-yard post route first, then the seam-read, then the wheel route, and finally the shoot route.

The wheel tag adjusts all of the receiver routes. The outside receiver will run the seam-read route, and the #2 receiver will run the seven-yard post route. The #3 receiver will run the wheel route, and the #4 receiver will run a shoot route. The #4 receiver in a bunch set is identified as the receiver lined up in the back, farthest from the line of scrimmage.

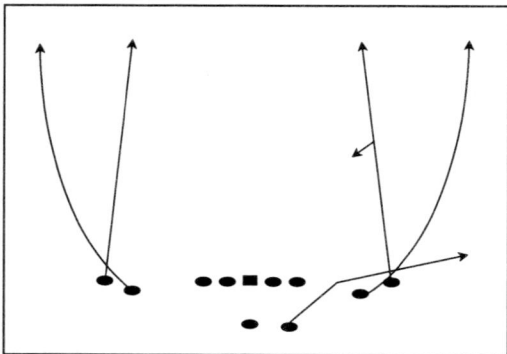

Figure 10-38. Vertical route with a wheel tag from a bunch 2 x 2 set

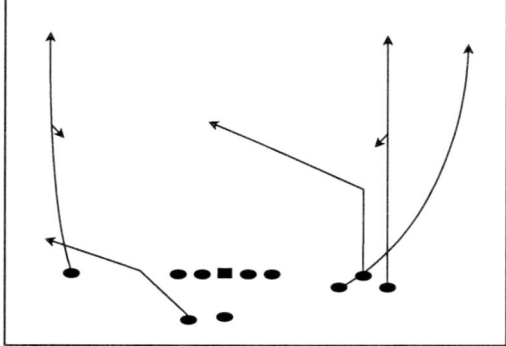

Figure 10-39. Vertical route with a wheel tag from a bunch 3 x 1 set

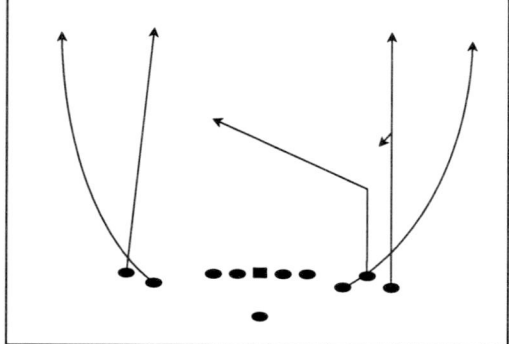

Figure 10-40. Vertical route with a wheel tag from a bunch 3 x 2 set

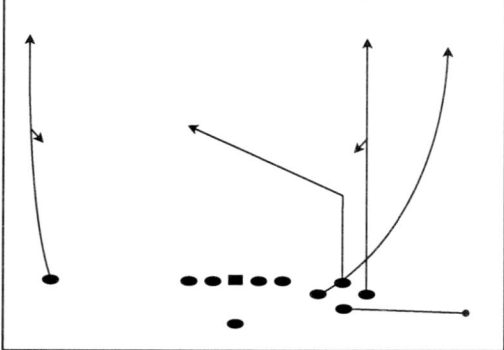

Figure 10-41. Vertical route with a wheel tag from a bunch 4 x 1 set

11

Choice Routes

Introduction

The quarterback will pick a side and will read the route outside in. He will throw to the choice route until it is taken away, and then he will attempt to throw to the next receiver inside on the seam-read route. If there is only one receiver tagged as the choice route, the quarterback will work the choice route first and then progress from the choice route back across the field.

Play #58: The Choice Route

The choice route is a good route for attacking man-to-man coverage as well as cover 3 zone and cover 4 zone defenses. The route can also be tagged to a single receiver, which allows the coach more control from the sideline.

The running back will be in protection if he is aligned in the backfield. He will run a shoot route, looking back over his outside shoulder after three steps, if he is lined up as a receiver.

In a 2 x 2 set, when both outside receivers are tagged, the route is mirrored. Each outside receiver will run the choice route. The technique on the choice route is just like the technique on the speed-out route, with the exception that the break is at 10 yards instead of at four steps with the speed-out route. The inside receivers each run a seam-read route. If the inside receivers get to 10 yards and are open, they will hook up and make themselves available to the quarterback. The inside receivers will need to use the hash marks as their landmarks, so in a 2 x 2 set, each inside receiver will hook up on the hash mark to their side. In a 3 x 1 or a 3 x 2 set, the inside receiver on the strongside of the formation drives seven yards and then breaks across the field to the far hash. If there is a #4 receiver, which would be the running back, he will run a shoot route.

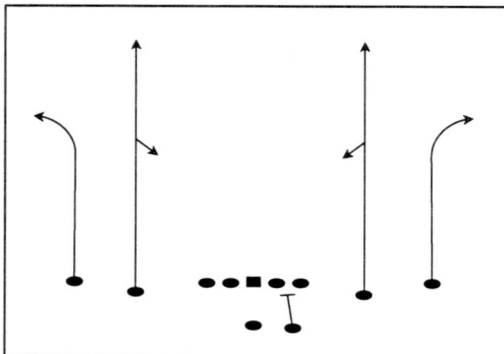

Figure 11-1. Choice route in a 2 x 2 set

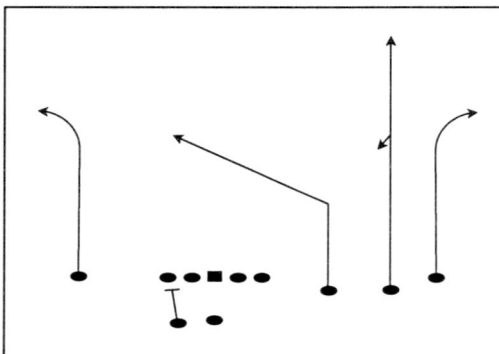

Figure 11-2. Choice route in a 3 x 1 set

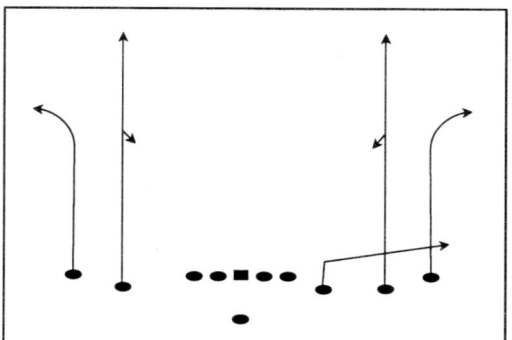

Figure 11-3. Choice route in a 3 x 2 set

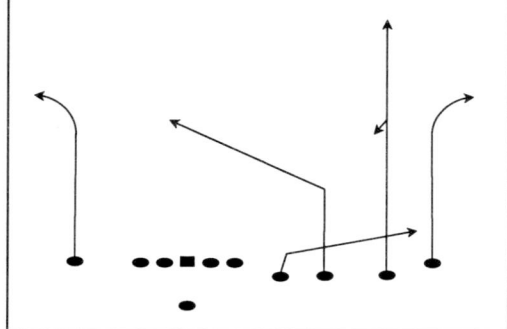

Figure 11-4. Choice route in a 4 x 1 set

Play #59: The Choice Route With a Switch Tag

The switch tag is designed to let the quarterback read a specific receiver on the choice route and then progress across the field to two backside receivers running vertical read routes. This route gives the offense a high-completion route with the choice, as well as a vertical threat on the backside. The switch tag exchanges the routes of the #1 and the #2 receivers.

The quarterback will read the tagged receiver first, and if he can complete the choice route, he will take it. If not, he will pivot and read the backside receivers inside out.

The running back will be in protection if he is aligned in the backfield. He will run a shoot route if he is lined up as a receiver.

The tagged receiver will run the choice route. The backside #1 and #2 receivers away from the choice route will run the switch route off of the vertical route package. The outside receiver will run a seam-read. He will drive inside to the hash and work vertical to 10 yards. If he can keep running without being covered, he will keep running vertically down the hash. If not, he will hook up at 10 yards. The inside receiver will run a go-read. The inside receiver technique is very similar to the wheel route technique, with two exceptions. He doesn't have to sell the shoot route first, and he has to read the defense. If the defense is staying on top of his route, he will hook up at 10 yards deep, seven yards from the sideline.

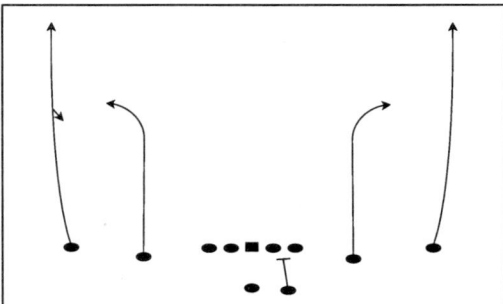

Figure 11-5. Choice route with a switch tag in a 2 x 2 set

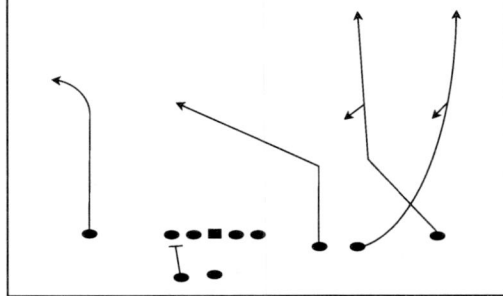

Figure 11-6. Choice route with a switch tag in a 3 x 1 set

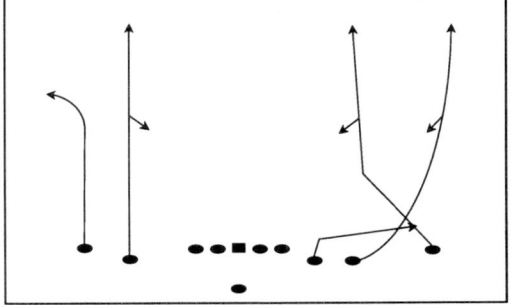

Figure 11-7. Choice route with a switch tag in a 3 x 2 set

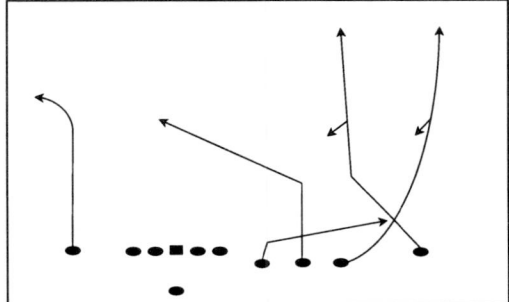

Figure 11-8. Choice route with a switch tag in a 4 x 1 set

Play #60: The Choice Route With a Swap Tag

The swap tag exchanges the routes of the #2 and the #3 receivers. The swap tag creates a rub for the inside receiver running the seam read. One receiver can be tagged on the choice route, or both outside receivers can be tagged with choice routes.

The quarterback will read this tag like the normal choice route unless he sees blitz or man-to-man defense. Then he can look inside to the seven-yard post to the seam-read. If the quarterback sees a zone defense, he will pick a choice route to which he can throw. If the choice is covered, the quarterback will then read the seven-yard post to the seam-read route.

The running back will be in protection if he is aligned in the backfield. He will run a shoot route if he is lined up as a receiver.

The swap tag tells the #2 receiver to drive seven steps vertically and then to break across the field. The #3 receiver releases outside and scrapes off the backside of the #2 receiver. He will then execute his seam-read route. All other routes stay consistent with the base choice route package.

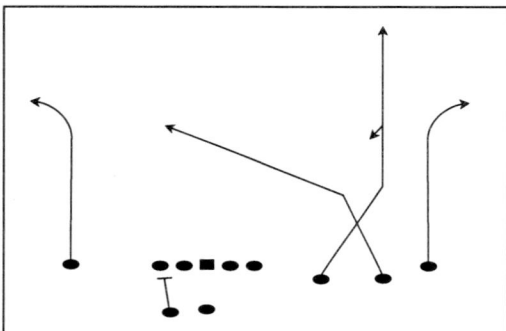

Figure 11-9. Choice route with a swap tag in a 3 x 1 set

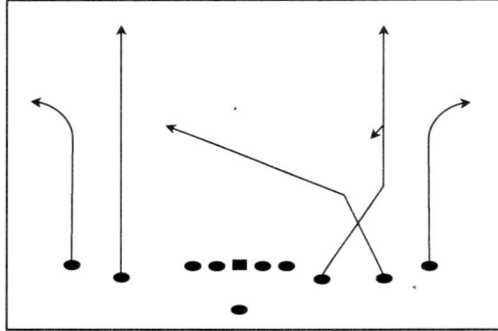

Figure 11-10. Choice route with a swap tag in a 3 x 2 set

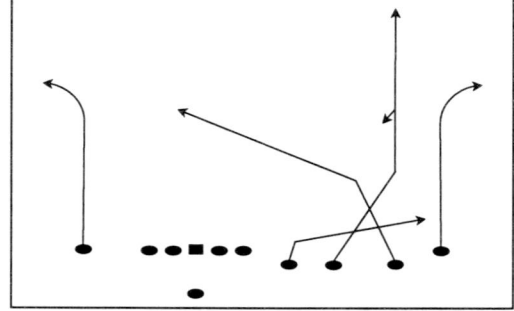

Figure 11-11. Choice route with a swap tag in a 4 x 1 set

Play #61: The Choice Route With a Corner Tag

The corner tag is a good addition to the choice route package. It is used primarily in third-down-and-long situations.

The quarterback will read the #1 defender. If he holds on the choice route, the quarterback will throw to the corner route. If the #1 defender keeps working for depth to the corner route, the quarterback will throw to the choice route.

The running back will be in protection if he is aligned in the backfield. He will run a shoot route if he is lined up as a receiver.

On this tag, the inside receivers will run the corner routes. Their technique is to push vertically to 10 yards, dip the inside shoulder to the post, and break to the corner, aiming 25 yards deep at the sideline. All other routes stay consistent with the base choice route package.

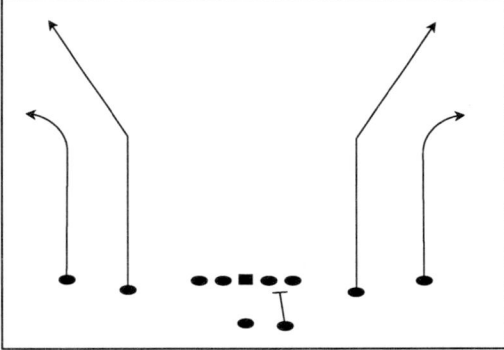

Figure 11-12. Choice route with a corner tag in a 2 x 2 set

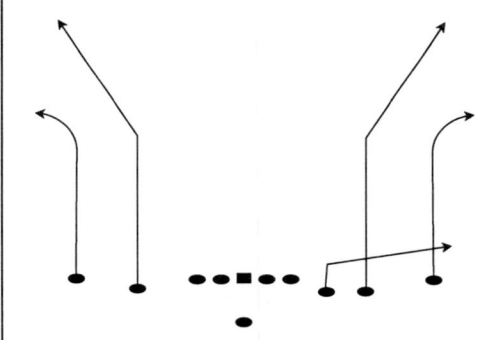

Figure 11-13. Choice route with a corner tag in a 3 x 2 set

Play #62: The Choice Route With an Under Tag

The under tag is used to flood a side of the field with three or four receivers. It is an excellent tag to use versus a blitzing defense, as the under route can come free with a lot of open space to run.

If the quarterback sees blitz or man-to-man coverage, he will throw to the under route. If the defense is playing zone coverage, the quarterback will read the choice route to the seam-read route.

The running back will be in protection if he is aligned in the backfield. He will run a shoot route if he is lined up as a receiver.

All routes will remain consistent with the base choice route package except for the tagged receiver, who will run the under route. The receiver running the under route will take two steps up the field and then break inside, parallel to the line of scrimmage.

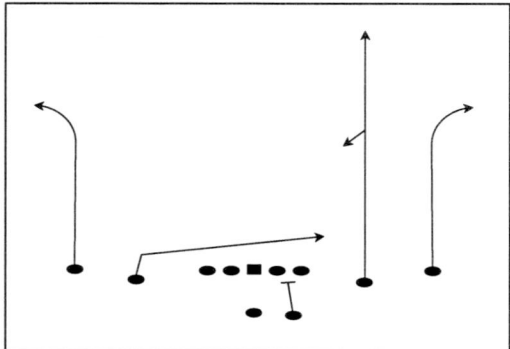

Figure 11-14. Choice route with a under tag in a 2 x 2 set

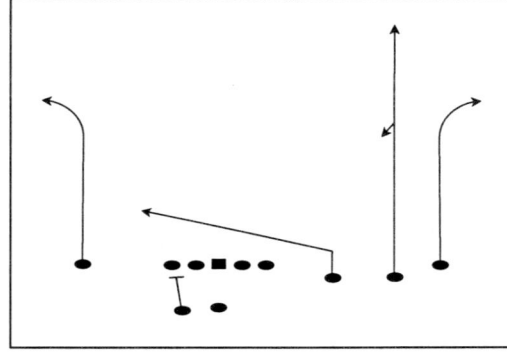

Figure 11-15. Choice route with a under tag in a 3 x 1 set

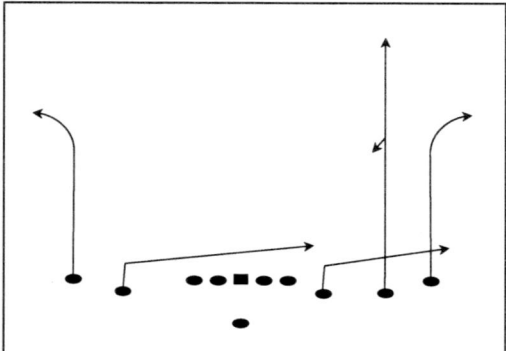

Figure 11-16. Choice route with a under tag in a 3 x 2 set

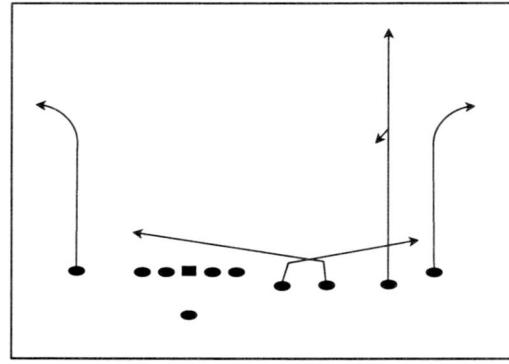

Figure 11-17. Choice route with a under tag in a 4 x 1 set

12

Pivot Routes

Introduction

The quarterback will need to identify the defender over the pivot route. The quarterback will pick a side and read the defender to this side.

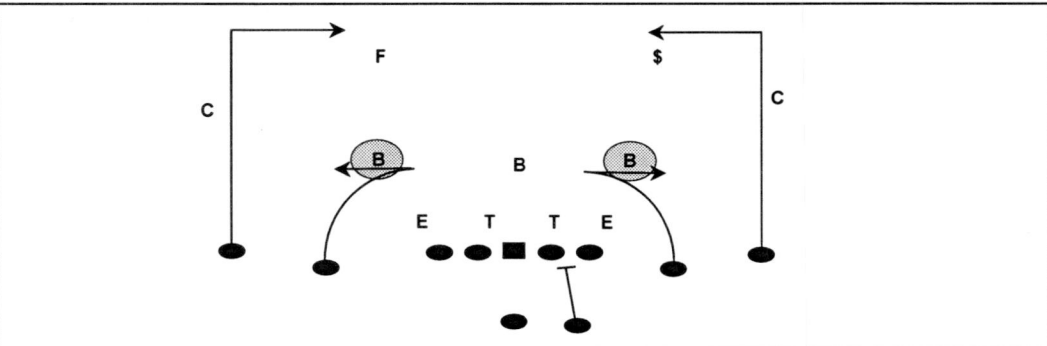

Figure 12-1. Pre-snap identification of the read key versus a cover 2 defense

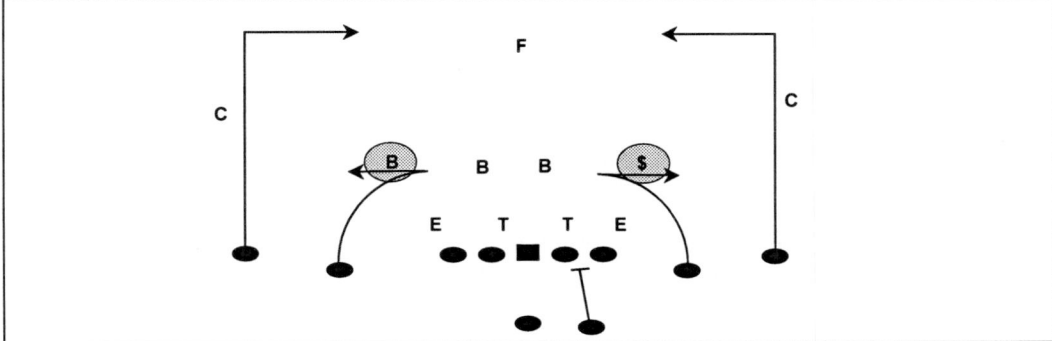

Figure 12-2. Pre-snap identification of the read key versus a cover 3 defense

Play #63: The Pivot Route

The pivot route is a good route to use on any down, as it features short throws and a simple read for the quarterback.

The quarterback will try to make the defender wrong. If the defender covers the whip route, the quarterback will throw the football to the dig route. If the defender does not react out to the whip route, the quarterback will throw the football to the whip route. The only time the football will be thrown to the post route is versus a cover 4 zone defense, with the safety trying to take the dig route away.

In a 2 x 2 set, the route is mirrored. The outside receivers will run dig routes at 10 yards. The technique will be to burst vertically for 10 yards and then make a 90-degree cut inside. The receiver will settle in the first open area after making his break. The inside receivers run a whip route. They will drive inside at a 45-degree angle for five steps and then pivot back outside parallel to the line of scrimmage at a depth of three to five yards from the line of scrimmage.

In any three- or four-receiver side of the formation, the #1 receiver will run a post route, breaking at 10 yards. The #2 receiver will run the 10-yard dig route. The #3 receiver will run the whip route, and the #4 receiver, if there is one, will run a four-step slant route. If there is a single receiver on the backside, he will run a four-step slant route.

The running back will be in protection if he is aligned in the backfield. He will follow receiver rules if he is lined up as a receiver.

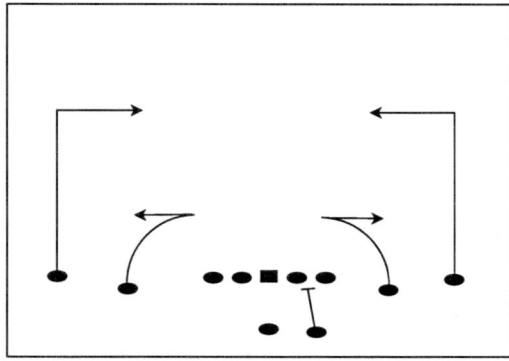

Figure 12-3. Pivot route in a 2 x 2 set

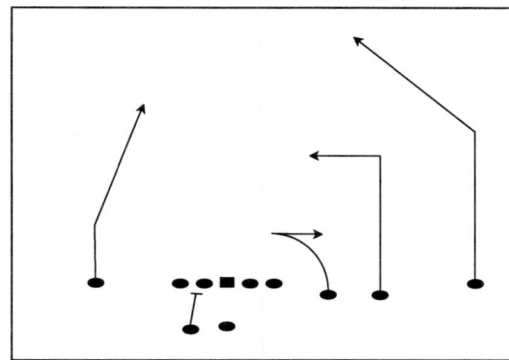

Figure 12-4. Pivot route in a 3 x 1 set

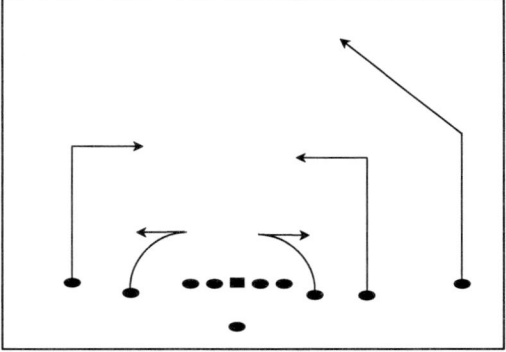

Figure 12-5. Pivot route in a 3 x 2 set

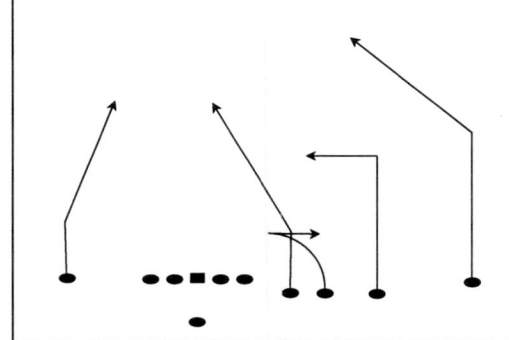

Figure 12-6. Pivot route in a 4 x 1 set

Play #64: The Pivot Route With an Under Tag

The under tag is a good route to use versus man-to-man defense. It also has the ability to beat zone defenses with a strongside flood and a weakside dig route.

The quarterback will read the #2 defender to the strongside of the formation. If he takes away the shoot route by the running back, the quarterback will look inside to the under route, by the backside inside receiver. The quarterback will then progress from the dig route to the other under route. If the #2 defender doesn't take away the shoot route by the back, the quarterback will throw the football to the running back.

Several changes are necessary for this route. The running back will always run a shoot route, no matter where he lines up. The strongside #1 receiver will run a corner route. The two receivers closest to the offensive tackles (except the running back, who runs the shoot route), will run the under routes. The receiver that comes from the side of the formation with the most receivers will be the deeper receiver. This setting is called the depth of the mesh. The other inside receiver rubs underneath. The remaining receiver will run the dig route.

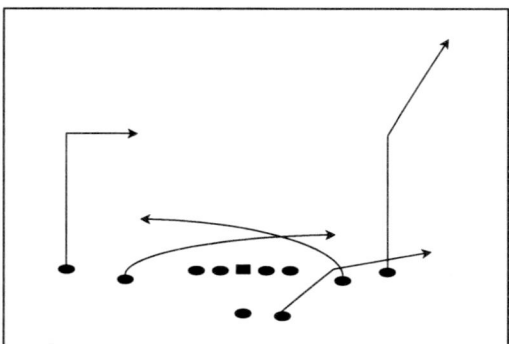

Figure 12-7. Pivot route with an under tag in a 2 x 2 set

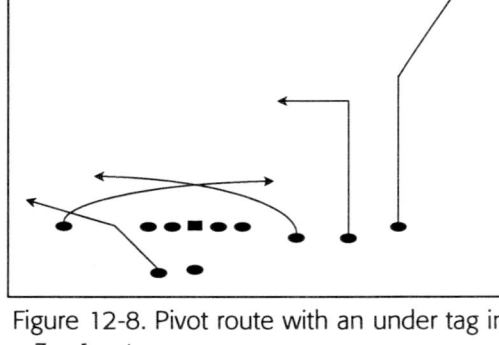

Figure 12-8. Pivot route with an under tag in a 3 x 1 set

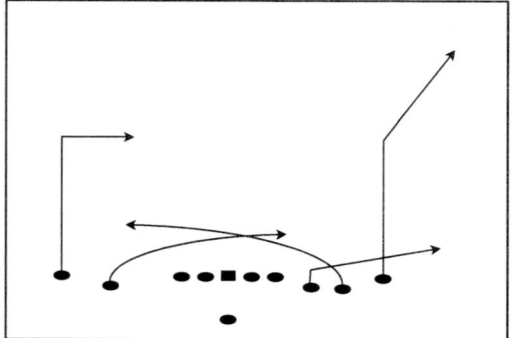

Figure 12-9. Pivot route with an under tag in a 3 x 2 set

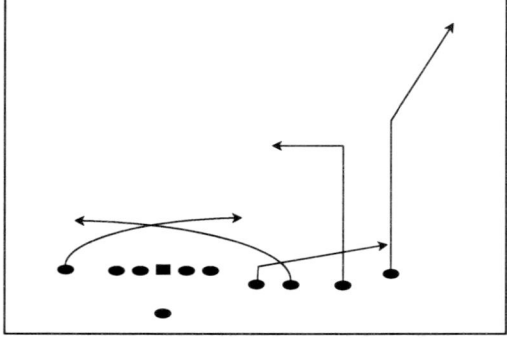

Figure 12-10. Pivot route with an under tag in a 4 x 1 set

13

Stick Routes

Introduction

The quarterback will need to identify the #2 defender to the strongside of the formation because the #2 defender is the quarterback's first read on the stick play.

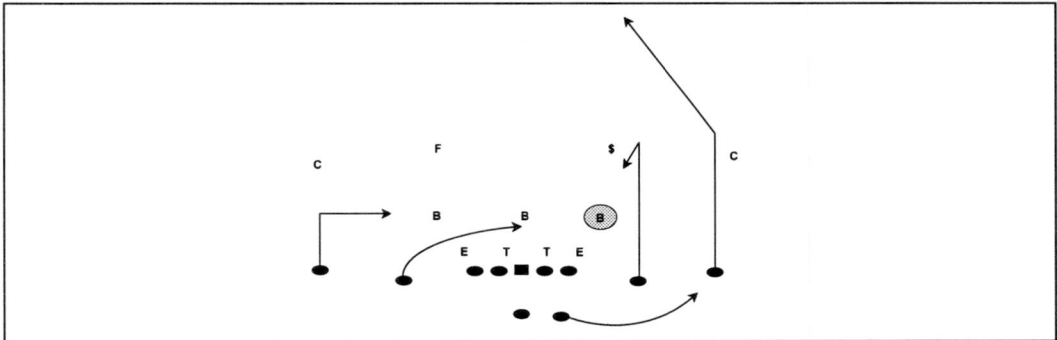

Figure 13-1. Pre-snap identification of the read key versus a cover 2 defense

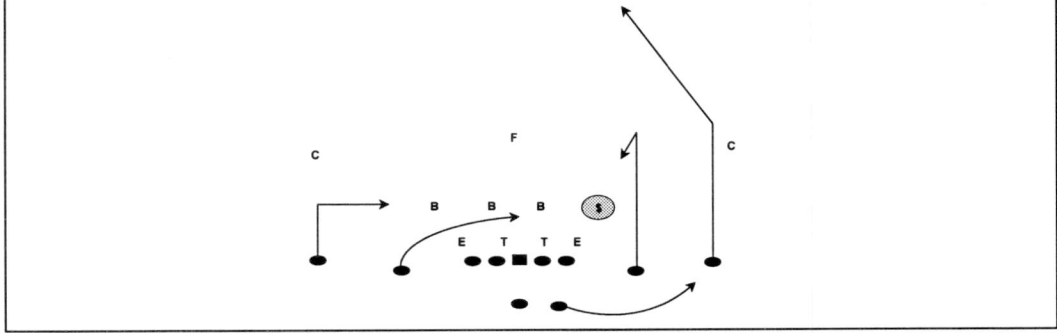

Figure 13-2. Pre-snap identification of the read key versus a cover 3 defense

Play #65: The Stick Route

The stick route is a good way to attack cover 3 and cover 4 zone defenses. It also has built-in man beaters on the backside of the formation.

The quarterback will read the #2 defender and try to make him wrong. If the defender covers the bubble route, the quarterback will throw the football to the stick-curl route. If the defender does not react out to the bubble route, the quarterback will throw the football to the bubble route. The only time the football will be thrown to the post route is versus a cover 4 zone defense, with the safety trying to take the stick-curl route away. If the bubble and stick routes are covered, the quarterback will progress back across the field to the middle hunt route, followed by the four-step in route on the backside.

The stick route is set up to be a strongside play, and all routes work from the strongside #1 receiver. Therefore, the route does not mirror. The strongside outside receiver will run a 10-yard post route. The #2 receiver will run a 10-yard stick-curl. The #3 receiver, either a receiver or the running back out of the backfield, will run a bubble route. The #4 receiver will run a middle hunt route five to eight yards deep over the strongside offensive tackle. The #5 receiver runs a four-step in route. If the #4 receiver is on the strongside, he will run a whip route in order to hit the same landmark he would if he were on the backside of the formation running the hunt route.

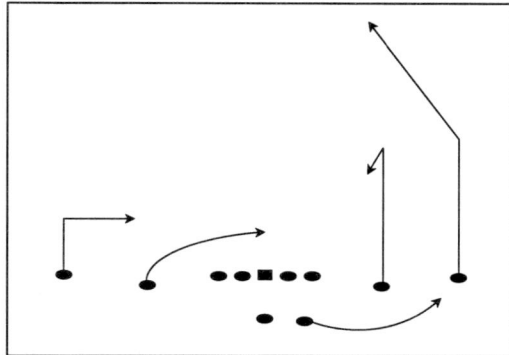
Figure 13-3. Stick route in a 2 x 2 set

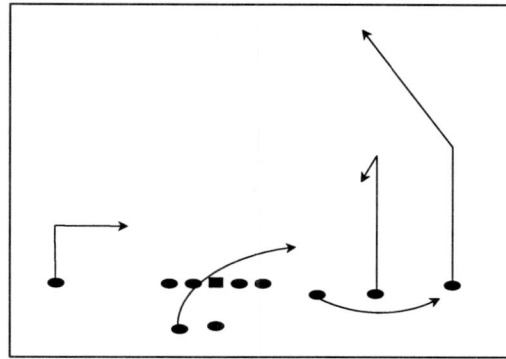
Figure 13-4. Stick route in a 3 x 1 set

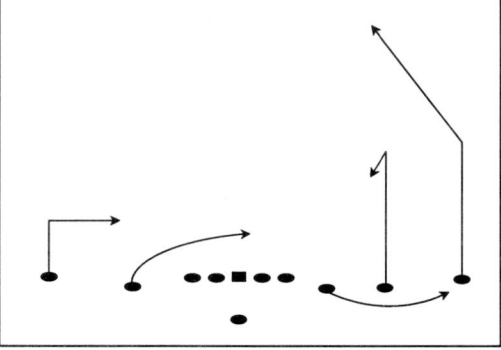
Figure 13-5. Stick route in a 3 x 2 set

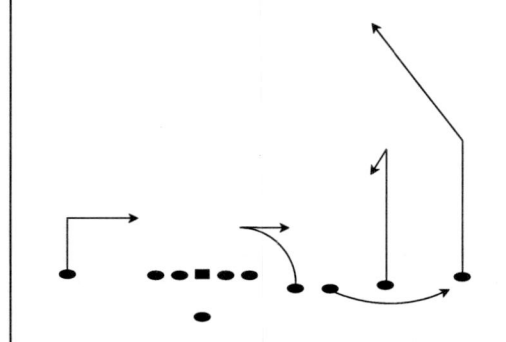
Figure 13-6. Stick route in a 4 x 1 set

Play #66: The Stick Route With a Wheel Tag

The wheel tag, a good addition to the stick route, is good for taking advantage of man-to-man coverage teams. The quarterback will still read the #2 defender, and if he runs with the shoot-to-wheel route, the quarterback can either stay with the wheel route, or he can work the backside of the formation. The only adjustment on the wheel route is the bubble. The bubble becomes a shoot route for five steps and then turns into a wheel route up the sideline.

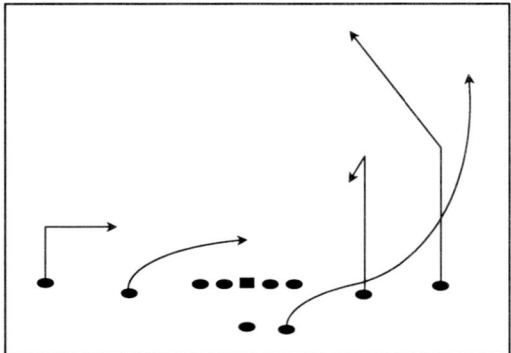

Figure 13-7. Stick route with a wheel tag in a 2 x 2 set

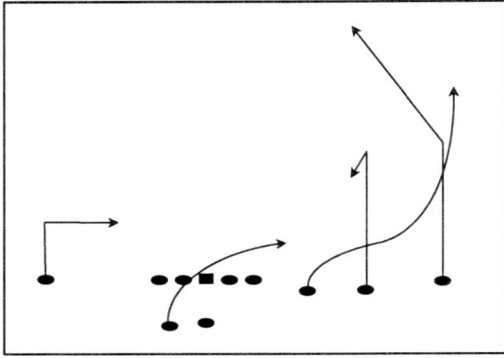

Figure 13-8. Stick route with a wheel tag in a 3 x 1 set

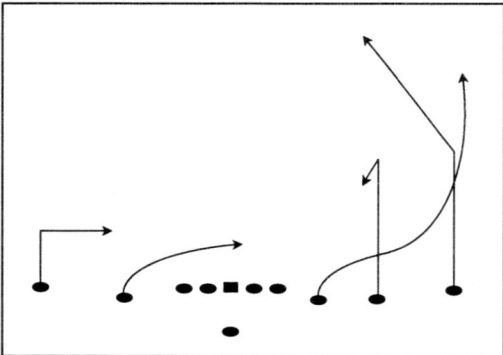

Figure 13-9. Stick route with a wheel tag in a 3 x 2 set

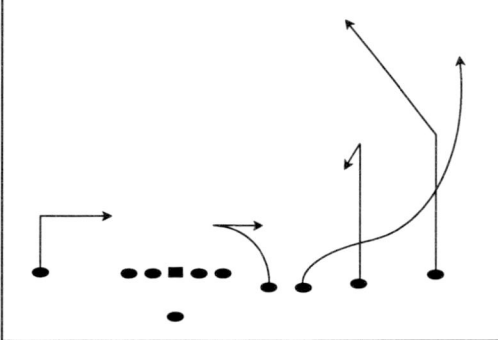

Figure 13-10. Stick route with a wheel tag in a 4 x 1 set

14

Drag Routes

Introduction

The quarterback will need to identify and read the #2 defender to the weakside of the formation.

Play #67: The Drag Route

The drag route is a good cover 2 zone beater. It is also a good route to use versus man-to-man defenses. The drag route is a good complement to many other drop-back routes in that the quarterback will be reading the #2 defender to the weakside of the formation instead of reading the #2 defender to the strongside of the formation.

After the quarterback identifies the #2 defender, he will react to his movement. If the #2 defender blitzes, the quarterback will throw the football to the dig route, who will be converting his route to a four-step slant. If the defender opens and runs with the dig route, the quarterback will be patient and throw the football to the drag route after the drag has cleared the tackle box. If the defender collisions the dig and then sits to wait for the drag route, the quarterback will stare at the drag route, reset his feet, and throw to the dig route behind the #2 defender.

The running back will run a shoot route every time, whether he is lined up in the backfield or lined up as a receiver.

In a 2 x 2 set, the strongside outside receiver will run a 10-yard post route. The weakside outside receiver will run a vertical route. The inside receivers will run a dig or a drag. A good rule is to tag the receiver to run the drag route. It is also a good rule to have the receiver to the side of the back run the drag route. The remaining inside receiver will then run the 10-yard dig route. The dig route will always come from the opposite side of the drag route. The receiver will convert the dig route to a four-step slant versus blitz on his side of the formation.

In any three- or four-receiver side of the formation, the two receivers closest to the offensive tackles will run the dig and drag routes, unless that position is filled by a running back, who runs the shoot route. The remaining receivers will, outside in, run a vertical route, a post route, and a four-step slant route.

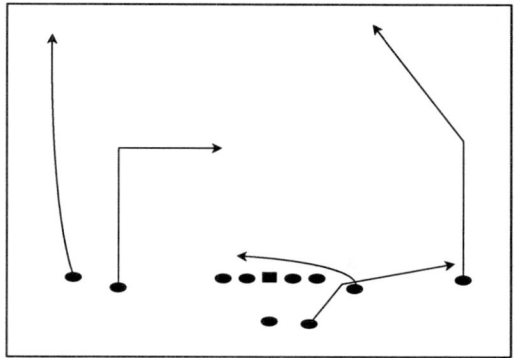

Figure 14-1. Drag route in a 2 x 2 set

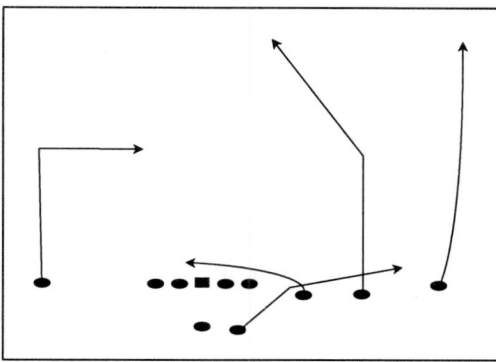

Figure 14-2. Drag route in a 3 x 1 set

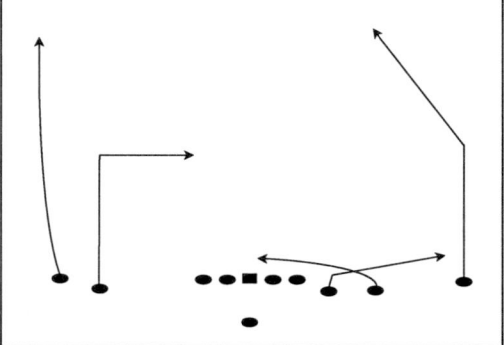

Figure 14-3. Drag route in a 3 x 2 set

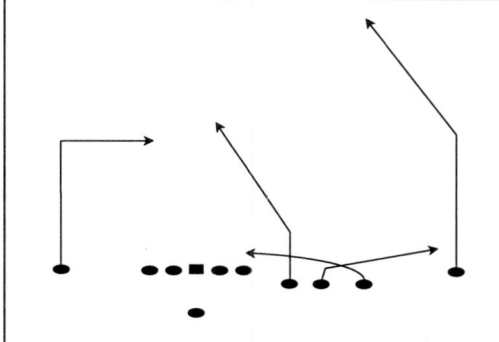

Figure 14-4. Drag route in a 4 x 1 set

Play #68: The Drag Route With a Wheel Tag

The wheel tag is a good way to attack man-to-man coverage. It is especially good to use when the running back is clearly faster than the defender covering him. When the wheel tag is called, it is expected that the offense has a favorable matchup between the running back and the defender covering him. The quarterback will look to the wheel route first, and then come back down to the drag-dig read. The wheel tag is for the running back. Instead of running the shoot route, he will run the shoot for five steps and then turn the route into a wheel route up the sideline. All other routes for the receivers will stay the same, just like the base drag route package.

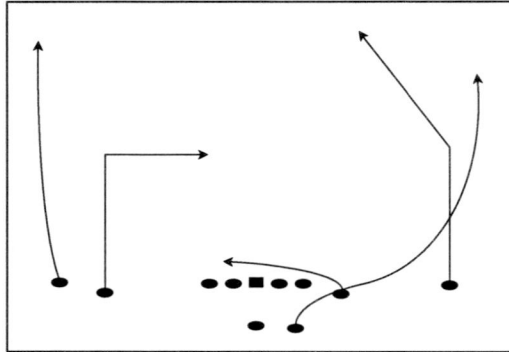

Figure 14-5. Drag route with a wheel tag in a 2 x 2 set

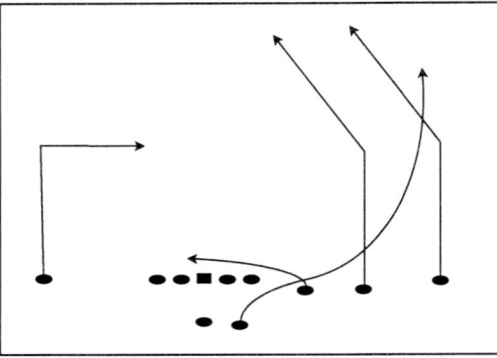

Figure 14-6. Drag route with a wheel tag in a 3 x 1 set

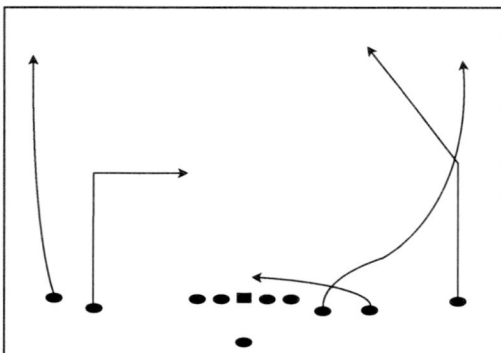

Figure 14-7. Drag route with a wheel tag in a 3 x 2 set

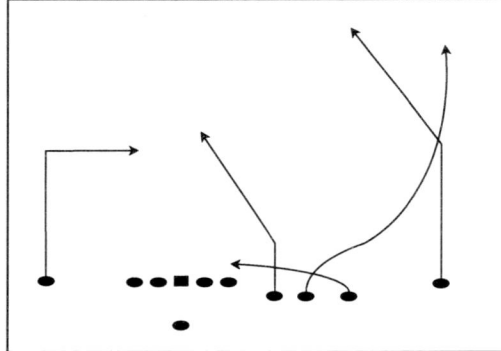

Figure 14-8. Drag route with a wheel tag in a 4 x 1 set

Play #69: The Drag Route With a Curl Tag

The curl tag is another good addition to the drag route package, as it gives the quarterback a good option to work versus cover 3 zone defense.

The quarterback will pre-snap read the defense, and if he sees the defense in a cover 2 zone or in man-to-man defense, he will work his read just as if there wasn't a tag. If the defense is in cover 3 zone, the quarterback will read the route like the curl package. He will read the #3 defender to the strongside of the formation, and then work the flat-curl combination.

All routes will stay the same as the base drag route package with the exception of the strongside outside receiver. He will run a post-curl route at 12 yards.

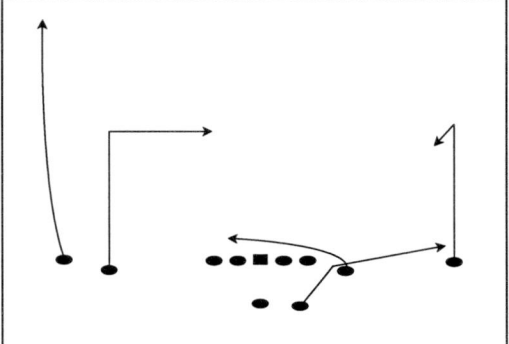

Figure 14-9. Drag route with a curl tag in a 2 x 2 set

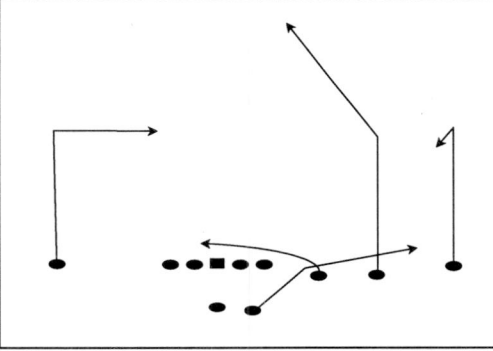

Figure 14-10. Drag route with a curl tag in a 3 x 1 set

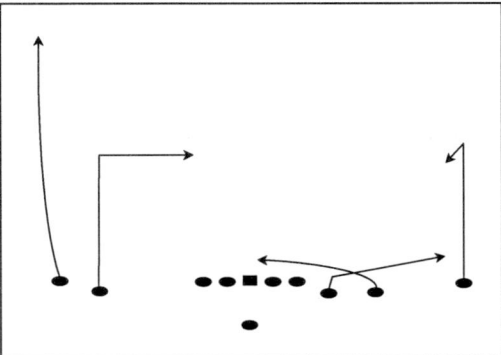

Figure 14-11. Drag route with a curl tag in a 3 x 2 set

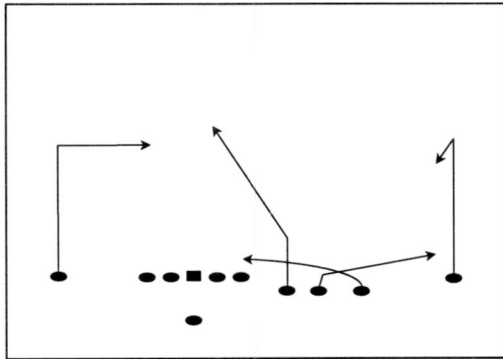

Figure 14-12. Drag route with a curl tag in a 4 x 1 set

15

Drive Routes

Introduction

The quarterback will need to identify the read key, who on this route is the defender lined up over the receiver running the drive route.

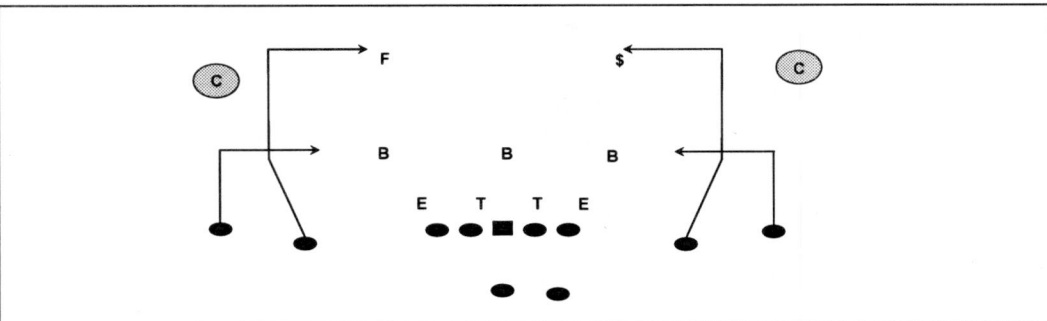

Figure 15-1. Pre-snap identification of the read key in a 2 x 2 set

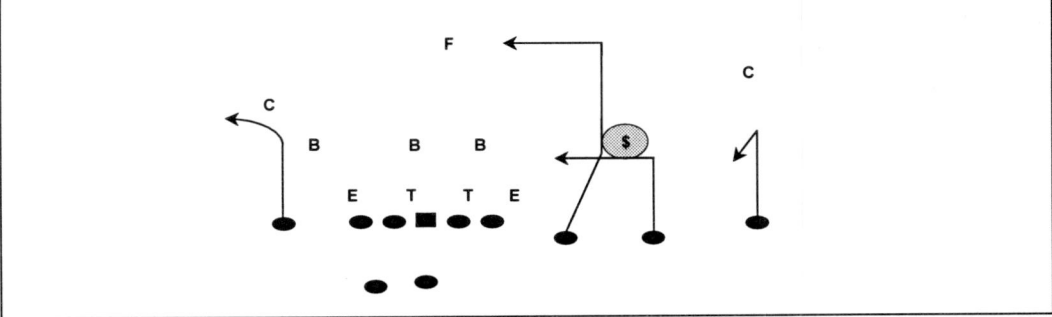

Figure 15-2. Pre-snap identification of the read key in a 3 x 1 set

Play #70: The Drive Route

The drive route is a fairly new route to football. It is a great possession route, and has the potential for big plays when it's used with tags such as seam, corner, and swap, which are all discussed in this chapter.

The quarterback will read the defender over the drive route. A good rule for the quarterback is to throw to the drive route every time until the defense clearly takes the drive route away. If the defense takes the drive route away, the quarterback will then work to the dig. Then, if there is a hitch route to that side, he will try to deliver the football there, late.

The running back will be in protection if he is aligned in the backfield. He will follow receiver rules if he is lined up as a receiver.

In 2 x 2 sets, the route is mirrored. The outside receiver will run a drive route, with the technique being to drive four steps up the field, plant, and then break inside, parallel to the line of scrimmage. The receiver should look for the football right off of the break. If the receiver feels a man following, he will continue to run away from the defense. If he is not being chased, he will settle and make himself available to the quarterback. The inside receivers will run a rub-dig route. The receiver's first job is to rub for the drive route; his second job is to run the dig route at 10 yards.

In any three- or four-receiver side of the formation, the #2 receiver will run the drive route, and the first receiver inside of the drive route will run the rub-dig route. The next receiver inside, if there is one, will run a four-step slant route. The receiver outside of the drive route will run a hitch route.

The outside receiver on the opposite side of a three- or four-receiver side will run a four-step speed-out route. If there is an inside receiver, he will run a seam route. The outside receiver is an especially good option versus blitz or if there is a positive matchup between the outside receiver and the #1 defender.

The drive route can be run out of several different formations within the spread offense, including 2 x 2 sets, 3 x 1 sets, 3 x 2 sets, and 4 x 1 sets.

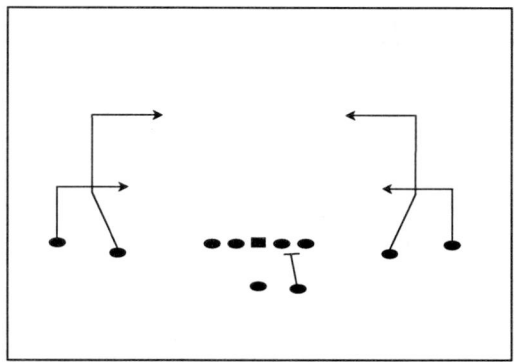

Figure 15-3. Drive route in a 2 x 2 set

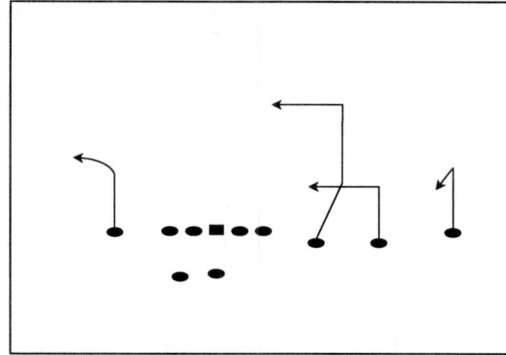

Figure 15-4. Drive route in a 3 x 1 set

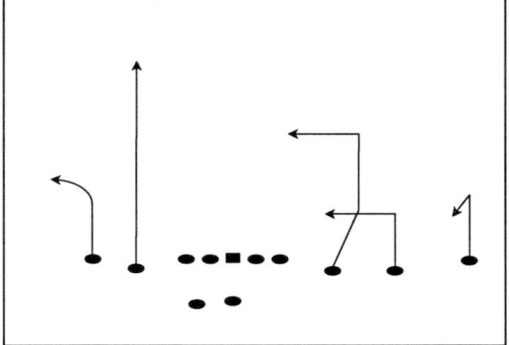

Figure 15-5. Drive route in a 3 x 2 set

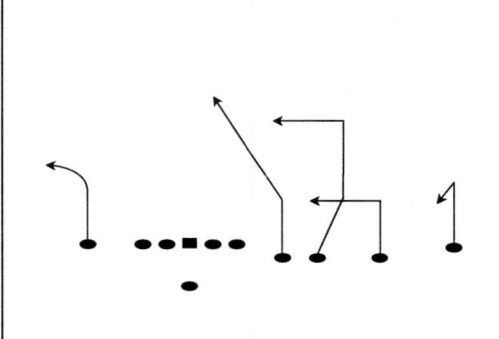

Figure 15-6. Drive route in a 4 x 1 set

Play #71: The Drive Route With a Seam Tag

The seam tag is used with the drive route to give the offense an option of a vertical route within the package.

The read for the quarterback will be the same. He will still try to throw the drive route first; then he will progress to the seam route; and finally he will look to the hitch route by the outside receiver, if there is one.

The running back will be in protection if he is aligned in the backfield. He will follow receiver rules if he is lined up as a receiver.

This route is also mirrored in 2 x 2 sets. The only change on this route is by the first receiver inside the drive route. Instead of running a rub-dig route, he will run a rub-seam route. All other routes stay consistent with the base drive route, in all formations.

The drive route with the seam tag can be run out of several different formations, including 2 x 2 sets, 3 x 1 sets, 3 x 2 sets, and 4 x 1 sets.

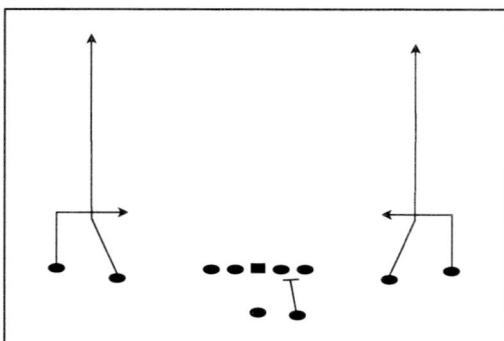

Figure 15-7. Drive route with a seam tag in a 2 x 2 set

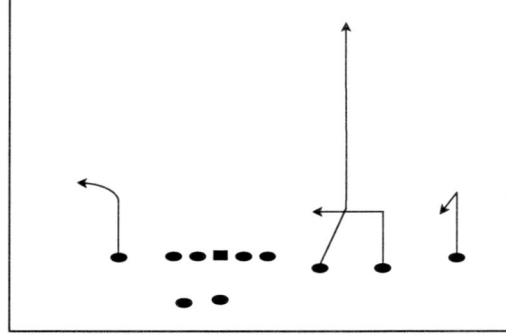

Figure 15-8. Drive route with a seam tag in a 3 x 1 set

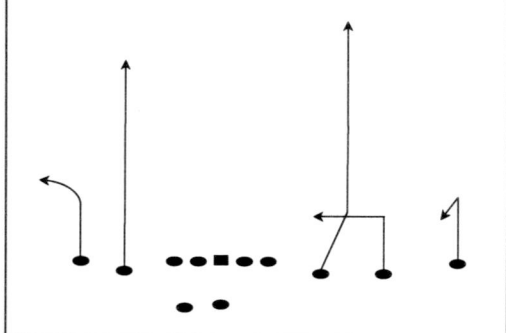

Figure 15-9. Drive route with a seam tag in a 3 x 2 set

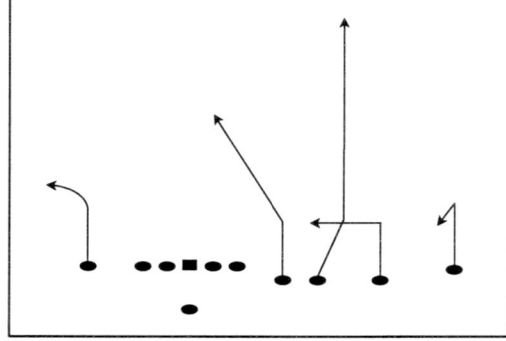

Figure 15-10. Drive route with a seam tag in a 4 x 1 set

Play #72: The Drive Route With a Corner Tag

The corner tag is used with the drive route to give the offense an option of a corner route within the package. It is good for attacking man-to-man defense as well as cover 2 zone defense.

The read for the quarterback will be the same. He will still try to throw the drive route first; then he will progress to the corner route; and finally he will look to the hitch route by the outside receiver, if there is one.

The running back will be in protection if he is aligned in the backfield. He will follow receiver rules if he is lined up as a receiver.

This route is also mirrored in 2 x 2 sets. The only change on this route is by the first receiver inside the drive route. Instead of running a rub-dig route, he will run a rub-corner route. All other routes stay consistent with the base drive route, in all formations.

The drive route with the corner tag can be run out of several different formations, including 2 x 2 sets, 3 x 1 sets, 3 x 2 sets, and 4 x 1 sets.

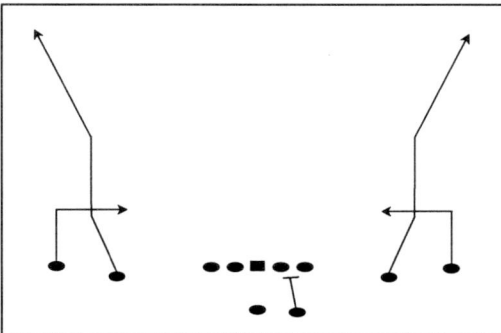

Figure 15-11. Drive route with a corner tag in a 2 x 2 set

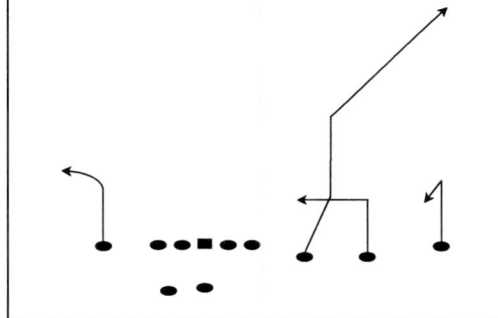

Figure 15-12. Drive route with a corner tag in a 3 x 1 set

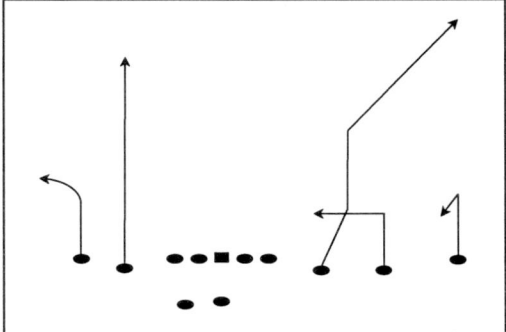

Figure 15-13. Drive route with a corner tag in a 3 x 2 set

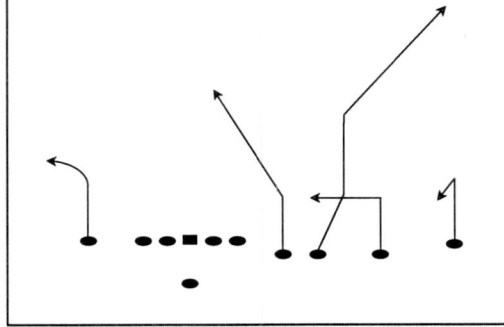

Figure 15-14. Drive route with a corner tag in a 4 x 1 set

Play #73: The Drive Route With a Swap Tag

The swap tag exchanges the routes of the #2 and the #3 receivers. This route is a good way to get the drive route to come open quickly, without the clutter of another receiver trying to rub a defender.

The read for the quarterback will be the same. He will still try to throw the drive route first; then he will progress to the dig route and finally he will look to the hitch route by the outside receiver, if there is one.

The running back will be in protection if he is aligned in the backfield. He will follow receiver rules if he is lined up as a receiver.

The only change on this route is the #2 receiver will run the dig route, and the #3 receiver will run the drive route. All other routes stay consistent with the base drive route, in all formations.

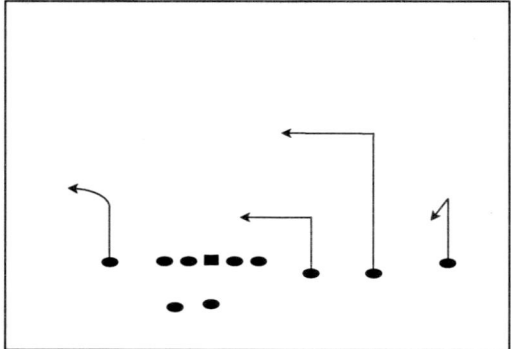

Figure 15-15. Drive route with a swap tag in a 3 x 1 set

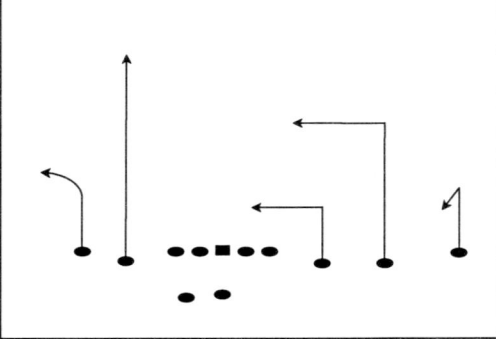

Figure 15-16. Drive route with a swap tag in a 3 x 2 set

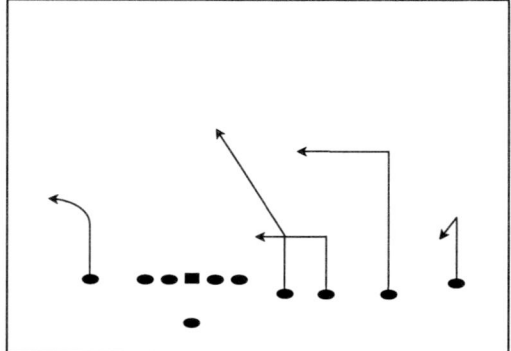

Figure 15-17. Drive route with a swap tag in a 4 x 1 set

16

Scat Routes

Introduction

It is important for the quarterback to identify his read key when using the scat route. It is also important for the quarterback to be able to see the leverage that the receivers have on the read key.

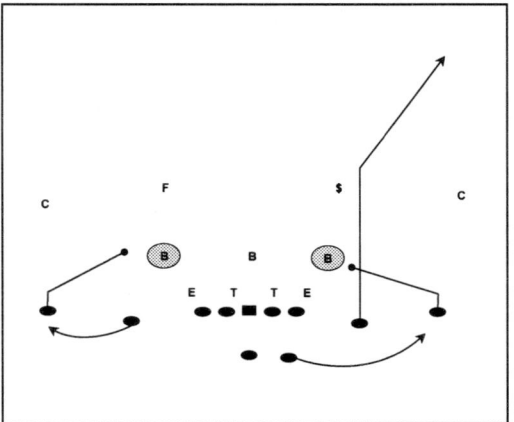

Figure 16-1. Pre-snap identification of the read key in a 2 x 2 set

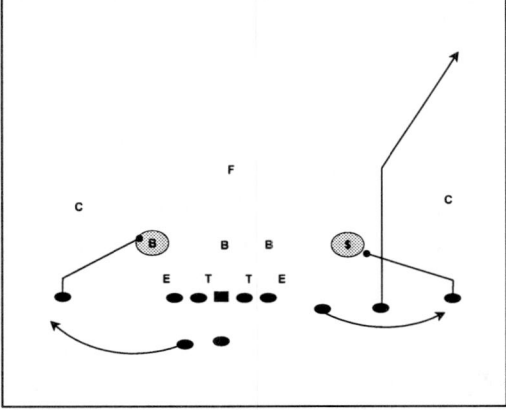

Figure 16-2. Pre-snap identification of the read key in a 3 x 1 set

Play #74: The Scat Route

The scat route is a good way to be able to get the ball to a variety of receivers based on the quarterback's read and the coverage employed by the defense. The route also has built-in answers to beat various coverages.

The quarterback will read the #2 defender. If the defender works outside to cover the swing or bubble route of the receiver or running back, the quarterback will throw the football to the outside receiver on the slant-sit route. If the defender holds inside on the slant-sit route by the outside receiver, the quarterback will throw the football to the swing or bubble route. The corner route is a good option versus man-to-man defenses.

The running back will run a swing route, looking back for the football over his inside shoulder after his third step. If lined up as a receiver, the running back will follow receiver rules.

The receivers will always have a three-man side and a two-man side, unless the offense is lined up in a 4 x 1 set.

On the three-man side, the outside receiver will run a slant-sit route. The technique is to drive two steps forward, then break inside at a 45-degree angle, and accelerate to a finishing point of one step inside the #2 defender. The #2 receiver on the three-man side will run a corner route. He will push vertically to 10 yards, dip his shoulder to the post, and break to the corner, aiming 25 yards deep at the sideline. The #3 receiver will run a bubble route. If the #3 receiver is the running back in a 2 x 2 set, he will run a swing route. On the two-man side, the #1 receiver mirrors the three-man side receiver's slant-sit route. The #2 receiver runs a bubble route. If there is a #4 receiver, he will run a four-step slant route. If there is a single receiver on a side without a running back to his side, he will still run the two-step slant-sit.

The scat route can be run out of several different formations within the spread offense, including 2 x 2 sets, 3 x 1 sets, 3 x 2 sets, and 4 x 1 sets.

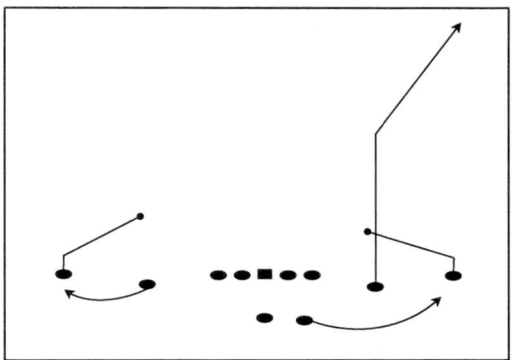
Figure 16-3. Scat route in a 2 x 2 set

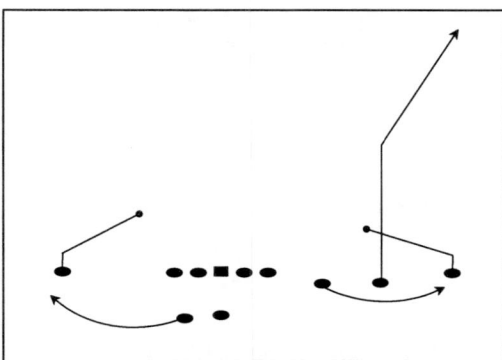
Figure 16-4. Scat route in a 3 x 1 set

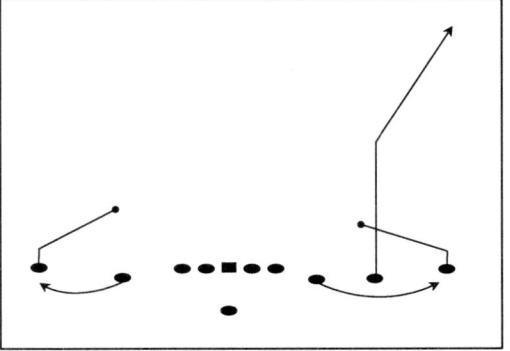
Figure 16-5. Scat route in a 3 x 2 set

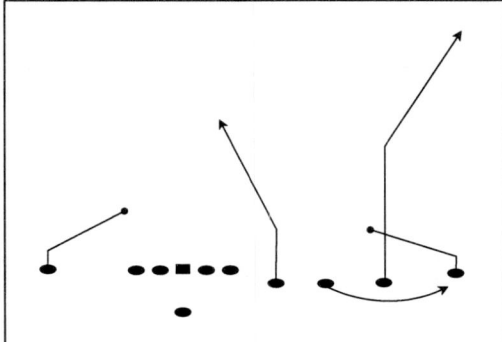
Figure 16-6. Scat route in a 4 x 1 set

Play #75: The Scat Route With a Trail Tag

The trail tag is a good way to attack switch man-to-man or bracket defenses. The trail tag should only be used to a three or a four-receiver side of a formation.

The quarterback will look first to the outside receiver on the under route, then to the inside receiver on the trail route.

All receiver rules remain intact with the exception of the #1 and #3 receivers to the three- or four-man side. The outside receiver will run a two-step under route. He cannot sit his route down versus zone defense, as the trail route is following him. The #3 receiver will run his normal bubble route for five steps. Then he will plant and cut back inside, following the under route. This same rule applies for the running back. In a 2 x 2 set, he will run the trail route. If there is a #4 receiver, he will run a four-step slant route. If there is a single receiver on a side without a running back to his side, he will still run the two-step slant-sit.

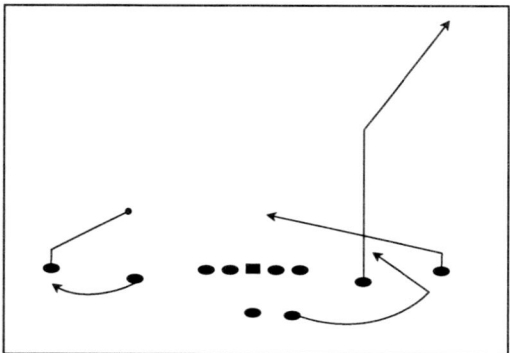

Figure 16-7. Scat route with a trail tag in a 2 x 2 set

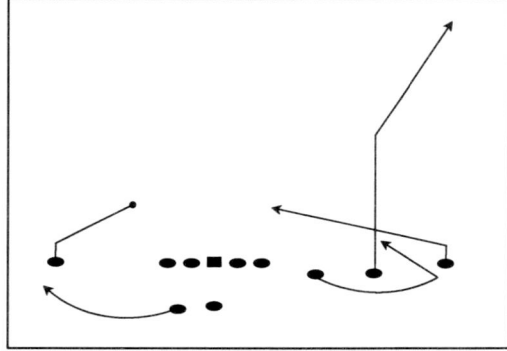

Figure 16-8. Scat route with a trail tag in a 3 x 1 set

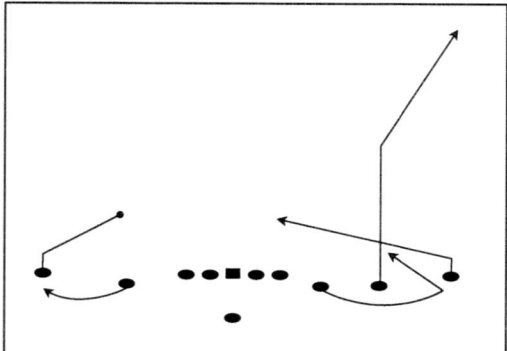

Figure 16-9. Scat route with a trail tag in a 3 x 2 set

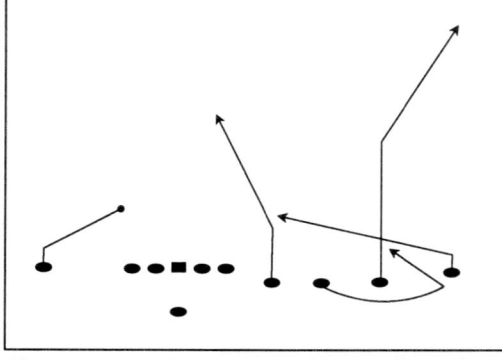

Figure 16-10. Scat route with a trail tag in a 4 x 1 set

Play #76: The Scat Route With an Under and Dig Tag

The under and dig tags are solid additions to the scat route. They allow the route to be more effective versus man-to-man defenses. The under and dig tags also give the offense the opportunity to attack the middle of the defense more effectively.

The quarterback will read the #2 defender to the strongside of the formation. If he takes away the swing route by the running back or the bubble route by the receiver, the quarterback will look inside to the under route, by the backside receiver. The quarterback will then progress to the dig route, and to the other under route. If the #2 defender doesn't take away the swing route by the back, or the bubble route by the receiver, the quarterback will throw the football to the swing or bubble route.

Several changes are necessary on the route. The running back will still run a swing route if lined up in the backfield. He will follow the receiver rules when lined up as a receiver. The under tag tells the outside receivers to convert their slant-sit routes into under routes. They will cross the formation at three to four yards deep. The receiver lined up on the side of the formation with the most receivers will be the deeper of the two under routes. The dig tag tells the #2 receiver to run a dig route at 10 yards instead of the corner route. If there is a #4 receiver, he will run a four-step slant route.

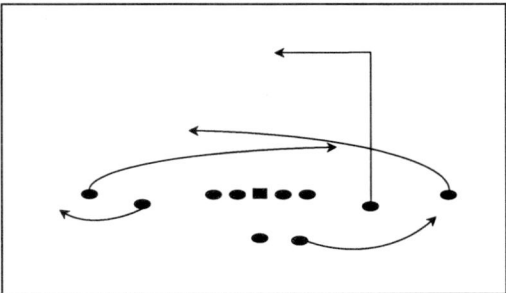

Figure 16-11. Scat route with an under and a dig tag in a 2 x 2 set

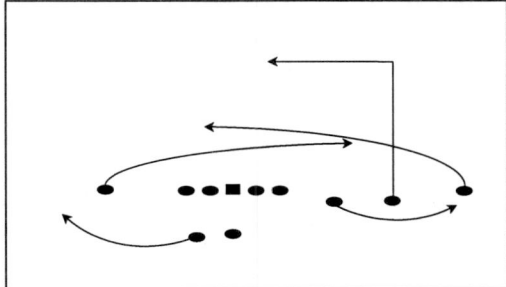

Figure 16-12. Scat route with an under and a dig tag in a 3 x 1 set

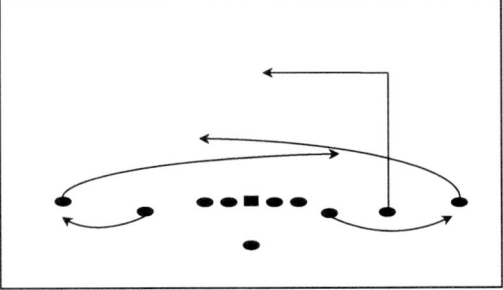

Figure 16-13. Scat route with an under and a dig tag in a 3 x 2 set

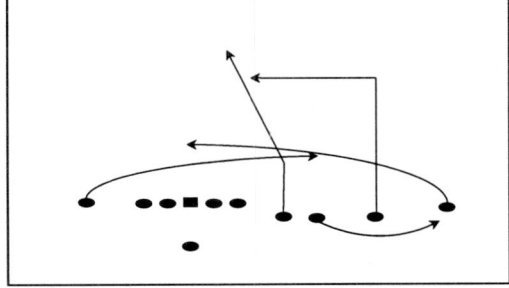

Figure 16-14. Scat route with an under and a dig tag in a 4 x 1 set

Play #77: The Scat Route From a Bunch Set

The scat route from a bunch set gives the route an entirely new personality. This route becomes a very good route for attacking any coverage. The route does, however, take time to implement, based on the releases of the receivers from a compressed set.

The quarterback will read the strongside of the formation. He will execute a progression read. Versus man-to-man defense, the quarterback will look to the shoot route first, followed by the corner route, and finally the whip route. Versus cover 3 zone defense, the quarterback will look to the shoot route first, followed by the whip route and finally the corner route. Versus cover 4 zone defense, the quarterback will look to the shoot route first, followed by the whip route, and finally the corner route. Versus cover 2 zone defense, the quarterback will look to the corner route first, followed by the whip route.

The basic rules by the receivers will stay the same, with minor adjustments to their individual techniques. The outside receiver will run a whip route and will aim to run over the feet of the #3 defender versus man-to-man coverage. When running his route against zone defense, he will release inside, run at the next defender inside, selling the under route, and then he will pivot back outside. The #2 receiver will run the same corner route with no changes. The #3 receiver will run a pause-shoot route. He will hold in place for a count, then release on a shoot route, looking for the ball over his outside shoulder after his third step. In a 4 x 1 set, this receiver is lined up in the back, farthest away from the line of scrimmage. If there is a #4 receiver, he will run a four-step slant route. On this route, the #4 receiver is considered the receiver closest to the offensive tackle.

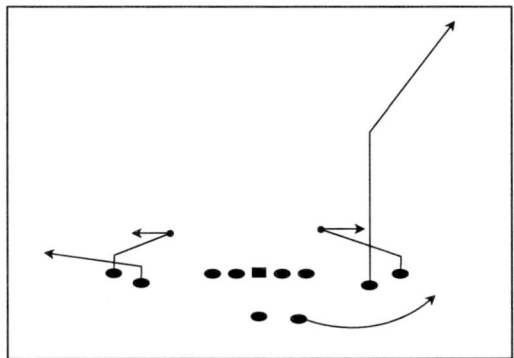

Figure 16-15. Scat route from a bunch 2 x 2 set

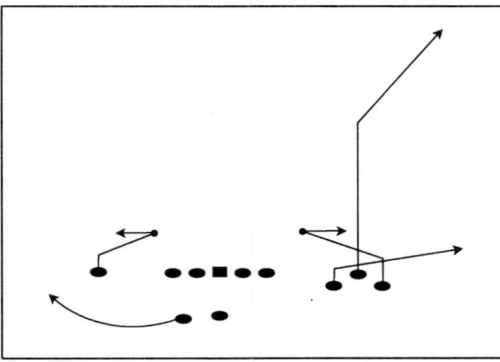

Figure 16-16. Scat route from a bunch 3 x 1 set

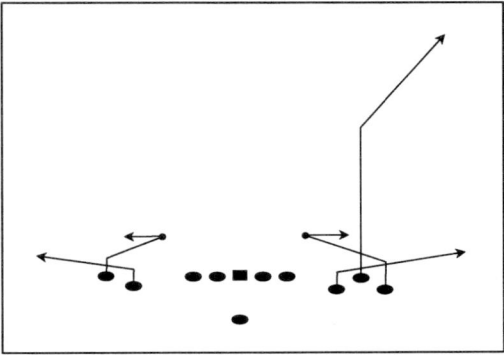

Figure 16-17. Scat route from a bunch 3 x 2 set

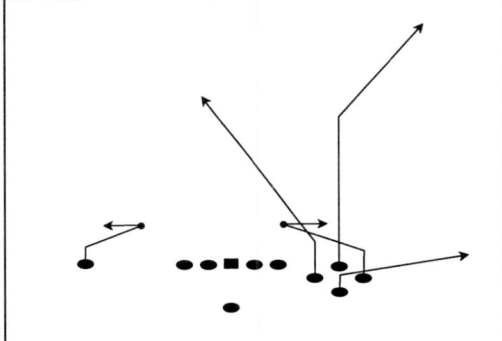

Figure 16-18. Scat route from a bunch 4 x 1 set

Section 3:
The Screen Passes

17

Bubble Screen

Introduction

The bubble screen can be used as an extension of the quick passing game as well as the running game. It is also an effective tool to keep the defense honest versus the run. By running the bubble screen, the defensive force players have to either play the pass or play the run. They cannot do both at the same time. In addition, the bubble screen is great to use any time there are more receivers aligned on one side of the formation than defenders. This screen is not effective versus tight man-to-man defense.

Play #78: The Bubble Screen

A good rule to use with offensive linemen is for the playside linemen (including the center) to reach block and the backside linemen to base block. An alternate way to block the bubble screen is to have all the linemen outside-zone block to the playside.

On the bubble screen, the quarterback will open and throw the ball as quickly as he can to the intended receiver. Speed of delivery and accuracy are paramount. A typical rule is to have the inside receiver be the designated receiver to catch the bubble screen.

The running back will fake a run away from the playside. Another way to use the running back is to have him lead on the playside force player of the defense.

The receiver to run the bubble will take three steps in place and then open up to the sideline and run as fast as he can to the sideline, while looking over his inside shoulder. He does not want to cross the line of scrimmage before he catches the football. The first receiver outside the bubble receiver will block the most dangerous man to the bubble route. The remaining receivers lined up on the playside will block the next players out from the most dangerous man. Backside receivers execute their normal backside run rules.

The bubble screen can be run out of several different formations, specifically anytime the offense has the defense outnumbered. Offensive sets include 2 x 2, 3 x 1, 3 x 2, and 4 x 1 sets.

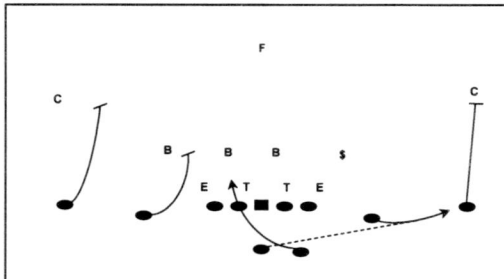

Figure 17-1. Bubble screen in a 2 x 2 set

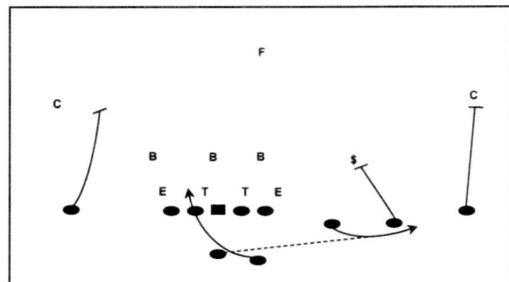

Figure 17-2. Bubble screen in a 3 x 1 set

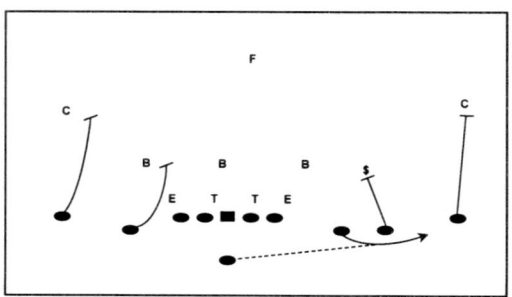

Figure 17-3. Bubble screen in a 3 x 2 set

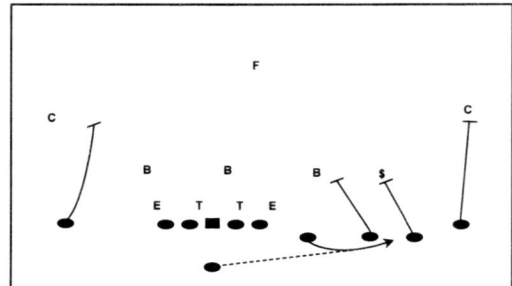

Figure 17-4. Bubble screen in a 4 x 1 set

Play #79: The Bubble Screen and Go

The bubble screen and go is good to use versus teams that are using defensive backs to aggressively stop the bubble screen.

The offensive line will be involved in quick pass protection.

The quarterback will open and fake the throw to the bubble screen, set his feet, and get the ball out as quickly as possible. He will look for the outside receiver first and then progress in.

The running back technique is identical to the bubble screen pass. He will be involved in pass protection if he is in the backfield, and involved in the route scheme if he is lined up as a receiver.

The bubble receiver will run the same bubble route, with no change in technique. The outside receiver will drive inside slightly to sell a block on the first defender inside of him, and then he will burst up the seam, staying away from the safety. The next receiver in will sell a block on the force defender and then sit down one step inside of this defender. If there is a fourth receiver on the playside, he will execute the same responsibility that the #3 receiver will execute in a three-receiver set. Backside receivers run the short route package.

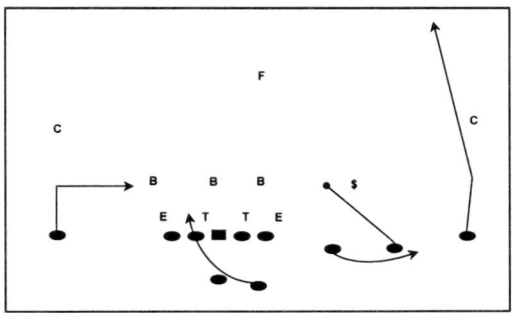

Figure 17-5. Bubble screen and go in a 3 x 1 set

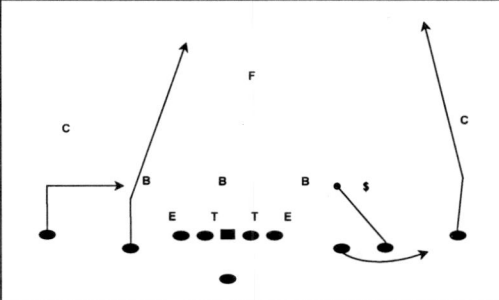

Figure 17-6. Bubble screen and go in a 3 x 2 set

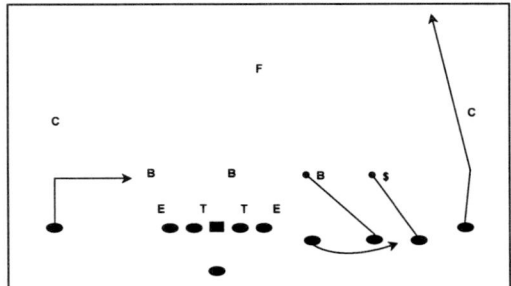

Figure 17-7. Bubble screen and go in a 4 x 1 set

18

Hitch Screen

Introduction

The hitch screen can be used as an extension of the quick passing game. It is also an excellent way to get the ball to the outside receivers. The hitch screen is great to use anytime there are more receivers aligned on one side of the formation than defenders. This screen is not effective versus tight man-to-man defense.

Play #80: The Hitch Screen

A good rule for the linemen to use on the hitch screen is to have the playside linemen (including the center) to reach block and the backside linemen to base block. An alternate way to block the hitch screen is to have the linemen all outside-zone block to the playside.

On the hitch screen, just like the bubble screen, the quarterback will open and throw the ball as quickly as he can to the intended receiver. Speed of delivery and accuracy are paramount. A typical rule is to have the outside receiver be the designated receiver to catch the hitch screen, but by tagging a receiver at the end of the play call, the intended receiver can be changed.

The rule for the running back is the same on the hitch screen as it is on the bubble screen. The running back will fake a run away from the playside. Another way to use the running back is to have him lead on the playside force player of the defense.

The receiver to run the hitch will take two steps forward, push back, and then open up to the quarterback. After catching the ball, the receiver will read the block of the next receiver inside on the defender over the hitch receiver. The first receiver inside the hitch receiver will block the most dangerous man to the hitch route. The remaining receivers lined up on the playside will block the next players in from the most dangerous man. Backside receivers execute their normal backside run rules.

The hitch screen can be run out of several different formations, specifically any time the offense has the defense outnumbered. Offensive sets include 2 x 2, 3 x 1, 3 x 2, and 4 x 1 sets.

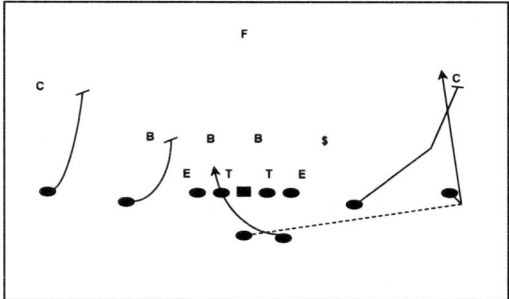

Figure 18-1. Hitch screen in a 2 x 2 set

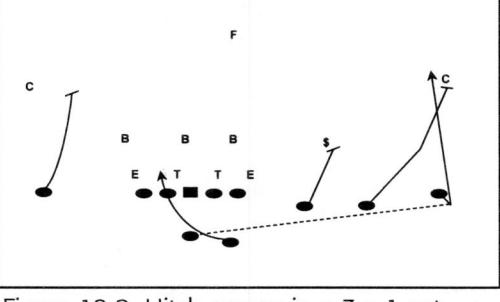

Figure 18-2. Hitch screen in a 3 x 1 set

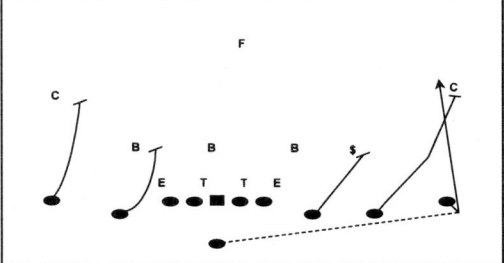

Figure 18-3. Hitch screen in a 3 x 2 set

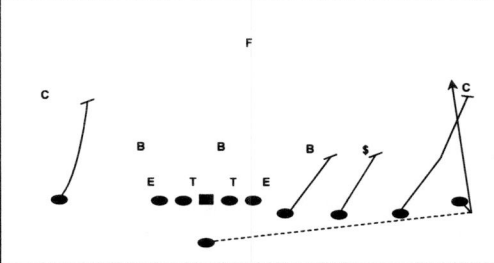

Figure 18-4. Hitch screen in a 4 x 1 set

Play #81: The Hitch Screen and Go

The hitch screen and go is good to use versus teams that are using both the #1 defender and safety to aggressively stop the hitch screen.

The offensive line will be involved in quick pass protection.

The quarterback will open and fake the throw to the hitch screen, set his feet, and get the ball out as quickly as possible. He will look for the outside receiver first and then progress in.

The running back technique is identical to the hitch screen pass. He will be involved in pass protection if he is in the backfield, and involved in the route scheme if he is lined up as a receiver.

The outside receiver will sell the hitch screen and then burst up the field on a vertical route. The receiver needs to avoid contact with the defender. The #2 receiver will run his path as if to block the #1 defender and then settle, getting his numbers to the quarterback. The remaining receivers inside will sell blocks on the nearest defenders inside of their alignment, and then turn back to the quarterback. Backside receivers run the short route package.

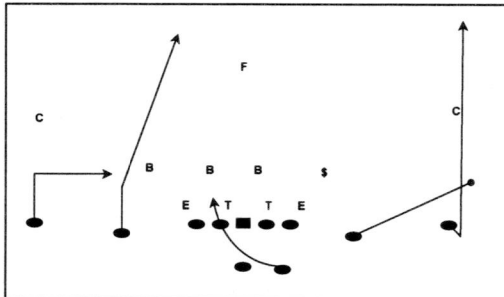

Figure 18-5. Hitch screen and go in a 2 x 2 set

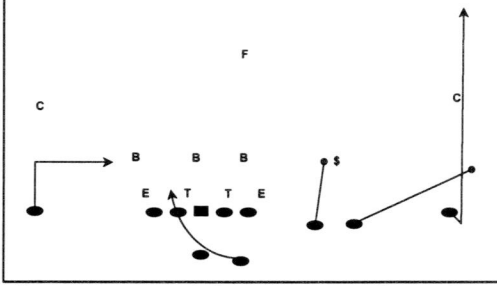

Figure 18-6. Hitch screen and go in a 3 x 1 set

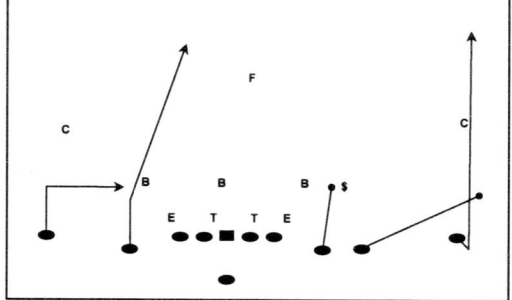

Figure 18-7. Hitch screen and go in a 3 x 2 set

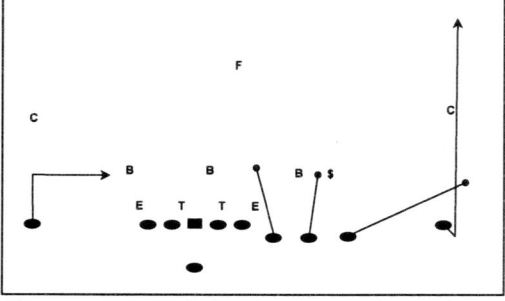

Figure 18-8. Hitch screen and go in a 4 x 1 set

Play #82: The Hitch Screen and Wheel

The hitch screen and wheel is good to use versus teams that are using both the #1 defender and safety to aggressively stop the hitch screen. This route is just another way to attack the quick reaction to the hitch screen by the defense.

The offensive line will be involved in quick pass protection.

The quarterback will open and fake the throw to the hitch screen, set his feet, and get the ball out as quickly as possible. He will look for the wheel route first, then to the hitch route by the outside receiver, and then progress in.

The running back technique is identical to the hitch screen pass. He will be involved in pass protection if he is in the backfield, and involved in the route scheme if he is lined up as a receiver.

The outside receiver will sell the hitch screen and then wait for the football. The #2 receiver will run his path as if to block the #1 defender and then burst up the field seven yards from the sideline on a wheel route. The remaining receivers inside will sell blocks on the nearest defenders inside of their alignment, and then turn back to the quarterback. Backside receivers run the short route package.

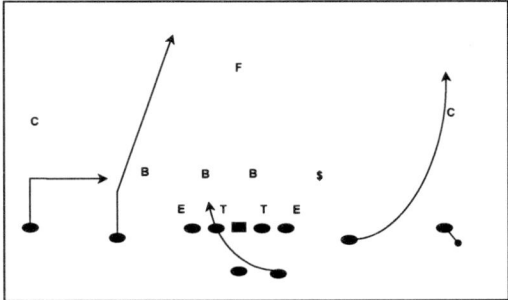

Figure 18-9. Hitch screen and wheel in a 2 x 2 set

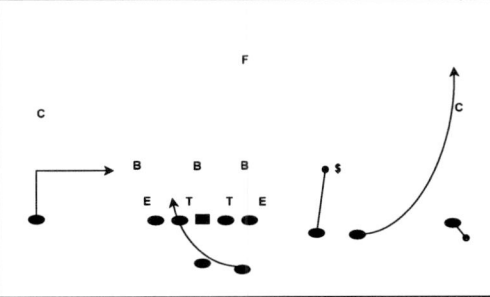

Figure 18-10. Hitch screen and wheel in a 3 x 1 set

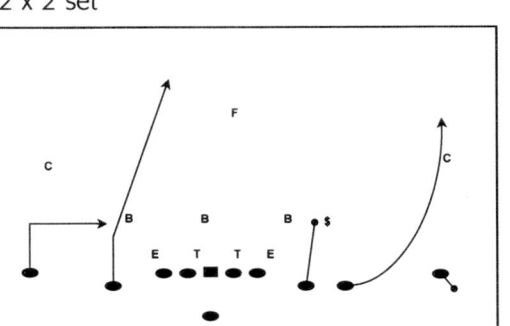

Figure 18-11. Hitch screen and wheel in a 3 x 2 set

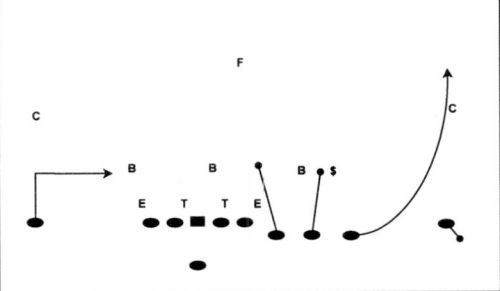

Figure 18-12. Hitch screen and wheel in a 4 x 1 set

19

Double Screen

Introduction

The double screen is a great way to handle a dominant defensive end without blocking him. The double screen allows the quarterback to read the defensive end and throw the football to two different receivers, based on the reaction of the defensive end. This screen is also a great screen to run versus teams that blitz regularly.

Play #83: The Double Screen

Offensive lineman rules for the double screen:

- PST: Pass sets the defensive end, avoids contact, pulls flat to the outside and kicks out the #1 defender.
- PSG: Pass sets for one count, then releases to block the free safety.
- C: Pass sets for one count, then releases to block the backside linebacker.
- BSG: Pass sets for one count, then releases to block the backside linebacker.
- BST: Pass sets for one count, then releases to block the backside outside linebacker.

On the double screen, the quarterback will catch the snap, take a three-step drop, and read the playside defensive end. If the defensive end rushes the passer, the quarterback will open and throw the football to the running back on a swing route. If the defensive end releases to cover the running back, the quarterback will take a shuffle step back, pivot and throw the ball to the receiver coming in from the backside.

The running back will release on a swing route. The back will need to look back for the football over his inside shoulder after his third step.

The playside receivers all crack block one man inside, leaving the #1 defender for the playside offensive tackle to block.

The backside outside receiver will drive two steps forward, retrace his steps, and work inside. It is important for this receiver to get and keep a good sight line with the quarterback. This receiver would like to catch the ball five yards outside the tackle and two yards behind the line of scrimmage.

Any remaining receivers on the backside will block out one man, so the backside tackle will block the first defender outside the tackle box.

This screen is great to run out of multiple formations, as shown in Figures 19-1 through 19-6.

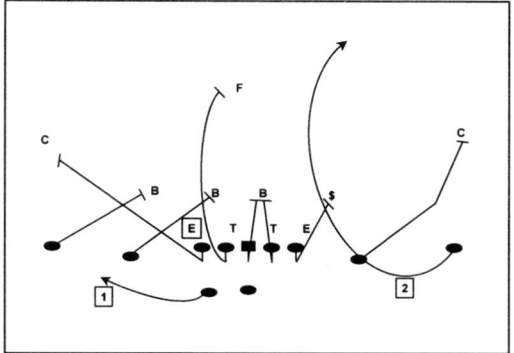

Figure 19-1. Double screen in a 2 x 2 set

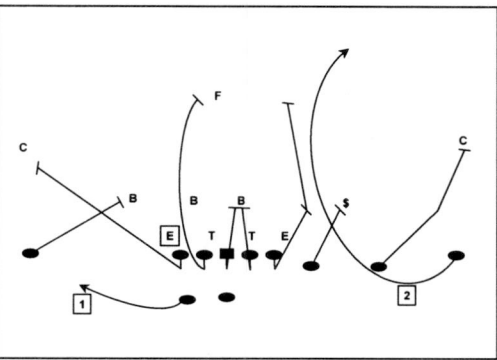

Figure 19-2. Double screen in a 3 x 1 set

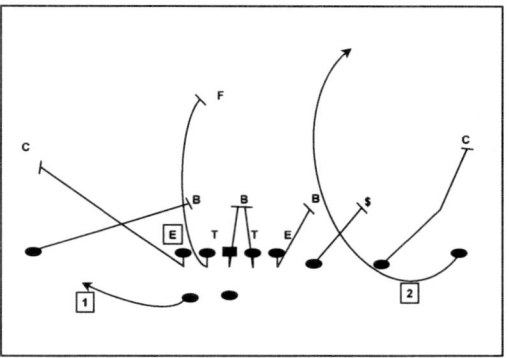

Figure 19-3. Double screen in a 3 x 1 set

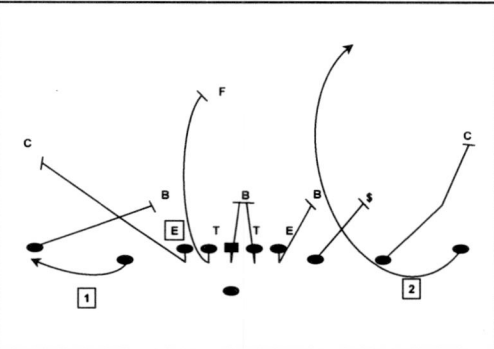

Figure 19-4. Double screen in a 3 x 2 set

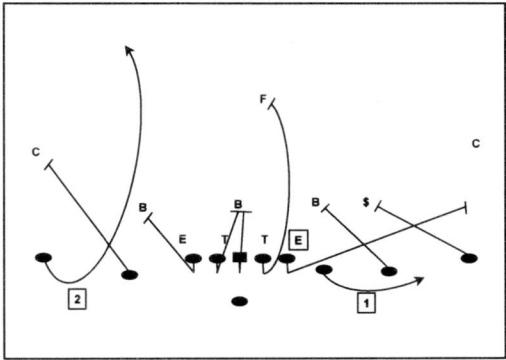

Figure 19-5. Double screen in a 3 x 2 set

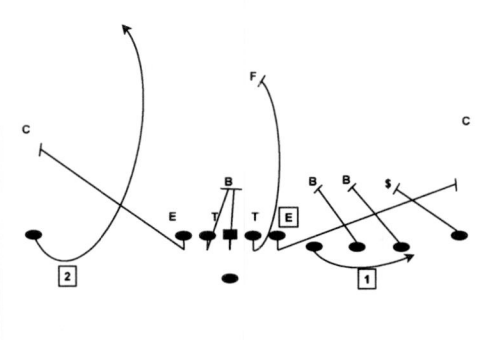

Figure 19-6. Double screen in a 4 x 1 set

20

Tunnel Screen

Introduction

The tunnel screen is good screen to throw versus the defensive blitz. It is a great misdirection play.

Play #84: The Tunnel Screen

Offensive lineman rules for the tunnel screen:

- PST: Rips inside one step, selling sweep, then pivots and pulls flat to the playside to kick out the first defender seen.
- PSG: Rips inside two steps, selling sweep, then pivots and pulls flat to the playside and turns back inside to seal in the first defender seen.
- C: Rips inside two steps, selling sweep, then pivots and pulls flat to the playside and leads up in between the blocks of the PST and the PSG.
- BSG: Reach blocks to the backside, just like sprint-out pass his way.
- BST: Reach blocks to the backside, just like sprint-out pass his way.

On the tunnel screen, the quarterback will catch the snap, sell sprint-out pass to the backside for three steps, pivot to the playside, and throw the ball to the intended receiver.

The running back will sell sprint-out pass protection to the backside.

The tunnel screen receiver will drive two steps forward, retrace his steps, and work inside. It is important for this receiver to get and keep a good sight line with the quarterback. After catching the football, the receiver needs to get vertical as quickly as possible. Any receivers on the playside outside of the tunnel receiver will stalk block the defender over them. Any receivers on the playside inside of the tunnel receiver will block one man out. All backside receivers will execute their responsibilities on the smash route package.

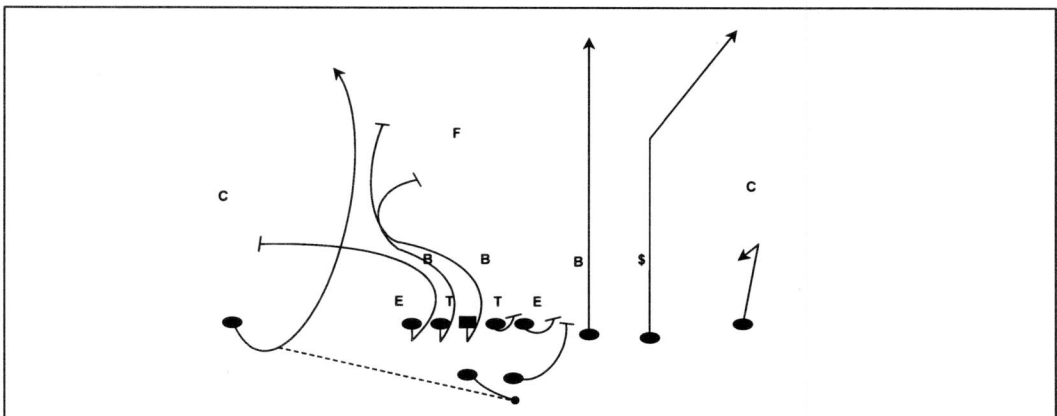
Figure 20-1. Tunnel screen in a 3 x 1 set

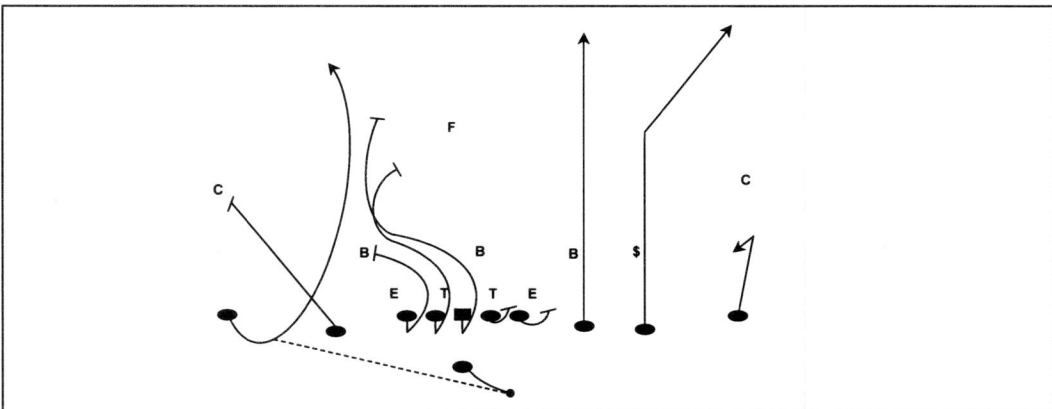
Figure 20-2. Tunnel screen in a 3 x 2 set

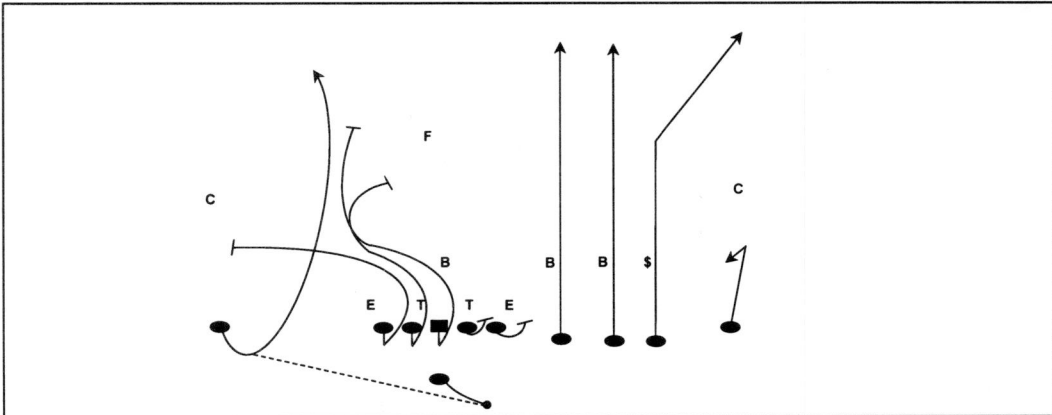
Figure 20-3. Tunnel screen in a 4 x 1 set

21

Slip Screen

Introduction

The slip screen is a quick-hitting screen that attacks the middle of the defense. This screen is a good screen to run out of multiple formations, and it has easy rules for linemen to learn.

Play #85: The Slip Screen

The rules for the offensive lineman on the slip screen are: Inside gap down, linebacker. If the lineman has a defensive player in his backside gap, he will block down on that player. If he doesn't have a player in his backside gap, he will release to the playside and block the first linebacker lined up to playside.

On the slip screen, the quarterback will catch the snap, take a three-step drop, and continue to fade back. The quarterback will need to throw the football between his third and fifth step.

The running back will either run a swing route to the backside, be lined up as a receiver and follow receiver rules, or be the intended receiver. If the running back is the intended receiver from the backfield, he will attack the playside defensive end, make contact, and spin away from the pressure by the defensive end. He will turn to the quarterback, catch the ball, and get vertical as quickly as possible.

The slip screen receiver will open up to the inside and work inside. It is important for this receiver to get and keep a good sight line with the quarterback. After catching the ball, the receiver needs to get vertical as quickly as possible, working just inside the first kick-out block by the offensive lineman. Any receivers on the playside outside of the slip receiver will stalk block the defender over them. Any receivers on the playside inside of the slip receiver will block one man out. All backside receivers will follow backside run rules.

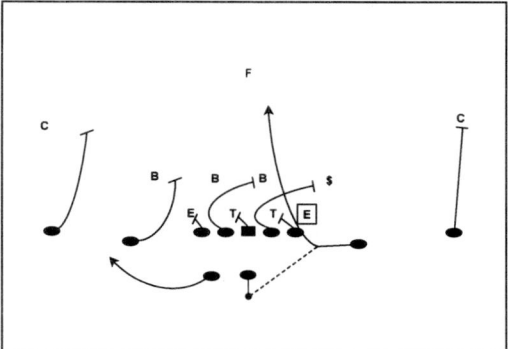
Figure 21-1. Slip screen in a 2 x 2 set

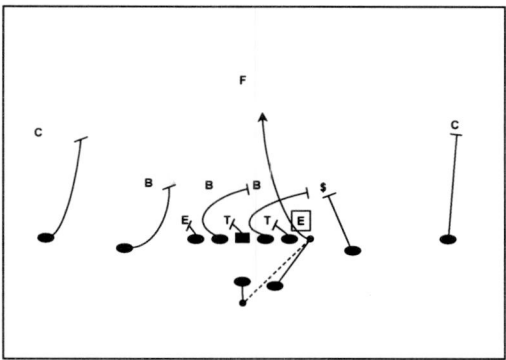
Figure 21-2. Slip screen in a 2 x 2 set

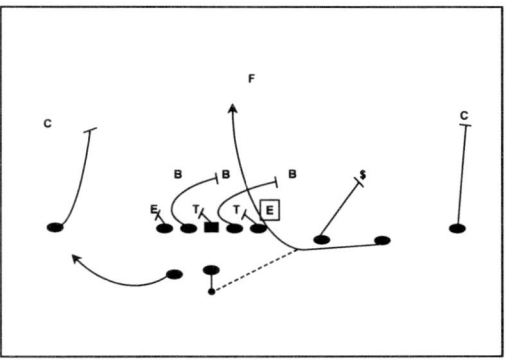
Figure 21-3. Slip screen in a 3 x 1 set

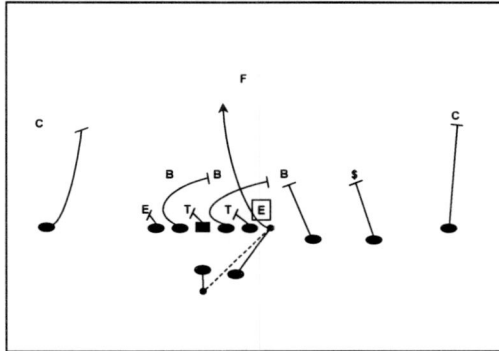
Figure 21-4. Slip screen in a 3 x 1 set

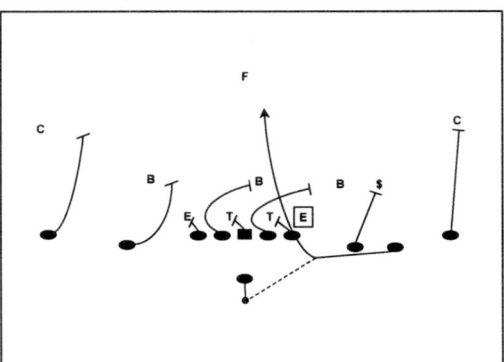
Figure 21-5. Slip screen in a 3 x 2 set

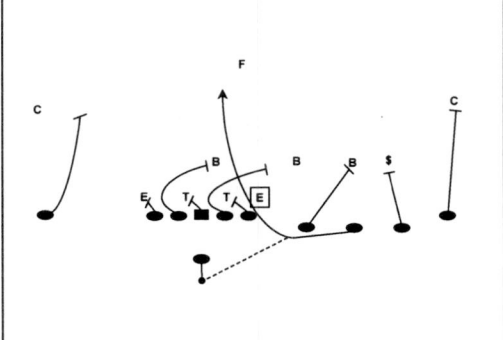
Figure 21-6. Slip screen in a 4 x 1 set

Section 4:
The Movement Passes

22

Movement Passes

Introduction

The movement passes are an important aspect of protecting the quarterback. The movement passes either move the pocket, simulate a run play, or both.

Play #86: Play-Action

A good way to play-action pass is to group the best run with several different pass routes. One way to do this is to call play-action for your linemen and backs, while calling pass routes for your receivers and quarterback.

When the offensive linemen hear play-action, they know it's grouped with the inside zone play, so they will try to sell the inside zone play, with their pads low.

The quarterback and running back will first make a great fake and then execute their pass responsibilities. The quarterback will mesh with the back, then take a quick drop and get his eyes on his read. The running back will make a great fake with his pads down and then block his responsibility in a six-man pass protection.

The receivers will run the routes called with their eyes up, recognizing what coverage the defense is playing.

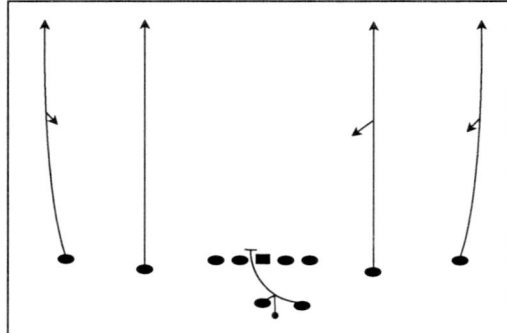

Figure 22-1. Play-action vertical route in a 2 x 2 set

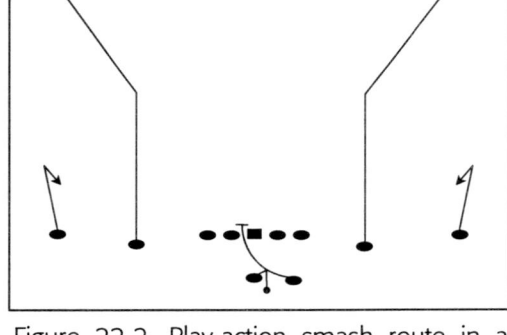

Figure 22-2. Play-action smash route in a 2 x 2 set

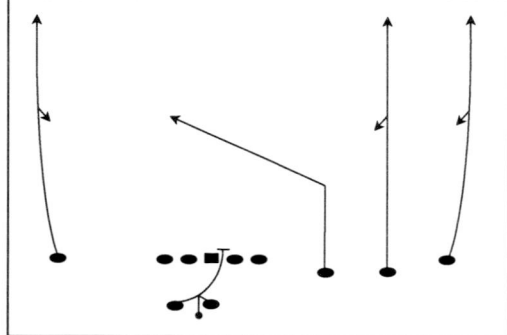

Figure 22-3. Play-action vertical route in a 3 x 1 set

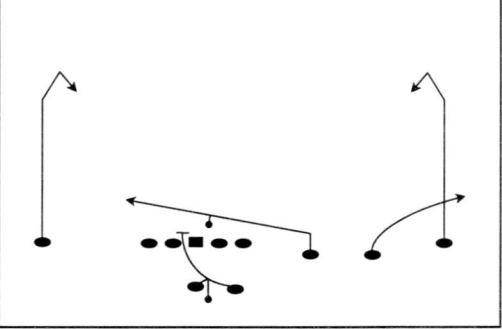

Figure 22-4. Play-action curl route in a 3 x 1 set

Play #87: Naked Action

Naked action is similar to play-action except it is full flow by the linemen. They will not be blocking the backside defensive end. It is important to know the defensive end is not responsible for contain to call this play. It is a great play because it moves the pocket quickly, gets the quarterback on the edge of the defense, and sells a run play.

All offensive linemen will try to reach the next gap to the playside without climbing to the second level.

The quarterback and running back will first make a great fake and then execute their pass responsibilities. The quarterback will mesh with the back, then burst past the defensive end, while keeping his depth. The running back will make a great fake with his pads down and then block his responsibility in a six-man pass protection.

The receivers will run the routes called with their eyes up, recognizing what coverage the defense is playing.

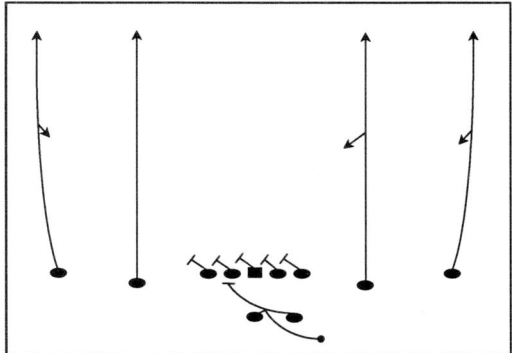

Figure 22-5. Naked action vertical route in a 2 x 2 set

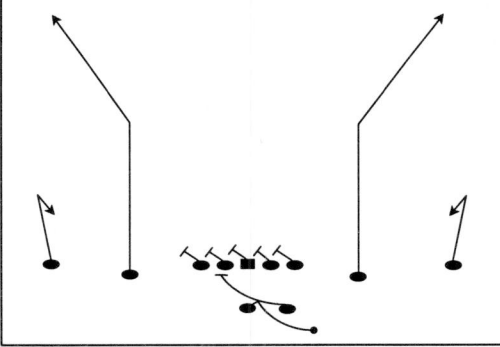

Figure 22-6. Naked action smash route in a 2 x 2 set

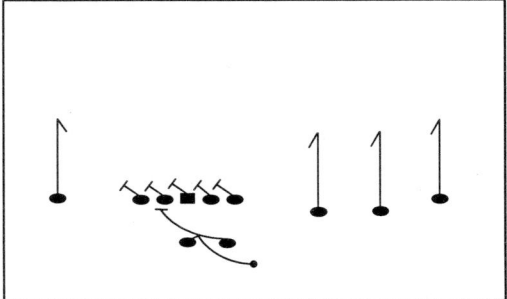

Figure 22-7. Naked action hitch route in a 3 x 1 set

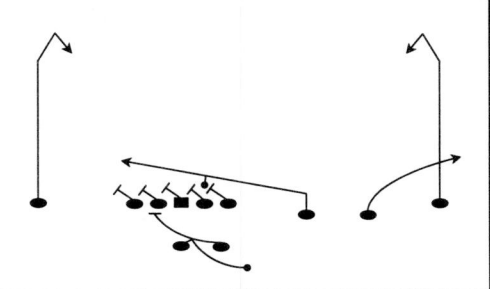

Figure 22-8. Naked action curl route in a 3 x 1 set

Play #88: Waggle Action

The waggle action is a great play-action because it pulls linemen and moves the pocket for the quarterback, helping him become a run threat. As with the play-action package, a good way to use the waggle package is to call the waggle and then call the route you want the receivers to execute.

Rules for the offensive line are as follows:
- PST: Blocks down to the first down lineman inside.
- PSG: Opens and pulls to seal in the playside defensive end.
- C: Blocks back for the pull of the BSG.
- BSG: Opens and pulls to be a personal protector for the quarterback.
- BST: Pass sets and backpedals in and back at a 45-degree angle.

The quarterback and running back will first make a great fake and then execute their pass responsibilities. The quarterback will mesh with the back, then push three steps at a 45-degree angle back and to the outside, while getting his eyes on his read. The running back will make a great fake with his pads down and then fit in between the center and the backside tackle for pass protection.

The receivers will run the routes called with their eyes up, recognizing what coverage the defense is playing.

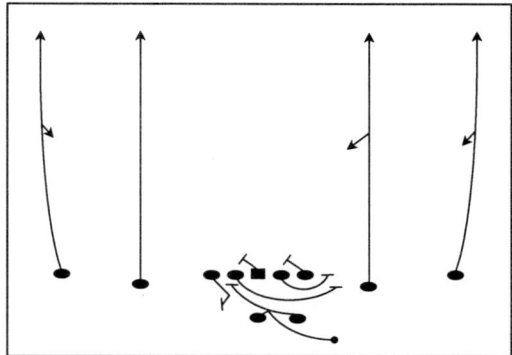

Figure 22-9. Waggle action vertical route in a 2 x 2 set

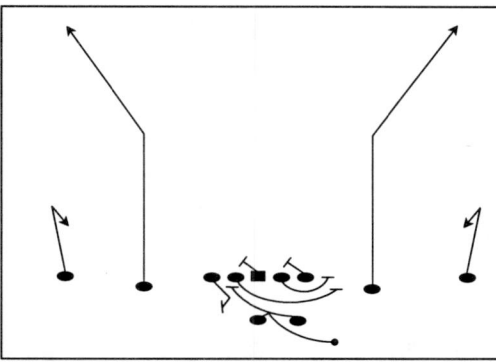

Figure 22-10. Waggle action smash route in a 2 x 2 set

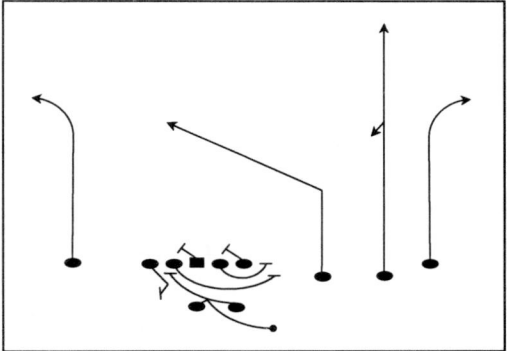

Figure 22-11. Waggle action choice route in a 3 x 1 set

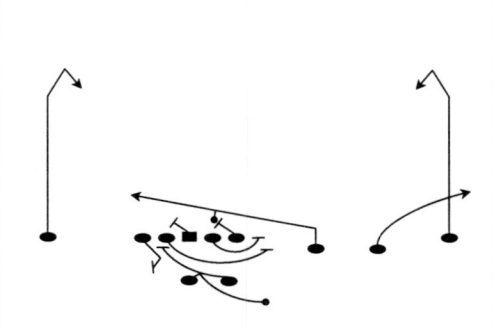

Figure 22-12. Waggle action curl route in a 3 x 1 set

Play #89: Sprint-Out Action

Sprint-out action is a great way to move the pocket for the quarterback. This play can make shorter throws for the quarterback, help improve his sight lines, and keep the defense guessing as to where he will be setting up. Defenses blitz to get to the launch point, and if the launch point is constantly being moved, it makes for a frustrating day for the defensive coaches.

A good rule to use for offensive linemen is to have the playside linemen reach and the backside linemen hinge. The center should be considered playside.

To sprint out with dropback routes, the quarterback will catch the snap and take three steps out and back to the playside at a 45-degree angle. He should set up behind the offensive tackle, seven to eight yards deep. He should be ready to throw after taking a hitch step.

To sprint out with a quick pass route, the quarterback will need to take three steps on his throwing-arm side and two steps on his non-throwing-arm side. The steps should be parallel to the line of scrimmage. The quarterback will need to be ready to throw the ball on his second or third step, depending on to which side he is sprinting out.

The running back, if he is aligned in the backfield, will be responsible for blocking the playside linebacker if he blitzes. If he doesn't blitz, the running back will help the offensive tackle by sealing in the defensive end.

The receivers will run the routes called with their eyes up, recognizing what coverage the defense is playing.

An alternate way to run these routes is to have rules for backside receivers. A typical rule is to have the backside inside receiver run a drag route and the backside outside receiver to run a post route, as shown in Figure 22-17.

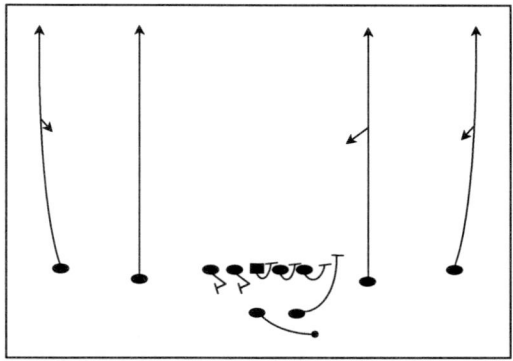

Figure 22-13. Sprint-out action vertical route in a 2 x 2 set

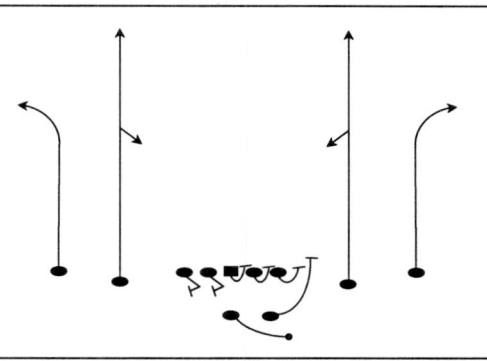

Figure 22-14. Sprint-out action choice route in a 2 x 2 set

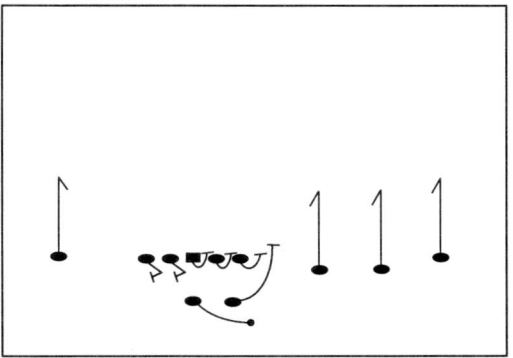

Figure 22-15. Sprint-out action hitch route in a 3 x 1 set

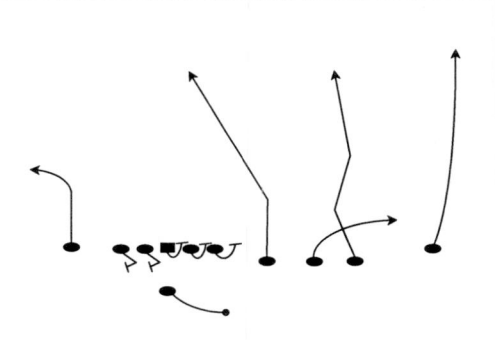

Figure 22-16. Sprint-out action out route in a 4 x 1 set

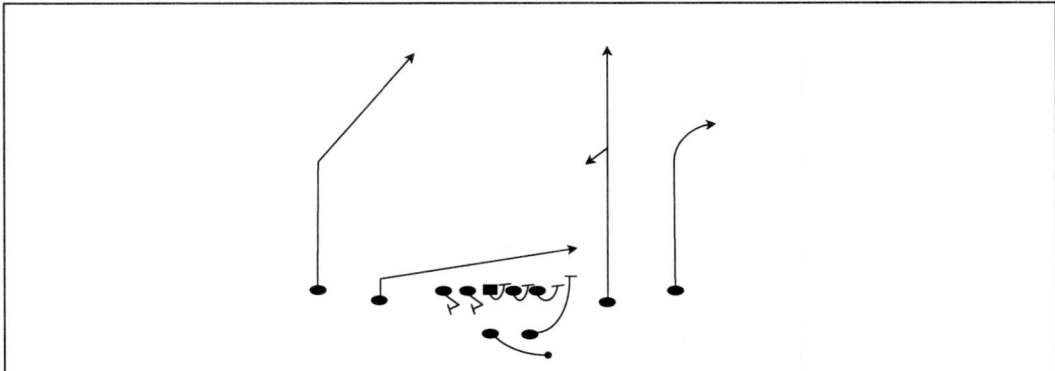

Figure 22-17. Sprint-out action choice route in a 2 x 2 set with alternate backside routes

Section 5:
The Run Game

23

The Sweep

Introduction

The sweep play is a good way to attack the perimeter of the defense. The sweep is particularly good versus a defense that blitzes in the A and B gaps. The sweep uses outside-zone blocking principles for the offensive linemen.

Play #90: The Fly Sweep

All offensive linemen follow outside-zone blocking rules. The basic principle is to block an area, not just a man. If two linemen next to each other are both covered, the lineman on the playside will be blocking one-on-one. If one lineman is covered and one lineman is not covered, they will work together to block the down lineman to the linebacker behind. All sweep plays will be blocked the same way by the offensive line and will only be described once, here.

On the fly sweep, the quarterback will start the tagged receiver in motion and have the ball snapped when the tagged receiver gets behind the offensive tackle. The quarterback must catch the snap, pivot, reach and mesh with the receiver, give the ball, then mesh with the running back and burst away from his last fake. If the quarterback is running this play from a no-back set, he will read the backside defensive end, just like a zone-read play. If the defensive end chases the receiver, the quarterback will pull the ball and burst past the defensive end and up the field. If the defensive end stays and plays contain, the quarterback will give the football to the receiver and try to burst past the defensive end.

The running back will pause at the snap then run through the mesh area under control. His aiming point is the far hip of the center. The back will sell his fake through the line of scrimmage to the linebacker.

The receivers that are not tagged to run the sweep will be responsible for blocking. A good rule to have receivers follow is to have the playside receivers stalk block and the backside receivers cut off block. If a receiver is lined up on the outside, he is considered the #1 receiver, and he will block the #1 defender. The receivers will count off the defenders in this manner, both on the playside and on the backside. For future reference, these rules will be called playside-backside rules for receivers.

The tagged receiver will, at the quarterback's signal, open and run full speed through the mesh with the quarterback, with the near elbow up. After receiving the hand off, the receiver will read the playside offensive tackle's block. If the tackle gets the defensive end reached, the receiver will continue his path outside. If the tackle can't get the defensive end reached, he'll try to work him outside as far as he can. The receiver will then cut up inside the tackle's block. The receiver will get up the field and then try to get back outside as quickly as possible.

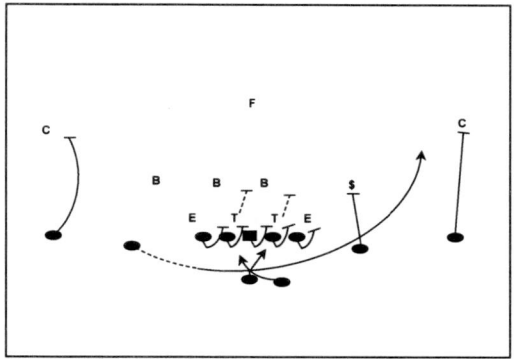

Figure 23-1. Fly sweep in a 2 x 2 set

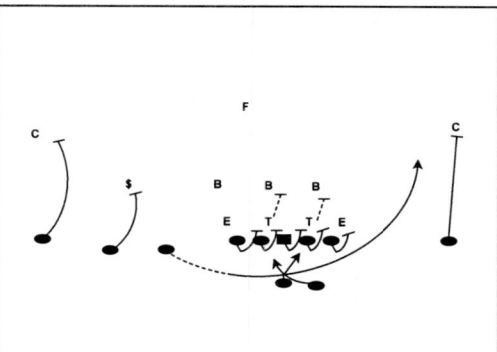

Figure 23-2. Fly sweep in a 3 x 1 set

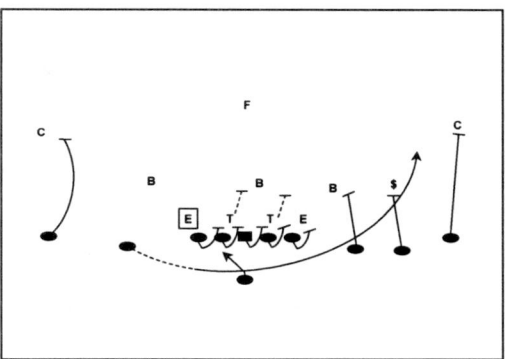

Figure 23-3. Fly sweep in a 3 x 2 set

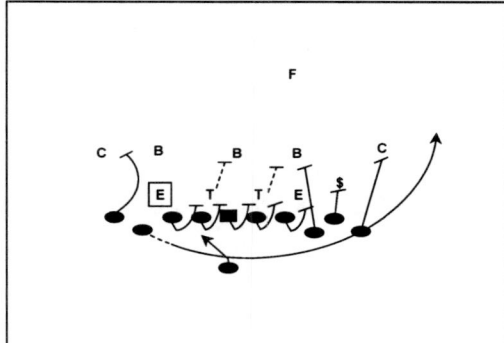

Figure 23-4. Fly sweep in a 3 x 2 nasty split set

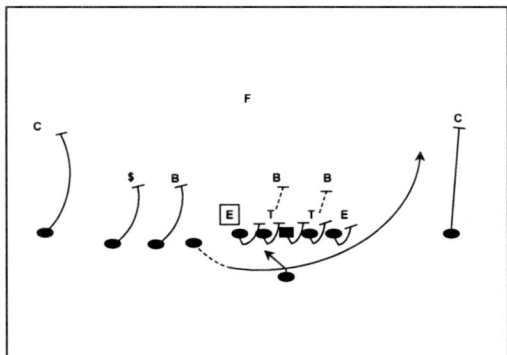

Figure 23-5. Fly sweep in a 4 x 1 set

Bonus Play: The Fly Sweep With Lead Blocking

The sweep play with a lead block allows the receivers to crack block inside and the running back to kick out on a defensive back.

All offensive linemen follow outside-zone blocking rules.

This play is just like the no-back fly sweep for the quarterback. He will read the backside defensive end for the give or the keep.

The running back, at the snap, will open up and lead the sweep to the playside. He will block out on the #1 defender.

The receivers on the backside will use normal backside rules. The playside receivers will block one man inside, leaving the #1 defender for the running back to block.

The tagged receiver's technique is no different than the regular fly sweep, with the exception that his read is now outside on the perimeter instead of on the defensive end.

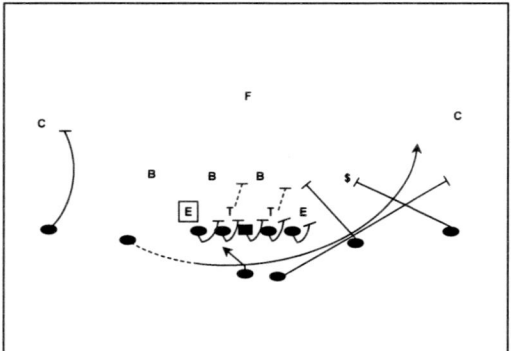

Figure 23-6. Fly sweep with lead blocking in a 2 x 2 set

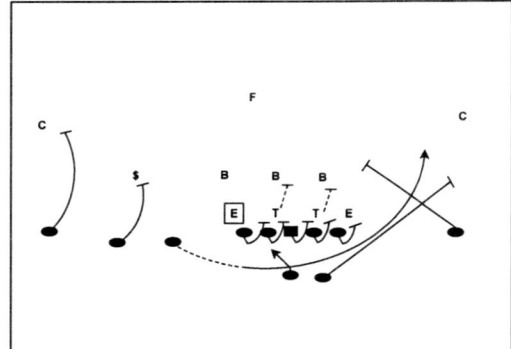

Figure 23-7. Fly sweep with lead blocking in a 3 x 1 set

Bonus Play: The Hand Sweep

The hand sweep play is another good way to attack the perimeter of the defense. It is a good way to attack strong versus zone defense and weak versus man-to-man defense.

All offensive linemen follow outside-zone blocking rules.

The quarterback will catch the snap, pivot, reach, and mesh with the running back while reading the backside defensive end. If the defensive end chases the back, the quarterback will pull the ball and burst past the defensive end and up the field. If the defensive end stays and plays contain, the quarterback will give the football to the running back and try to burst past the defensive end.

The running back, at the snap, will pause, then run through the mesh area under control. The running back is in charge of the mesh, so he needs to see the football, and he needs to run through it on his way to the line of scrimmage. His aiming point is the far hip of the playside offensive tackle. After receiving the hand off, the running back will read the playside offensive tackle's block. If the tackle gets the defensive end reached, the running back will continue his path outside. If the tackle can't get the defensive end reached, he'll try to work him outside as far as he can. The running back will then cut up inside the tackle's block. The running back will get up the field and then try to get back outside as quickly as possible. If the running back does not get the football, he will sell his fake through the line of scrimmage to the linebacker.

The receivers will follow playside-backside receivers' rules.

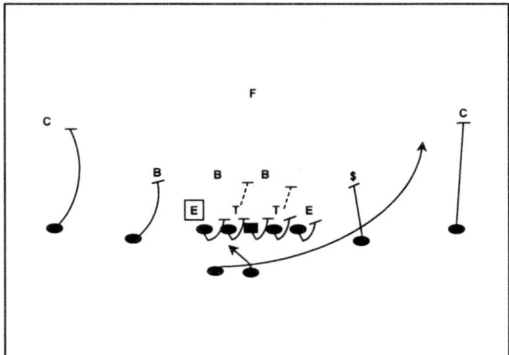

Figure 23-8. Hand sweep in a 2 x 2 set

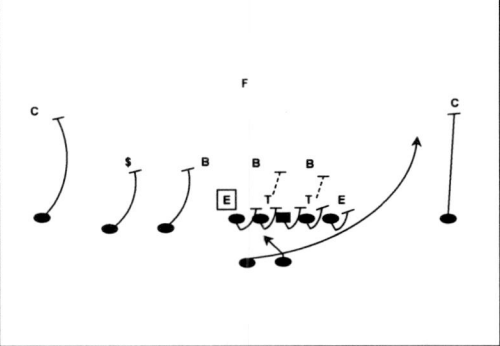

Figure 23-9. Hand sweep in a 3 x 1 set

24

Option Plays

Introduction

The option is a great way to slow down the defense. It is a great way to attack a defense by reading a player that otherwise would be difficult to block.

Play #91: The Speed Option

The speed option is great to run versus defenses that have the offense outnumbered between the tackles.

All offensive linemen (except the playside offensive tackle) follow outside-zone blocking rules. The playside offensive tackle will leave the end man on the line of scrimmage versus even fronts. He will reach the defensive end versus odd fronts.

The quarterback will catch the snap, pivot, and attack the end man on the line of scrimmage versus even fronts, and the linebacker versus odd fronts. The quarterback will attack the outside number of the defender. The read will happen fast versus an even front and slower versus odd fronts.

The running back will take three steps back and to the outside at a 45-degree angle, pivot, and start working forward into pitch path with the quarterback.

The receivers will follow playside-backside receivers' rules.

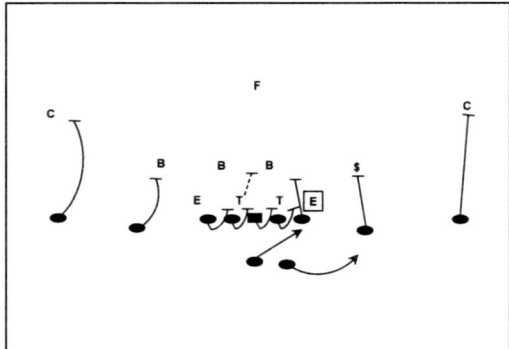

Figure 24-1. Speed option in a 2 x 2 set versus an even front

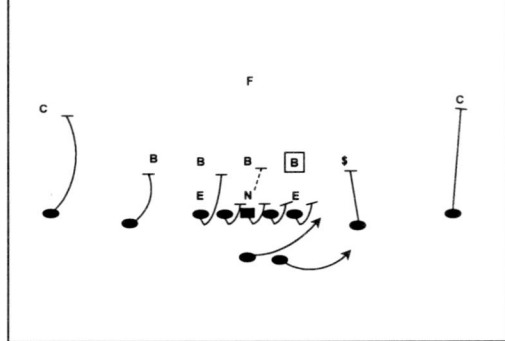

Figure 24-2. Speed option in a 2 x 2 set versus an odd front

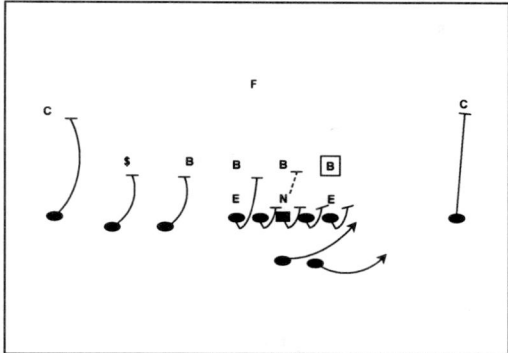

Figure 24-3. Speed option in a 3 x 1 set

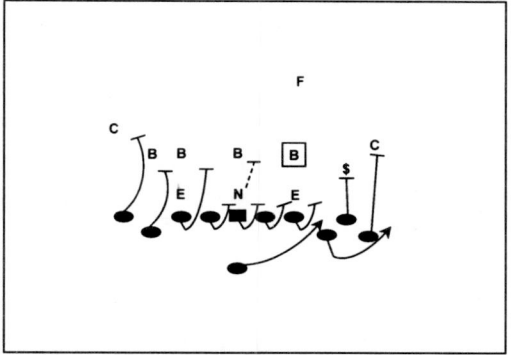

Figure 24-4. Speed option in a 3 x 2 nasty split set

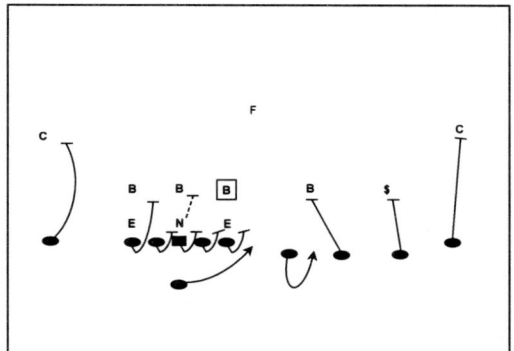

Figure 24-5. Speed option in a 4 x 1 set

Play #92: The Midline Option

The midline play is a good way to attack a defense that stunts and blitzes the majority of the time. It is also a good way to handle a dominant defensive lineman without blocking him. The only way to run this play is to read an A-gap down lineman, not a B-gap down lineman. The play can also be run out of no-back formations with the fly-sweep action.

The playside offensive linemen follow outside-zone blocking rules. The basic principle is to block an area, not just a man. If two linemen next to each other are both covered, the lineman on the playside will be blocking one-on-one. If one lineman is covered and one lineman is not covered, they will work together to block the down lineman to the linebacker behind.

The center, backside guard, and backside tackle have different rules. The A-gap down lineman will not be blocked, as he is the read key. The center is responsible for the playside linebacker in 4-2 front and a 3-2 front. He is responsible for the middle linebacker in a 3-3 front. He wants to put a hand on the down lineman before going to the linebacker. The backside guard is responsible for the backside linebacker. He also wants to get a hand on the down lineman before releasing to the linebacker. The backside tackle will base block the defensive end outside versus all fronts.

The quarterback will catch the snap, pivot, reach, and mesh with the running back while reading the backside-A-gap defensive lineman. If the defensive lineman chases the back, the quarterback will pull the ball and burst past the defensive lineman and up the field, inside the B gap. If the defensive lineman stays and honors the keep, the quarterback will give the football to the running back and try to burst past the defensive lineman. If running the midline out of a no-back set, the quarterback will need to snap the football earlier than normal to allow for a read on the down lineman.

The running back, at the snap, will pause and then run through the mesh area under control. The running back is in charge of the mesh, so he needs to see the football, and he needs to run through it on his way to the line of scrimmage. His aiming point is the far hip of the playside offensive tackle. After receiving the hand off, the running back will read the playside offensive tackle's block. If the tackle gets the defensive end reached, the running back will continue his path outside. If the tackle can't get the defensive end reached, he'll try to work him outside as far as he can. The running back will then cut up inside the tackle's block. The running back will get up the field and then try to get back outside as quickly as possible. If the running back does not get the football, he will sell his fake through the line of scrimmage to the linebacker.

The receivers will follow playside-backside receivers' rules.

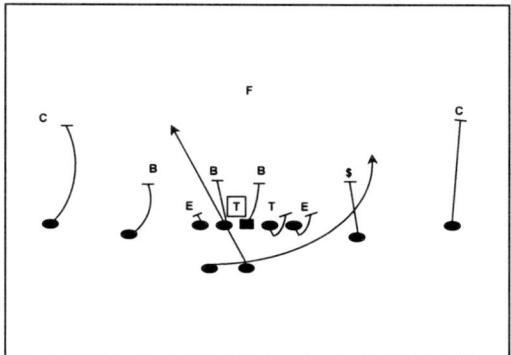

Figure 24-6. Midline option in a 2 x 2 set versus an even front

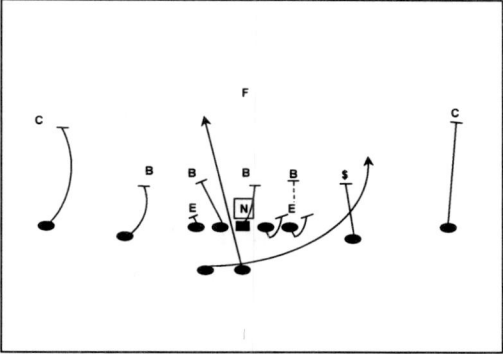

Figure 24-7. Midline option in a 2 x 2 set versus an odd front

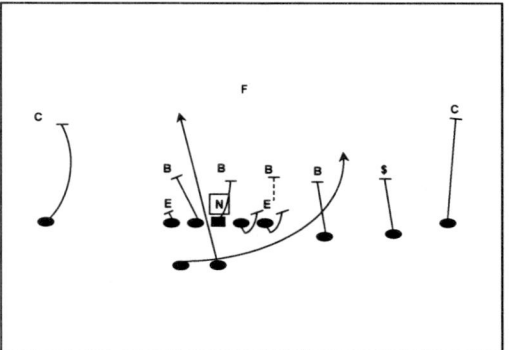

Figure 24-8. Midline option in a 3 x 1 set versus an odd front

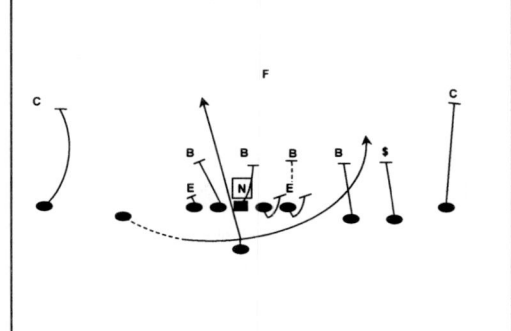

Figure 24-9. Midline option in a 3 x 2 set with fly motion versus an odd front

Play #93: The Inside Veer Option

The inside veer is a proven way to attack two defenders on one side of the formation without blocking them. The play requires time to work out the quarterback-running back mesh as well as the proper pitch relationship.

Linemen rules for a 4-2 front are as follows:
- PST: Combination blocks with the PSG to the playside linebacker.
- PSG: Combination blocks with the PST to the playside linebacker.
- Center and backside linemen: Inside zone block to the playside versus all fronts.

Linemen rules for a 3-3 front are as follows:
- PST: Blocks the inside linebacker.
- PSG: Blocks the middle linebacker.
- Center and backside linemen: Inside zone block to the playside versus all fronts.

Linemen rules for a 3-2 front are as follows:
- PST: Releases and blocks the playside safety.
- PSG: Blocks the playside linebacker.
- Center and backside linemen: Inside zone block to the playside versus all fronts.

The quarterback will meet the snap at four yards, pivot and mesh with the running back. The quarterback will read the playside defensive end for the give-keep read. If the quarterback gives the football, he will carry out his fake past the line of scrimmage, outside the defensive end. If the quarterback keeps the ball, he will burst past the defensive end and get vertical as quickly as possible. He will then option the next defender out for the pitch-keep read.

The running back will step in and toward the line of scrimmage at a 45-degree angle, mesh with the quarterback, and explode up the field, aiming for the middle of the playside guard's backside, through the line of scrimmage. He will then follow the block of the playside tackle.

The receivers will follow playside-backside receivers' rules, with the exception of the inside receiver to the playside. This receiver will get into pitch relationship with the quarterback after the mesh.

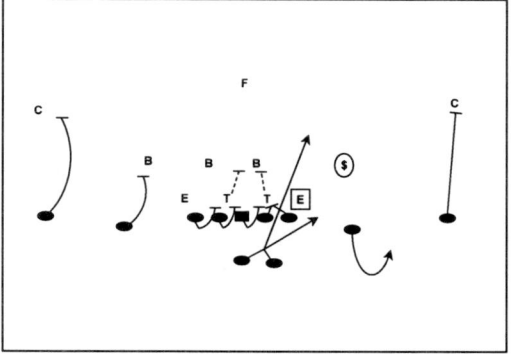

Figure 24-10. Inside veer option in a 2 x 2 set versus an even front

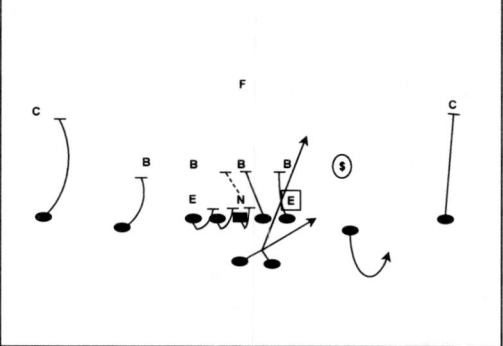

Figure 24-11. Inside veer option in a 2 x 2 set versus an odd front

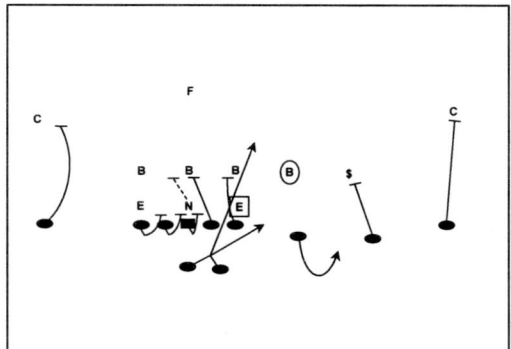

Figure 24-12. Midline option in a 3 x 1 set versus an odd front

Play #94: The Shovel Option

The shovel option is great to run versus defenses that have the offense outnumbered between the tackles. It is also a good play to run versus a dominant defensive end that cannot be consistently blocked.

The offensive linemen will block this play exactly like the speed-option play, with the exception that the playside tackle cannot block the playside defensive end. He must leave the defensive end and block the linebacker. An alternate way of blocking this play is to have the offensive line block the defense like a "power" running play, pulling the backside guard for the playside linebacker.

The quarterback will catch the snap, pivot, and attack the end man on the line of scrimmage, versus all fronts. The quarterback will attack the outside number of the defender. If the defensive end closes, the quarterback will pitch the football outside. If the defensive end slow plays the quarterback, the quarterback will attack outside and pitch underneath.

The playside pitchback will take three steps back and to the outside at a 45-degree angle, pivot, and start working forward into pitch relationship with the quarterback. The pitch relationship is flatter on the shovel-option play than on the normal speed-option play.

The backside pitchback will step forward and then follow two steps behind the quarterback. If the ball gets pitched to this back, he needs to get vertical immediately after catching the pitch.

The receivers will follow playside-backside receivers' rules, with the following exceptions. If no pitchback is on the backside of the quarterback, the inside receiver will become the inside pitchback. If no pitchback is aligned on the front side of the quarterback, the inside receiver to that side will become the outside pitchback.

This play can be run out of any formation, including no-back sets.

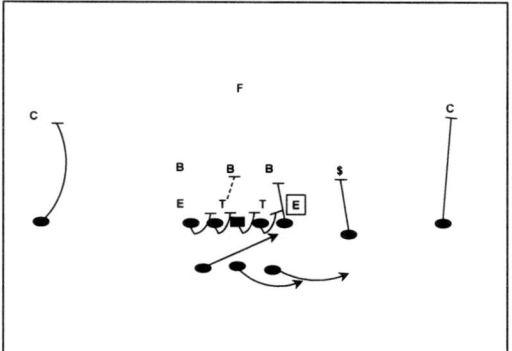

Figure 24-13. Shovel option in a 2 x 1 set versus an even front

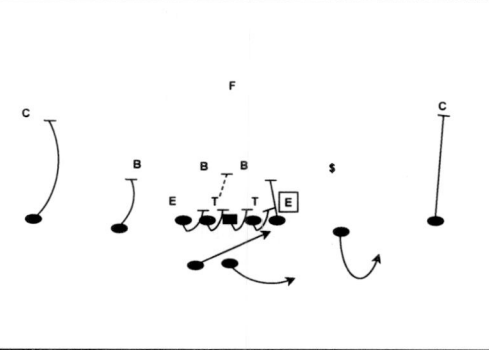

Figure 24-14. Shovel option in a 2 x 2 set versus an even front

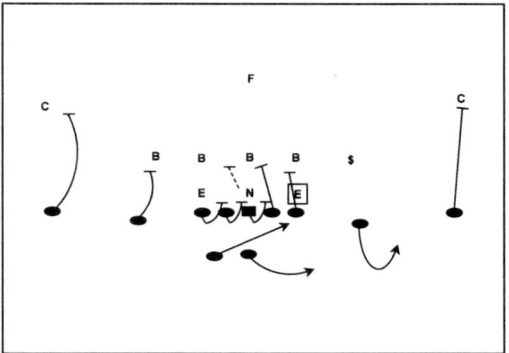

Figure 24-15. Shovel option in a 2 x 2 set versus an odd front

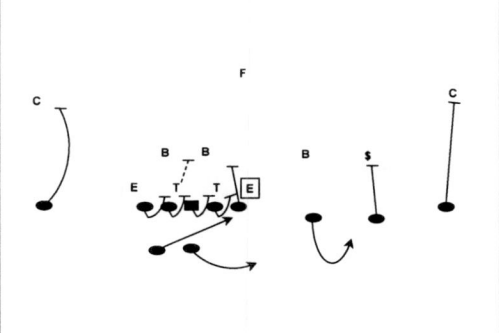

Figure 24-16. Shovel option in a 3 x 1 set versus an odd front

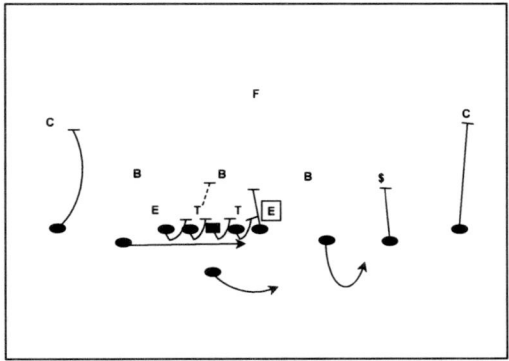

Figure 24-17. Shovel option in a 3 x 2 set versus an odd front

Play #95: The Shovel

The shovel play has proven to be a good way to option a dominant defensive end. It is also a good way to attack man-to-man coverage. However, it is not a great play to run against odd fronts.

All offensive linemen (except the playside offensive tackle) follow outside-zone blocking rules. The playside offensive tackle will leave the end man on the line of scrimmage in even fronts, and will block the defensive end versus odd fronts.

The quarterback will catch the snap, pivot, and attack the end man on the line of scrimmage. The quarterback will attack the outside number of the defender.

The running back will step forward and then follow two steps behind the quarterback. If the ball gets pitched to this back, he needs to get vertical immediately after catching the pitch.

The receivers will follow playside-backside receivers' rules.

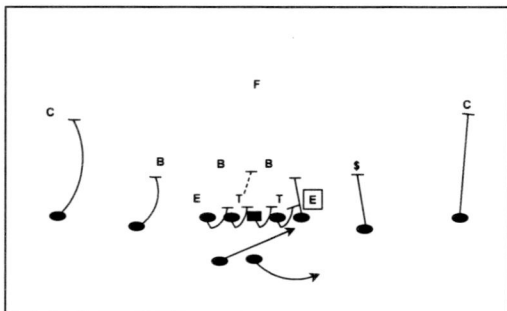

Figure 24-18. Shovel in a 2 x 2 set versus an even front

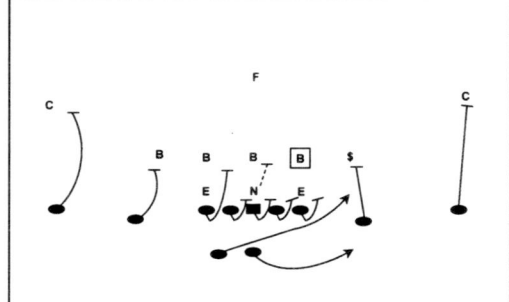

Figure 24-19. Shovel in a 2 x 2 set versus an odd front

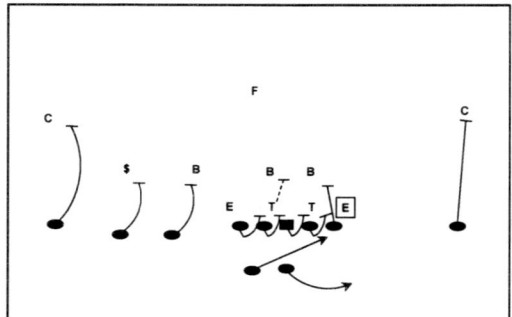

Figure 24-20. Shovel in a 3 x 1 set versus an even front

Play #96: The Lead Option

The lead option is a good change-up of blocking schemes by the playside receivers.

All offensive linemen (except the playside offensive tackle) follow outside-zone blocking rules. The playside offensive tackle will leave the end man on the line of scrimmage versus even fronts. He will reach the defensive end versus odd fronts.

The quarterback will catch the snap, pause, pivot, and attack the end man on the line of scrimmage. The quarterback will attack the outside number of the defender. The read will happen fast versus an even front and slower versus odd fronts.

Two backs will be in the backfield, a lead back and a pitchback. At the snap, the pitchback will open and run flat through the quarterback's heels until he gets to the correct pitch relationship with the quarterback. The lead back will open up to the playside and block out the #1 defender.

The backside receivers will follow their backside receivers' rules. The playside receivers will block one man inside, leaving the #1 defender for the lead back to block.

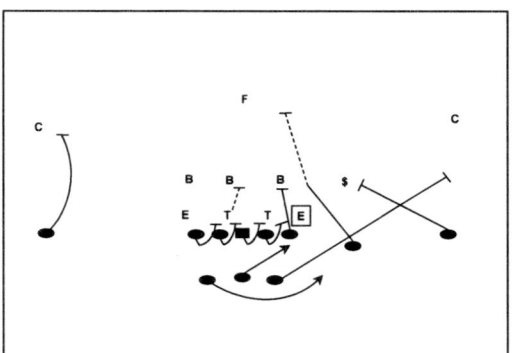

Figure 24-21. Lead option in a 2 x 1 set versus an even front

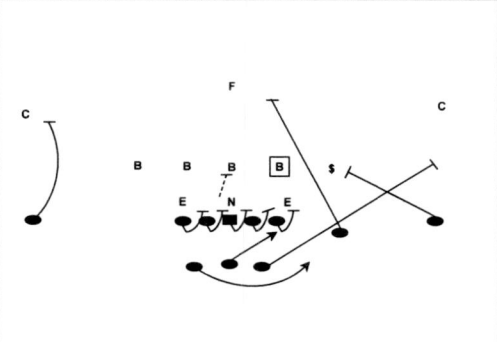

Figure 24-22. Lead option in a 2 x 1 set versus an odd front

25

Counter Plays

Introduction

The counter play is a good misdirection play, while at the same time being a downhill type of play to attack the defense. The play also allows a read by the quarterback on the backside defensive end.

Play #97: The Counter Trey

Linemen rules for a 4-2 front are as follows:
- PST: Combination blocks with the PSG to the backside linebacker.
- PSG: Combination blocks with the PST to the backside linebacker.
- C: Blocks back to the first defensive linemen to the backside.
- BSG: Pulls and kicks out the end man on the line of scrimmage versus all fronts.
- BST: Pulls and leads up on the playside inside linebacker versus all fronts.

Linemen rules for a 3-3 front are as follows:
- PST: Blocks the middle linebacker.
- PSG: Combination blocks with the center to the backside linebacker.
- C: Combination blocks with the PSG to the backside linebacker.
- BSG: Pulls and kicks out the end man on the line of scrimmage versus all fronts.
- BST: Pulls and leads up on the playside inside linebacker versus all fronts.

Linemen rules for a 3-2 front are as follows:
- PST: Releases outside and blocks the playside outside linebacker.
- PSG: Combination blocks with the center to the backside linebacker.
- C: Combination blocks with the PSG to the backside linebacker.
- BSG: Pulls and kicks out the end man on the line of scrimmage versus all fronts.
- BST: Pulls and leads up on the playside inside linebacker versus all fronts.

The quarterback will catch the snap, pivot, reach, and mesh with the running back while reading the backside defensive end. If the defensive end chases the back, the quarterback will pull the ball and burst past the defensive end and up the field. If the defensive end stays and plays contain, the quarterback will give the football to the running back and try to burst past the defensive end. If the play is run with fly-sweep action, the quarterback will not read the defensive end. He will start the receiver in motion, get the football snapped, mesh with the receiver, hand to the running back, and burst away from the play.

The running back, at the snap, will pause and then run through the mesh area under control. The running back is in charge of the mesh, so he needs to see the football, and he needs to run through it on his way to the line of scrimmage. His aiming point is the far A gap. After the running back runs through the mesh, his eyes go to the pulling guard's block. If the guard gets the kick-out block, the running back will cut inside and follow the pulling tackle. If the guard seals the defensive end in, the back will run outside this block and follow the pulling tackle.

The receivers will follow playside-backside receivers' rules.

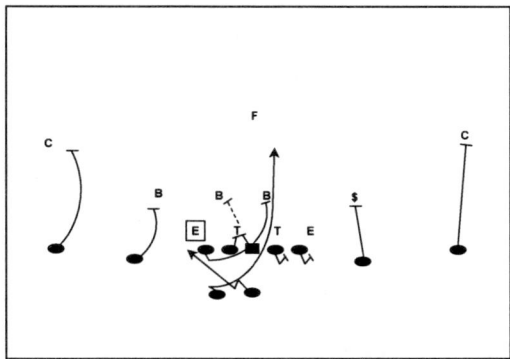

Figure 25-1. Counter in a 2 x 2 set versus a 4-2 front

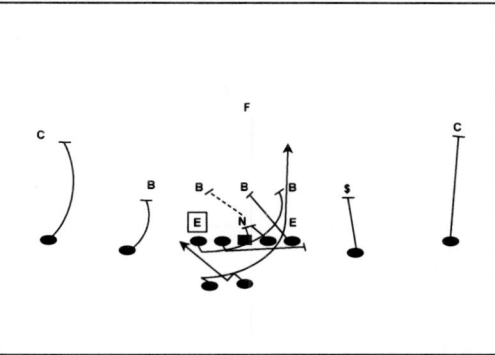

Figure 25-2. Counter in a 2 x 2 set versus a 3-3 front

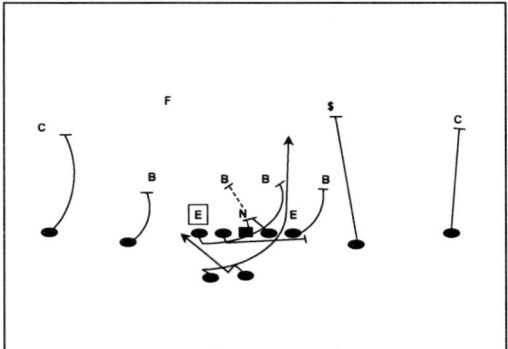

Figure 25-3. Counter in a 2 x 2 set versus a 3-2 front

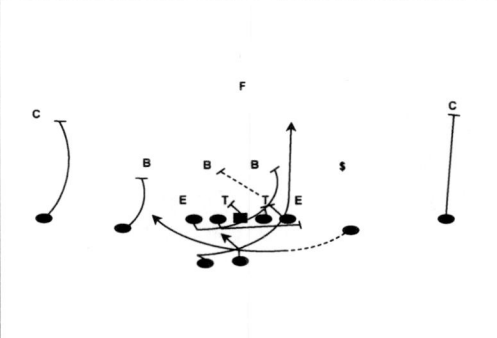

Figure 25-4. Counter with fly motion in a 2 x 2 set versus a 4-2 front

Bonus Play: The Same-Side Counter Trey

The same-side counter play is a good way to attack a defense that stunts on the side away from the running back's alignment.

The linemen follow their counter rules by front.

The quarterback will catch the snap, pivot, reach, and mesh with the running back while reading the backside defensive end. If the defensive end chases the back, the quarterback will pull the ball and burst past the defensive end and up the field. If the defensive end stays and plays contain, the quarterback will give the football to the running back and try to burst past the defensive end. This play is a more difficult play for the quarterback, as his hips and shoulders are turned away from the direction he will need to run, if he needs to keep the ball.

The running back, at the snap, will take three steps to the mesh, pivot, and then start downhill to his landmark. The running back is in charge of the mesh, so he needs to see the football, and he needs to run through it on his way to the line of scrimmage. His aiming point and reads are the same as the regular counter play. If the running back does not get the football, he will sell his fake through the line of scrimmage to the linebacker.

The receivers will follow playside-backside receivers' rules.

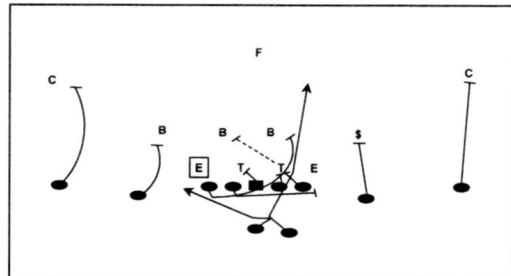

Figure 25-5. Same-side counter in a 2 x 2 set versus a 4-2 front

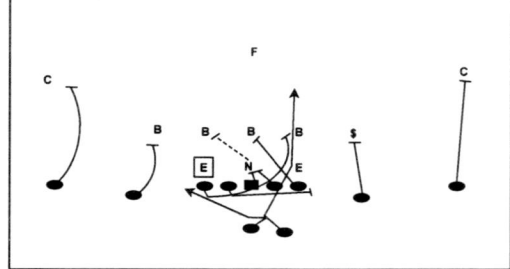

Figure 25-6. Same-side counter in a 2 x 2 set versus a 3-3 front

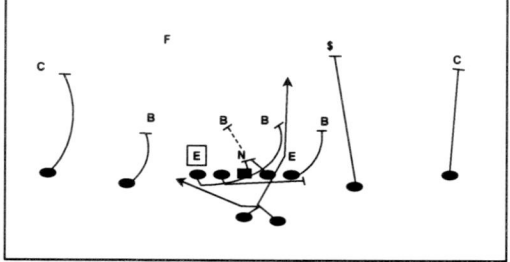

Figure 25-7. Same-side counter in a 2 x 2 set versus a 3-2 front

Bonus Play: The Quarterback Counter Trey

The quarterback counter trey is a great play to use versus defenses that are keying on the running back for their run fits. The quarterback counter trey is great misdirection and allows for six blockers, counting the running back. This play is not a read play. The play can also be run out of a no-back set with fly-sweep action.

The linemen follow their counter rules by front.

The quarterback will catch the snap, pivot, reach and fake with the running back. The aiming point for the quarterback is the A gap. After the quarterback fakes to the back, his eyes go the pulling guard's block. If the guard gets the kick-out block, the quarterback will cut inside and follow the pulling tackle. If the guard seals the defensive end in, the quarterback will run outside this block and follow the pulling tackle.

The running back will make a great fake and then block the backside defensive end. The back needs to keep the defensive end outside.

The receivers will follow playside-backside receivers' rules.

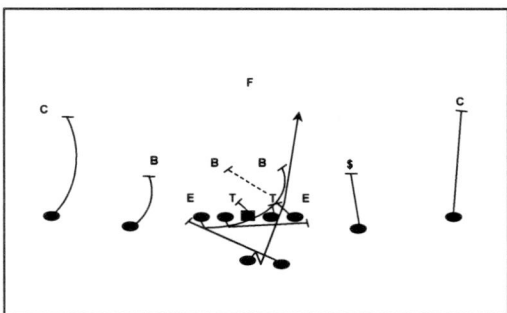

Figure 25-8. Quarterback counter in a 2 x 2 set versus a 4-2 front

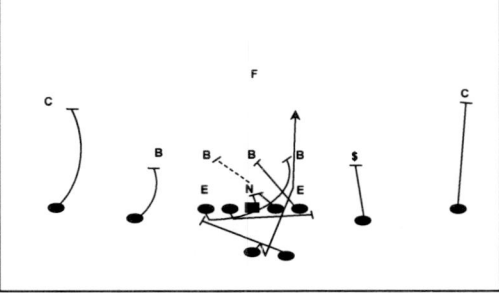

Figure 25-9. Quarterback counter in a 2 x 2 set versus a 3-3 front

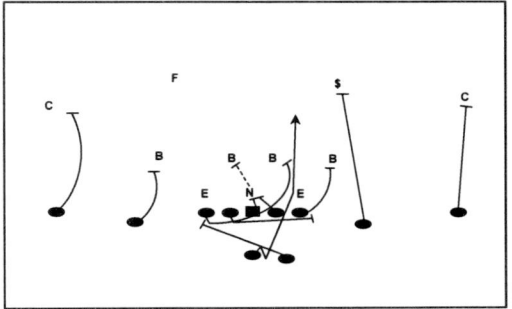

Figure 25-10. Quarterback counter in a 2 x 2 set versus a 3-2 front

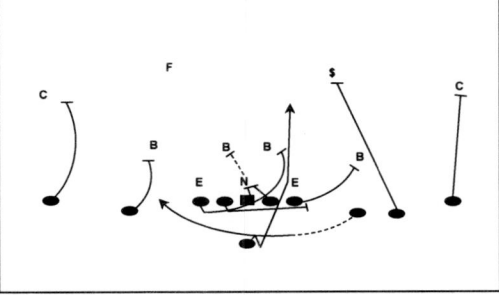

Figure 25-11. Quarterback counter with fly motion in a 3 x 2 set versus a 3-2 front

26

Wrap Plays

Introduction

The wrap play is a good misdirection play, while at the same time being a downhill type of play to attack the defense. The play also allows a read by the quarterback on the backside defensive end. The wrap is very similar to the counter play but has the added bonus of protecting against the linebacker run through, due to only having one pulling lineman.

Play #98: The Wrap

Linemen rules for a 4-2 front are as follows:

- PST: Pass sets the defensive end.
- PSG: Pass sets an outside technique, combination blocks with the center to the backside linebacker, if he has an inside technique.
- C: Combination blocks with the guard to the side of the A-gap down lineman to the backside linebacker.
- BSG: Pass sets an outside technique, combination blocks with the center to the backside linebacker, if he has an inside technique.
- BST: Pulls and leads up on the playside inside linebacker.

Linemen rules for a 3-3 front are as follows:

- PST: Pass sets the defensive end.
- PSG: Combination blocks with the center to the middle linebacker.
- C: Combination blocks with the PSG to the middle linebacker.
- BSG: Blocks the backside linebacker.
- BST: Pulls and leads up on the playside inside linebacker.

Linemen rules for a 3-2 front are as follows:

- PST: Releases outside and blocks the outside linebacker.
- PSG: Combination blocks with the center to the playside linebacker.
- C: Combination blocks with the BSG to the playside linebacker.
- BSG: Blocks the backside linebacker.
- BST: Pulls and kicks the playside defensive end..

The quarterback will catch the snap, pivot, reach, and mesh with the running back while reading the backside defensive end. If the defensive end chases the back, the quarterback will pull the ball and burst past the defensive end and up the field. If the defensive end stays and plays contain, the quarterback will give the football to the running back and try to burst past the defensive end. If the play is run with fly-sweep action, the quarterback will not read the defensive end. He will start the receiver in motion, get the football snapped, mesh with the receiver, hand to the running back, and burst away from the play.

The running back, at the snap, will pause and then run through the mesh area under control. The running back is in charge of the mesh, so he needs to see the football, and he needs to run through it on his way to the line of scrimmage. His aiming point is the far A gap. After the running back runs through the mesh, his eyes go the pulling tackle's block. He will cut off of the pulling tackle's block. If the running back does not get the ball, he will sell his fake through the line of scrimmage.

The receivers will follow playside-backside receivers' rules.

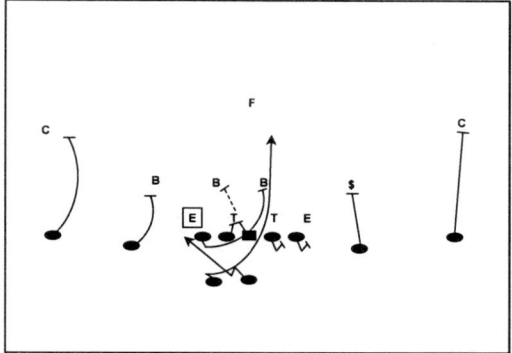

Figure 26-1. Wrap in a 2 x 2 set versus a 4-2 front

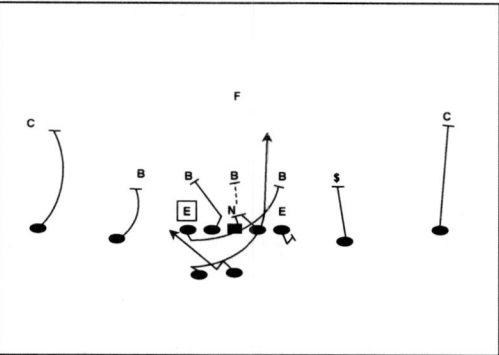

Figure 26-2. Wrap in a 2 x 2 set versus a 3-3 front

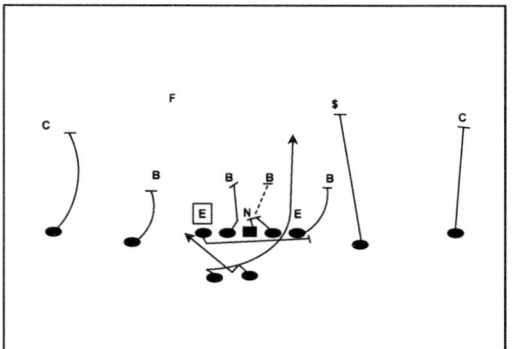

Figure 26-3. Wrap in a 2 x 2 set versus a 3-2 front

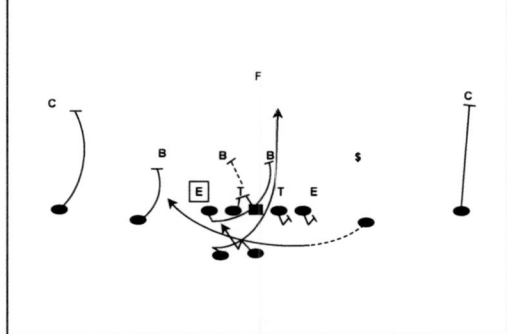

Figure 26-4. Wrap with fly motion in a 2 x 2 set versus a 4-2 front

Bonus Play: The Same-Side Wrap

The same-side wrap play is a good way to attack a defense that stunts on the side away from the running back's alignment.

The linemen follow their wrap rules by front.

The quarterback will catch the snap, pivot, reach, and mesh with the running back while reading the backside defensive end. If the defensive end chases the back, the quarterback will pull the ball and burst past the defensive end and up the field. If the defensive end stays and plays contain, the quarterback will give the football to the running back and try to burst past the defensive end. This play is a more difficult play for the quarterback, as his hips and shoulders are turned away from the direction he will need to run, if he needs to keep the ball.

The running back, at the snap, will take three steps to the mesh, pivot, and then start downhill to his landmark. The running back is in charge of the mesh, so he needs to see the football, and he needs to run through it on his way to the line of scrimmage. His aiming point and reads are the same as the regular wrap play. If the running back does not get the football, he will sell his fake through the line of scrimmage to the linebacker.

The receivers will follow playside-backside receivers' rules.

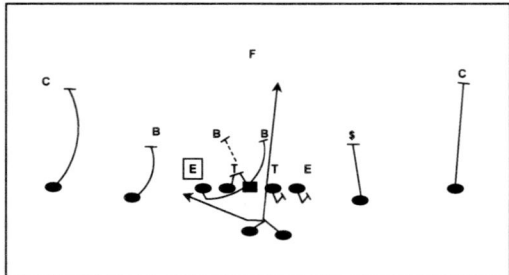

Figure 26-5. Same-side wrap in a 2 x 2 set versus a 4-2 front

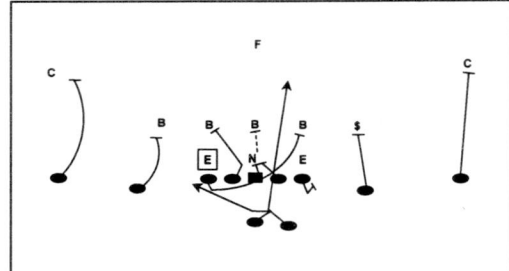

Figure 26-6. Same-side wrap in a 2 x 2 set versus a 3-3 front

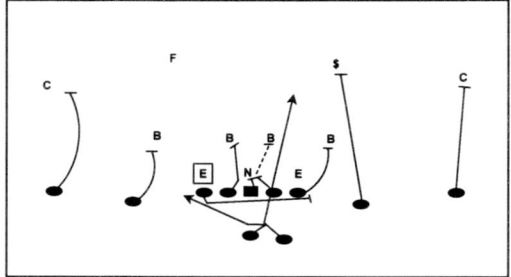

Figure 26-7. Same-side wrap in a 2 x 2 set versus a 3-2 front

Bonus Play: The Quarterback Wrap

The quarterback wrap is a great play to use versus defenses that are keying on the running back for their run fits. The quarterback wrap is great misdirection and allows for six blockers, counting the running back. This play is not a read play. The play can also be run out of a no-back set with fly-sweep action.

The linemen follow their wrap rules by front.

The quarterback will catch the snap, pivot, reach and fake with the running back. The aiming point for the quarterback is the A gap. After the quarterback fakes to the back, his eyes go the pulling tackle's block. His aiming point is the far A gap. He will cut off of the pulling tackle's block.

The running back will make a great fake and then block the backside defensive end. The back needs to keep the defensive end outside.

The receivers will follow playside-backside receivers' rules.

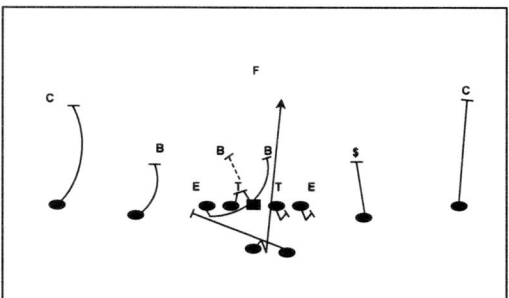

Figure 26-8. Quarterback wrap in a 2 x 2 set versus a 4-2 front

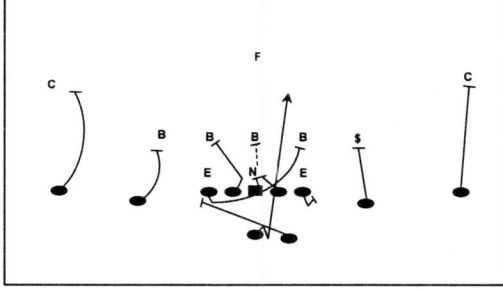

Figure 26-9. Quarterback wrap in a 2 x 2 set versus a 3-3 front

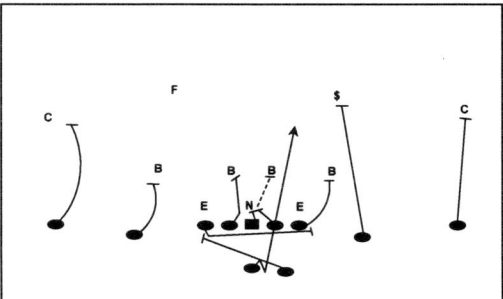

Figure 26-10. Quarterback wrap in a 2 x 2 set versus a 3-2 front

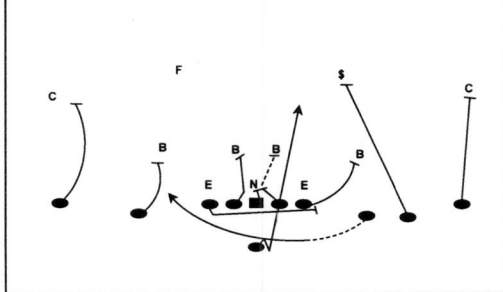

Figure 26-11. Quarterback wrap with fly motion in a 3 x 2 set versus a 3-2 front

27

The Trap Play

Introduction

The trap play is a good way to attack an up-the-field defensive lineman. It can be run versus an odd or even front.

Play #99: The Trap

- PST: Blocks the first linebacker in the box.
- PSG (even front): Pulls and kicks out the end man on the line of scrimmage.
- PSG (odd front): Combination blocks with the center, on the nose, to the first linebacker inside.
- C (even front): Blocks back on the first defensive lineman away from the hole.
- C (odd front): Combination blocks with the PSG, on the nose, to the first linebacker inside.
- BSG: Pulls and kicks out the first man on the line of scrimmage past the center versus all fronts.
- BST: Rips through the defensive end and blocks the backside inside linebacker.

On the running back trap play, the quarterback will meet the snap at four yards, pivot, give the ball to the running back, and drop back like a dropback pass. If it's a quarterback trap, the quarterback will catch the snap, fake to the running back, and get inside the pulling guard's block.

If the running back is the ball carrier, at the snap, he will meet the quarterback at four yards with his near elbow up, take the hand off, and get inside the pulling guard's block. If the quarterback is the ball carrier, the running back will make a quick fake and block the backside defensive end.

The receivers will follow playside-backside receivers' rules.

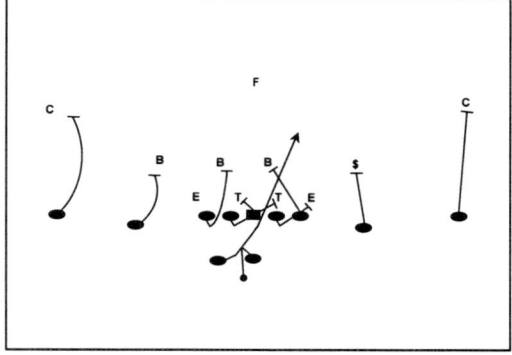

Figure 27-1. Trap in a 2 x 2 set versus an even front

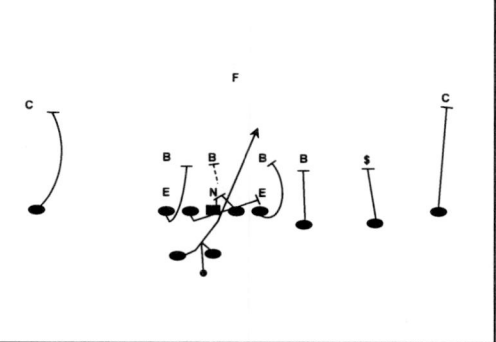

Figure 27-2. Trap in a 3 x 1 set versus an odd front

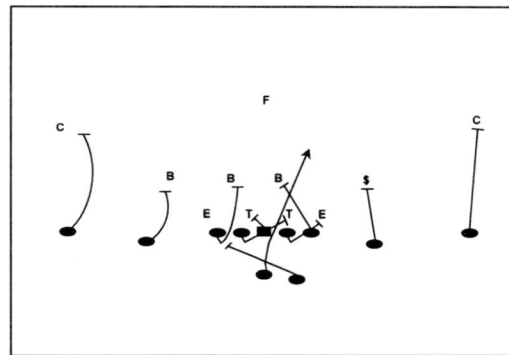

Figure 27-3. Quarterback trap in a 2 x 2 set versus an even front

28

The Isolation Play

Introduction

The isolation play is a good way to attack a defensive front that is rushing the passer without honoring the running game. It is also a good play to run versus linebackers that are dropping quickly to defend the pass. The play is timed and schemed like a draw play. It can be run versus an odd or even front.

Play #100: The Isolation

The offensive line rules are as follows:

- PST: Pass sets and stays on the defensive end.
- PSG: If he has a defensive lineman over him to the outside, pass sets him and stays on. If he is uncovered, or has an inside shade, works with the center to combination block the down lineman to the first linebacker inside him.
- C (even front): Combination blocks with the guard on the A-gap defensive lineman to the first linebacker backside.
- C (odd front): Combination blocks with the playside guard on the defensive lineman to the first linebacker backside.
- BSG (odd front): Blocks the backside linebacker.
- BSG (even front): If he has a defensive lineman over him to the outside, pass sets him and stays on. If he is uncovered, or has an inside shade, works with the center to combination block the down lineman to the first linebacker inside him.
- BST: Pass sets and stays on the defensive end.

The quarterback will catch the snap, open up to sell a quick pass to the flat, and follow the block of the running back. The running back will block the playside inside linebacker versus all fronts. The receivers will follow playside-backside receivers' rules.

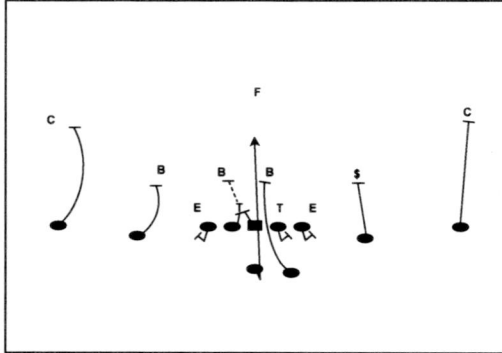

Figure 28-1. Quarterback isolation in a 2 x 2 set versus an even front

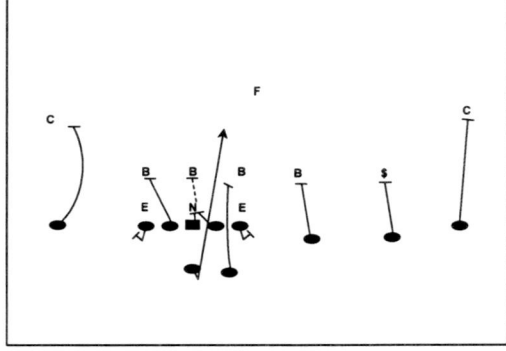

Figure 28-2. Quarterback isolation in a 3 x 1 set versus an odd front

29

Zone Plays

Introduction

The zone play is a good way to attack a defense that stunts and blitzes the majority of the time. It allows the linemen to pick up the stunts and keeps a defender from coming free untouched. It can be run versus an odd or even front.

Play #101: The Zone Play

All offensive linemen follow inside zone blocking rules. The basic principle is to block an area, not just a man. If two linemen next to each other are both covered, the lineman on the playside will be blocking one-on-one. If there is one lineman covered and one lineman not covered, they will work together to block the down lineman to the linebacker behind. All zone plays will be blocked the same way by the offensive line and will only be described once, here.

The quarterback will catch the snap, pivot, reach, and mesh with the running back while reading the backside defensive end. If the defensive end chases the back, the quarterback will pull the ball and burst past the defensive end and up the field. If the defensive end stays and plays contain, the quarterback will give the football to the running back and try to burst past the defensive end.

The running back will pause at the snap and then run through the mesh area under control. The running back is in charge of the mesh, so he needs to see the football, and he needs to run through it on his way to the line of scrimmage. His aiming point is the far hip of the center. After the running back runs through the mesh, his eyes go to the A-gap defender, then to the first down lineman inside of the A gap. If the A-gap defender gets reached, the running back will "bang" through the open gap. If the A-gap defender doesn't get reached, the running back will "bend" through the first gap behind the A-gap defender. If the running back does not get the football, he will sell his fake through the line of scrimmage to the linebacker.

The play can also be run with the fly-sweep motion as shown in Figure 29-4.

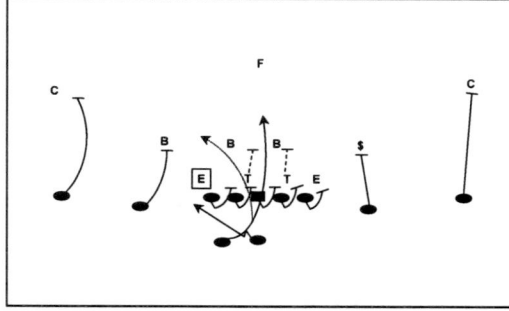

Figure 29-1. Zone in a 2 x 2 set versus a 4-2 front

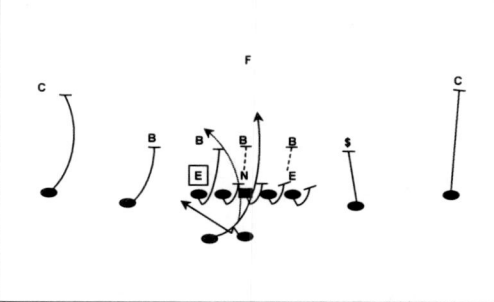

Figure 29-2. Zone in a 2 x 2 set versus a 3-3 front

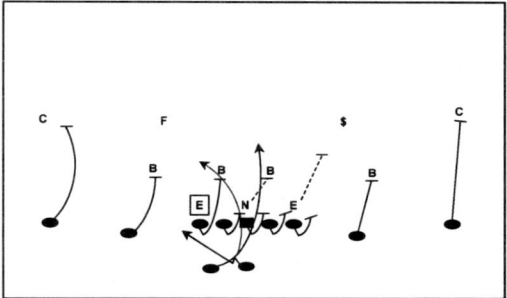

Figure 29-3. Zone in a 2 x 2 set versus a 3-2 front

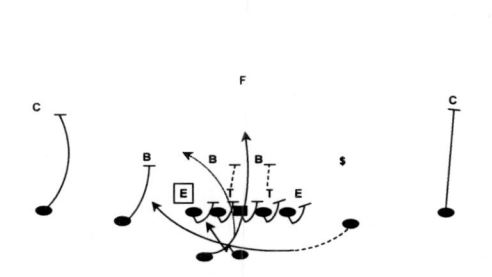

Figure 29-4. Zone with fly motion in a 2 x 2 set versus a 4-2 front

Bonus Play: The Same-Side Zone Play

The same-side zone play is another good way to attack a defense that stunts and blitzes the majority of the time. It allows the linemen to pick up the stunts and keeps a defender from coming free untouched. It can be run versus an odd or even front. The same-side zone play also allows the offense to attack the defense on the side in which the back is lined up.

The quarterback will catch the snap, pivot, reach, and mesh with the running back while reading the backside defensive end. If the defensive end chases the back, the quarterback will pull the ball and burst past the defensive end and up the field. If the defensive end stays and plays contain, the quarterback will give the football to the running back and try to burst past the defensive end. This play is a more difficult play for the quarterback, as his hips and shoulders are turned away from the direction he will need to run, if he needs to keep the ball.

The running back, at the snap, will take three steps to the mesh, pivot, and then start downhill to his landmark. The running back is in charge of the mesh, so he needs to see the football, and he needs to run through it on his way to the line of scrimmage. His aiming point is the far hip of the center. After the running back runs through the mesh, his eyes go to the A-gap defender, then to the first down lineman inside of the A gap. If the A-gap defender gets reached, the running back will "bang" through the open gap. If the A-gap defender doesn't get reached, the running back will "bend" through the first gap behind the A-gap defender. If the running back does not get the football, he will sell his fake through the line of scrimmage to the linebacker.

The receivers will follow playside-backside receivers' rules.

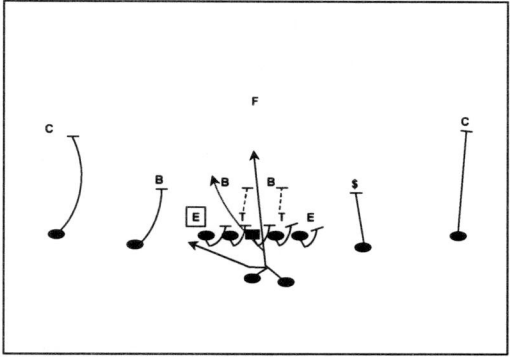

Figure 29-5. Same-side zone in a 2 x 2 set versus a 4-2 front

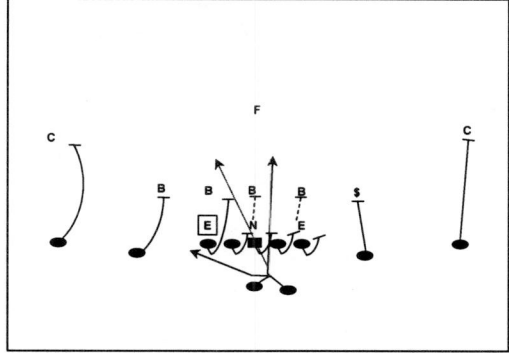

Figure 29-6. Same-side zone in a 2 x 2 set versus a 3-3 front

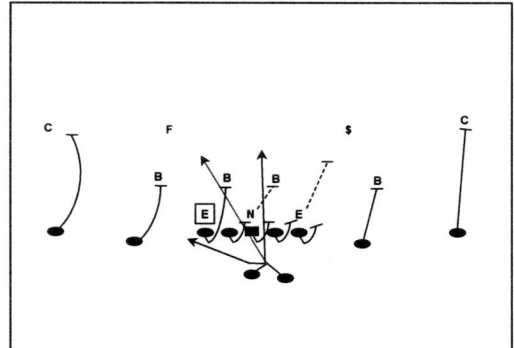

Figure 29-7. Same-side zone in a 2 x 2 set versus a 3-2 front

About the Author

Brent Eckley is the head football coach at Union High School in Union, Missouri—a position he has held since 2005. In that period, the Wildcats have won three district championships and two conference championships (2006), the school's first since 1992. Eckley is currently the winningest coach in the school's 40 year football history.

Eckley played college football in his home state of Iowa, at William Penn University, in Oskaloosa, Iowa, where he received his bachelor's degree in elementary education. He was a three-year letterman for the Statesmen football team, and was a two-year starter as a defensive lineman.

Eckley's first coaching assignment was as an assistant coach at Hickman Mills High School, in Kansas City, Missouri, in 1995 and 1996. From 1997 to 1999, Eckley was an assistant coach and the offensive coordinator at Warrensburg High School in Warrensburg, Missouri. Eckley was the head football coach at Montgomery County High School, in Montgomery City, Missouri, for five seasons (2000 through 2004) and finished with the highest winning percentage in the school's history. During his tenure, the Wildcats won three conference and three district championships, winning 28 of their last 33 games under Eckley. Eckley's overall record as a head coach is 73-24.

Known for his explosive offenses, Eckley has coached four different quarterbacks to throw for more than 2,000 yards in a season. He has coached two different quarterbacks that have recorded 40-plus touchdown pass seasons. Eckley has had four different teams average more than 45 points per game for the season. He also has had three teams average more than 500 yards per game in total offense for the season, including the 2007 Union High School team, which recorded a state record of 545 yards per game.

Coach Eckley has also developed four football videos, including videos on quarterback development and the quick passing game. In addition to video development, Eckley has spoken at numerous clinics across the Midwest.

Eckley and his wife, Sherene, an elementary teacher, live in Union, Missouri, with their five children, Hannah, Emily, Madison, Hillary, and Marquis.